CHASING RIVERS

Tamar
Glouberman

Chasing
Rivers

A
Whitewater
Life

Douglas & McIntyre

Douglas and McIntyre (2013) Ltd.
P.O. Box 219, Madeira Park, BC, V0N 2H0
www.douglas-mcintyre.com

Edited by Scott Steedman
Text design by Carleton Wilson
Printed and bound in Canada
Printed on stock made from 100% recycled fibers

Supported by the Province of British Columbia

Douglas and McIntyre acknowledges the support of the Canada Council for the Arts, the Government of Canada and the Province of British Columbia through the BC Arts Council.

LIBRARY AND ARCHIVES CANADA CATALOGUING IN PUBLICATION

Title: Chasing rivers : a whitewater life / Tamar Glouberman.
Names: Glouberman, Tamar, author.
Identifiers: Canadiana (print) 20220233187 | Canadiana (ebook) 20220233195 |
    ISBN 9781771623414 (softcover) | ISBN 9781771623421 (EPUB)
Subjects: LCSH: Glouberman, Tamar. | LCSH: Women adventurers—Canada—
    Biography. | LCSH: Adventure and adventurers—Canada—Biography. |
    LCSH: Outdoorswomen—Canada—Biography. | LCSH: Kayakers—Canada—
    Biography. | LCSH: Rafting (Sports) | LCGFT: Autobiographies.
Classification: LCC GV776.15.A2 G56 2022 | DDC 797.12/10971—dc23

This book is dedicated to my parents and sister for supporting my dream of being a writer even after they read this book, which, quite honestly, has a lot of stuff in it that no one really wants to know about their daughter or sister.

CONTENTS

AUTHOR'S NOTE

The events in this book have been retold to the best of my memory (along with a little help from emails I should probably have deleted long ago but hoarded away instead); however, I have changed some names and minor details to protect the privacy of individuals.

Both metric and imperial measurements are used in this story. Like many Canadians, I tend to use a mix of both. Even though I learned only the metric system in school, I've always thought of my height and weight in imperial. I generally think of temperature and driving distances in metric, except when I'm in the US and surrounded by people and signs that use imperial. I hope that staying true to how I think and speak about measurements in real life doesn't cause confusion in the written form.

CHAPTER 1

Chilko River, BC
July 2006

In the summer of 2006, I was thirty-three years old and single, and the closest thing I had to a permanent address was the licence plate number on my rusty hatchback. I was living the dream.

The rafting company I guided for advertised Lava Canyon as Class III–IV+, moderate to advanced whitewater. But it was bigger, pushier and more hazardous than most of the so-called Class V rapids I'd paddled outside of British Columbia. Lava Canyon crashed and boiled continuously for twenty-two kilometres, making it one of the longest uninterrupted stretches of whitewater on the continent. If a rafter fell out of the boat, there was high potential for a long, rough and possibly fatal swim. It was easy to think of reasons not to run Lava, yet when I wasn't, I was usually yearning to be.

All morning the four businessmen in my raft had been trying to one-up each other with tales of whitewater on rivers far more famous than the Chilko—stories of accidental swims in the Grand Canyon section of the Colorado River and a near flip on the Middle Fork of the Salmon in Idaho. I imagined their colleagues in Chris's raft had engaged in similar conversation. But as we scouted the upcoming section of whitewater, the eight men were silent. Lava Canyon had a habit of stealing words from even the most boisterous river runners.

Shielded from the glare of the July sun by his well-worn cowboy hat, my co-worker scanned the rapid for dangers. As was his habit when concentrating, Chris caressed his long red beard into two sections, emphasizing the part caused by an old scar on his chin.

The glaciers all around us were warming, sending meltwater streaming down mountainsides and filling rivers to the top of their banks. Like many of those rivers, the Chilko was roaring along with some of its highest water of the season.

Chris, our eight guests and I were on a high ridge overlooking Bidwell, the first drop of Lava Canyon. From there we had a good view of the three massive holes churning along the rapid's left side. Unlike the dryland version of the word, "holes" on rivers are far from empty voids—instead, they are filled with foaming white froth. River holes form when water pours over large obstructions, usually rocks, then leaves a cavity as it rushes downstream. Due to the laws of physics, the water turns back on itself to fill that cavity, creating a recirculating current. Some holes can be fun places to purposely surf a raft or kayak and still exit the hole safely. Other less-forgiving holes can pose a serious danger. The three holes on the left side of Bidwell, known unimaginatively as the Three Sisters, fell into the latter category. Each of the Sisters contained rocks sharp enough to puncture the tough PVC fabric of our rafts. Each had enough size and power to flip our heavily loaded eighteen-foot boats. But most concerning was that each hole had the potential to hold someone underwater longer than any of us could survive without air.

We were high enough above the rapid that its thundering was dulled to a low rumble. When I shifted my weight I could hear the dry, tall grass scratch against my dry suit. To break the silence I said, "We'll follow those downstream Vs to the right of centre."

Heavy waves pounded down from almost every direction, but as rough and wild as it looked, the route I pointed to was clear of any real hazards. The foaming white of rapids forms when water crashes up against rocks or other currents. As the water churns it mixes with air, like milk being frothed for a latte. Cutting through the white of Bidwell's froth were large V-shaped sections of green water where the current continued to push downstream. Those Vs were what we would aim for. If we stayed on that route, we would avoid the Sisters entirely. Reading the line at Bidwell was easy. Sticking to it was the challenge. Water was rushing through the gorge at more than 200 cubic metres per second—and most of it would be pushing anything in its path toward the rabid mouths of the Three Sisters.

Chris started into the talk we always gave the guests. "There are three components to survival," he told the men. "First is the guides' experience and training. Second is our passing on that information to you so that you understand what you need to do. And third is something Tamar and I can't do anything about. It's how you act on that information."

It was important guests understood they weren't on an amusement park ride and that we guides had only so much control. They needed to understand the river had potentially deadly consequences and that by agreeing to run it, they were taking on some of the responsibility for their own survival. Once they understood that, it was also important to give them a choice.

"Close your eyes," Chris said. "On the count of three give me a thumbs-up if you're in, thumbs-down if you're not. There's no shame in deciding this isn't your day to run Lava.

"One. Two. Three."

The eight guests stood with eyes closed and thumbs up. I'd never had someone change their mind at that point, and although it would suck to get someone out of there by land, I was a strong supporter of giving them the option. Whitewater comes with risks. Chris and I each had many years of experience successfully navigating those risks, but we both knew how easily clean records could change. Chris wore his "lucky" hat on every river we ran. "I'd rather be lucky than good," he'd say. "Because eventually we all have a day where we're not good enough."

We made our way back down to the large placid eddy where we'd left our boats. Chris nodded to me and I nodded back. My raft would go first. His would follow close behind. We'd stay tight together, constantly keeping an eye out for each other. We had no need to discuss it. To say Chris and I knew each other well was an understatement. Together we'd rowed hundreds of kilometres of remote rivers and driven thousands of kilometres of highways and logging roads getting to those rivers. Together we'd cooked meals, debated politics, read aloud from books and occasionally even admitted to each other how scared we were. Co-workers and guests sometimes made innuendos about our close friendship. I suppose I could have told them we were "just friends," but I never used those words. There was nothing "just" about friends who relied on each other in the way we did, but I liked the less-intense way Chris explained our relationship: "We're like an old married couple. We bicker all the time and don't have sex."

Our rafts were set up so that the guide rowed from the centre with two guests paddling in the bow and two in the stern. I checked that my guests' helmets and life jackets were properly buckled, then looked over at Chris. His palm rested flat on his head, the signal he was ready to go. I paused to take inventory of the moment: a sunny day, a strong and experienced crew, a rising river and twenty-two kilometres of prime whitewater ahead. A day so perfect it could have been cut and pasted from a raft guide's wet dream. Too bad I felt like I was going to puke.

Who do you think you are? The Indiana Jones of whitewater? You're just a short Jewish chick from Montreal who nearly failed high-school gym. You don't have the skills to guide people down a river like this. Apparently it was far too nice a day for my inner critic to stay home. To calm my nerves, my mind backpaddled to a morning several years earlier.

New York State's Adirondack Park. A fragrant bouquet of wet dog and unwashed long underwear permeates the old vw van. I'm riding in the back while my two kayaking buddies up front sip gas station coffee and eat mini-doughnuts. Drifter, the driver and my off-and-on lover, holds the doughnut box out to me but I don't take it.

"You need to eat," he says. "It's gonna be a big day."

"Ha," says our buddy Conway, wiping powdered sugar from his goatee. "As if our little health freak would start her day with doughnuts."

Drifter puts down the box, feels around in his grocery bag and produces an apple. I shake my head. "I feel like I'm going to puke."

Drifter pulls the van onto the gravel shoulder. "Please not in my van."

"Keep driving," Conway says. I can't see his face, but in his voice I hear his eyes roll. "She's not really going to throw up. All Tamar's best days start with her feeling that way."

In the rearview mirror, Drifter's almond-shaped eyes look to me, awaiting confirmation. For a moment I'm too surprised to say anything. I'm often the only female in the group when kayaking challenging rivers—leaving it to fall on my bra-strapped shoulders to prove a person doesn't need balls to be brave. I hate getting called out for being scared. Showing fear feels like letting down woman paddlers everywhere. On the other hand, I instantly recognize Conway is right: thinking I'm going to puke is exactly how all my best days start, and I feel lucky to have friends who know me better than I know myself. I nod to Drifter to keep driving.

This is going to be my first time paddling the bottom section of the Moose River and I'm not sure I have the skills to run it. Once we get on the water, though, every cell in my body buzzes with excitement as we kayak steep drops, launch over waterfalls and feel like key players in each other's lives. At the take-out I say, "We've got to do this again tomorrow."

If my memory of that day were a physical photograph, it'd be worn around the edges and stained with drink rings from all the times I'd taken it out to examine it. And thanks to Conway pointing out what he thought was obvious, from that day forward I'd been able to recognize that my fears were also letting me know that the day ahead could turn into a great one. My mind returned to the present, and in the eddy above Lava Canyon I placed my hand flat on my head to let Chris know I was ready.

Rowing across the eddy, I was visited by my usual onslaught of images, sounds and words slamming against each other in the mosh pit of my mind. Theme songs from eighties TV shows, memories of my grandparents, thoughts of dinner, fantasies about the cute-but-married guy in my boat all collided with river-specific imaginings: my boat being swept into the Three Sisters, the raft over-turning, a guest being sucked under the water and not resurfacing. The mental shindig grew louder and louder until my bow crossed the eddy line into the main flow of the river. Then all that internal noise stopped dead. The world outside the river ceased to exist, as though I'd put my life into an image-editing program, increased the sharp-ness of Lava Canyon and cropped out everything else. No other feeling came close to the focus I found when running big rapids.

To see as much of the rapid as possible, I stood while I rowed. The terrain on both sides of the river was steep and rocky, and dotted with towering conifers. From its perch high in a spruce tree, a bald eagle turned its white head to watch us. I felt the push of the current on my oar blades as clearly as if the water were push-ing against my own body. Manoeuvring around the first rocks and holes, we made our way from the left side of the river toward the right. A wall of lava rock came into view. The rock's bumps and divots held stories of thousands of years of eruption and ero-sion. But my real interest in the rock lay in the fact that inside this sprawling rapid it acted as a landmark, letting me know it was time to point the bow downstream and line us up for our first big hit.

"All forward," I yelled.

Four paddles drove through the water alongside my oars. Ahead, a giant wave towered.

"Get down!"

The guests hunkered down but I continued to stand. Although the force of the river could unclench my grip from the oars and send me flailing into the water, I didn't fear that—why should I, when the oars felt like an extension of my body? We slammed into the wave. The bow bent backward. Aerated water crashed over the raft, burying us upright in a world of white. The river had pulled us into its heart. I felt as much a part of the river as the water itself. Then the heart beat again and pumped us through to the other side of the wave.

"Get up! All forward," I yelled.

The two men in front clambered up from the floor to sit on the side tubes of the raft—just like they were supposed to for a strong paddle stroke. I turned to check on the two in back. They were also sitting high on the tubes, none of the hiding-on-the-floor-and-not-really-paddling that guests often melted into after that first hit.

"Look at this team! You guys are a well-oiled machine!"

The raft bucked and bounced as waves hit us from all angles. The current tried to coax us from our line, wanting to push us toward where the Three Sisters drooled hungrily in anticipation. But with oars and paddles we drove through the crashing waves and stayed our course.

"Take a break!"

The cute guy up front looked back at me. "This is huge!"

"Sweet, isn't it?" My earlier fears felt like ancient history. Before he could say more, I called, "All forward!"

We were coming up to a dead fir stretching out horizontally from the right shore. Trees in the river create dangerous strainers: water passes through the branches while solid objects like rafts and humans can get caught. A wave smashed us sideways, pushing us closer to the tree.

"Take a break!" I realigned the boat. Once again, the break was short-lived. "All forward!"

We powered into our strokes and passed safely to the left of the strainer. Then safely to the right of a potential pinning rock. Despite the dousing of glacial water, a white heat glowed inside me as if all the energy of the sun had somehow squeezed into my heart. We humans are a strange bunch: when life throws us challenges, we complain and call them problems; when life doesn't give us challenges, we seek them out and call them adventures. I knew the pursuit of adventure made no sense, but damn, it was fun.

After the trip, I would likely never see these men again, but in that moment I felt we were five-fifths of the same whole, wringing as much excitement from our lives as we could. I wanted the sensation to never end.

I yelled out exactly how I felt: "I fucking love my job!"

19

CHAPTER 2

Chilko River, BC
June 2002

My inaugural trip down the Chilko was in the spring of 2002. I
was on a "familiarization" trip, getting to know the river before
starting to guide it. Along with me on the trip were several other
newbies, all recent graduates of the company's guide school. After
dinner on our first evening everyone was hanging out around the
fire when one of the veteran guides asked: "Any of you know about
Ron Thompson?"

None of us did. The guide leaned forward in his camp chair,
eager to share his tale. "Back in the summer of '87 a raft guide
named Ron Thompson and his group of guests camped at this site,
just like us, and probably sat in this very same spot around the
fire."

He spoke like he was starting into a ghost story, and I suppose
in a way it was. The story of Ron Thompson would haunt me for
far longer than any other scary campfire tale I'd ever been told.

"The group was made up of eleven executives on a boys' retreat.
They wanted to run Lava together in the same raft so that everyone
in the group could have the same experience. So, in the morning,
Ron left behind his second raft and his other guide and took all
eleven of them himself."

Our storyteller didn't need to spell out that this decision was
a bad idea. First, the weight of a dozen men would make a raft
difficult to steer (especially in those days before self-bailing rafts).

And second, if things don't go as planned on the river, a second boat and guide can make all the difference between adventure and disaster.

The veteran guide went on to tell us how Thompson also wasn't strict about his guests' personal gear. Some weren't properly dressed in wetsuits despite the icy water, and some wore their life jackets much more loosely than flotation devices ought to be worn. But Thompson had over two hundred successful Lava Canyon runs under his belt, so why would anyone have imagined this trip would be any different?

Thompson's heavy raft crashed through the waves of Bidwell, avoiding the bubbling cauldrons of the Three Sisters. From the bottom of that drop, he rowed his crew into a stretch of medium-sized waves and then into the White Mile—a frothy chaos of overhead waves crashing down at different angles. Soon they came to a sharp bend where the current pushes powerfully toward a boulder on the outside of the turn. On the inside of that same turn, water pours over a sharp ledge that should be avoided. Thompson aimed his raft between the two obstacles, but the current pushed his heavy boat toward the outside of the turn.

He pulled hard on his oars, but the raft slammed sideways into the boulder they'd been trying to avoid. As the right side of the raft slid vertically up the rock's slippery surface, Thompson yelled for a highside. He needed everyone to move to the side of the raft that was rising, to help level out the boat. But Thompson's command went unheeded and the raft continued its climb until it was perpendicular to the river. Eleven of the twelve men, including Thompson, were swept into churning glacial water.

That section of river flows swiftly past steep banks and rocks, making it difficult to get out of the water. Still, Thompson got himself to shore and saw that three of his guests had managed to haul themselves out on the opposite bank. With those men accounted for, he began running the obstacle course of the river's edge, looking for the other eight. When that search failed, adrenaline helped him climb out of the canyon, run back to camp and launch his second raft to row the river hunting for the missing men. By the end of the day, three more guests had been rescued.

Around the campfire of my familiarization trip, we were all silent as our storyteller paused, making sure we understood the math. "The remaining five never made it home."

Being told this story while sitting in the same spot Thompson's group had sat the night before their deadly run made it all the more real to us. For a few moments, the only sounds were the fire popping and hissing and the river gurgling past, while we considered the risks involved in this whitewater life we all wanted so badly to be part of.

"There were twelve rafting deaths in BC that season," our storyteller continued, "including one more on Lava Canyon only three days after Ron Thompson's trip."

Because of that summer's death toll, the provincial government had introduced regulations to prevent us from making many of the same mistakes. Those laws had undoubtedly saved lives in the years since. But although I was new to the Chilko, I'd been guiding rivers long enough to know that no matter how many laws were passed and how much we learned from Thompson's story and others like it, the river is more powerful than any guide. And no matter how hard we try, we always run the risk of not being able to get a raft where it needs to go.

Shortly after the accident, Thompson was quoted as saying, "I just spent thirteen years of my life doing something that I felt was a good thing for people and society in general, and I have to wonder now if it was worth it."

I thought about Thompson every time I was at the top of Bidwell. I thought about him many other times as well. I clearly didn't think he had wasted his time helping people experience the joy and excitement of rivers. But every time I thought of him I did wonder if it was possible for a guide to make peace with themselves after an accident like that. Although no one officially blamed Thompson— the two lawsuits that followed were against the company that had organized the trip—I couldn't imagine not blaming myself if I'd been the one holding the oars.

I hoped Thompson had forgiven himself. I hoped he'd been able to continue living a fulfilling life. I feared if I were ever in his situation, I wouldn't be strong enough to carry on. In my search for adventure I pushed that fear aside over and over, not knowing that with each push, my time to test that strength was drawing closer.

CHAPTER 3

Hudson River, NY
May 2007

Saturday morning at the Hudson River put-in was like a three-ring circus with hungover ringleaders. State regulations allowed for a maximum of one thousand people on the river each day, and on Saturdays those slots were almost always full. Despite having stayed up too late drinking too much, there was grace in how guides from eleven companies avoided stepping on each other's toes while launching all those people within the short window of time when water was being released from the dam. The frenzied scene was poles apart from launching on remote rivers out west. On those western rivers we looked at schedules in terms of days, not hours, and certainly not minutes. Out there we had no dam releases to contend with, or even other humans at the put-in—only wilderness wrapping its arms around us, drawing us away from civilization. Despite their differences, the put-ins for all the rivers I worked on had two things in common: they held the promise of a great river journey ahead and they made me feel I truly belonged.

That Saturday on the Hudson, I'd been assigned a stag-party group of six. Rafting stags were popular and my boss had taken to giving me many of them. He'd realized no matter who I had in my boat, I usually ended up telling dirty jokes. The stags were a safer bet for him than the camp and church groups we got so many of, especially since a few of my dirty jokes involved nuns. Some stag days began with the men surprised to have a female guide.

And although five of the guys that day appeared unconcerned with my gender, the sixth seemed to feel his group had drawn the short straw. The sixth guy also stood out from his crew in other ways. While the others laughed together at inside jokes, spoke jovially about common friends and were all of small to medium build, number six didn't seem to get the jokes, only made negative comments and looked like he spent all day doing upper-body reps at the gym. The words "steroid monkey" came to mind. I guessed he was either a childhood friend the groom had stayed in touch with despite having grown apart or the bride's brother.

I gave a pre-trip briefing that Steroid Man barely listened to, then we all picked up the raft and walked it into line for the put-in eddy. A weekender guide I'd been friends with for years made his way through the crowd. He was taller than any of my stag-party crew and broader than all but Steroid Man. He had a dark beard, a handlebar moustache, a gruff voice and, for reasons no one could quite put their finger on, a remarkably policeman-like air. He hoisted me into a hug that left my feet dangling and asked his usual cheesy question, "How can you be so tiny on land but such a giant on the river?"

He set me down, looked at my crew and, in his low, steady voice, said: "You boys are lucky to have Tamar as a guide. She's one of the best. Listen up to what she says." He stared at them for a moment, letting that sink in.

I'm sure my friend assumed both my size and lady parts were a disadvantage for guiding. It didn't bother me that the assumption was sexist, I appreciated having friends who cared. I also thought his telling people to pay attention to me likely did more harm than good—after all, who wants to listen to a guide who needs someone else to stand up for them? That, however, didn't bother me either. At thirty-four years old, I was the most confident and comfortable I'd ever been in my skin. If people didn't listen to me, I had my own way to deal with it.

Afloat in the big put-in eddy, I shouted out practice commands. Five of the crew were on it, while Steroid Man paddled with all the force of a sleepy kitten. I tried to coax him into paddling in time with everyone else. We didn't need his power—I'd run good lines with ten-year-old Girl Scouts—we needed unison. But Steroid Man made a point of dragging his paddle and messing up the group's synchronization. That problem was exacerbated by his sitting up front, as the guys behind were supposed to follow his tempo. The good news was that his choosing to sit up front also made my plan easier.

The trip leader blew his whistle. I raised my paddle along with the other guides, signalling we were ready. The Hudson trip actually began on a tributary of the Hudson called the Indian River (as I'd explained to one curious guest from India, the name didn't stem from a special connection between the Adirondacks and her homeland, but from the widespread repercussions of Columbus's navigational error). Unlike the Chilko where there was open space between trees, the understory along the Indian was a dense tangle. The forest here paid little attention to boundaries between water and land, allowing its mix of deciduous and coniferous limbs to sag freely over and into the river. In addition to the usual rafting commands, on the Indian I taught guests that "Tree!" meant duck to avoid getting knocked out of the boat. The river itself was rocky and fairly narrow, making it a perfect trap for fallen trees to create strainers. But although the Indian had potential dangers, it was essentially straightforward, easy Class III water.

I turned our raft to hit the first wave sideways, soaking everyone on my side including Steroid Man. He didn't appreciate it as much as the others. The next big hit was Guides Hole—if you hit the hole forward, the raft kicked up in the stern and many guides (myself included) had at some point been tossed into the drink there. Although I generally ran it forward, as a special for Steroid Man I spun the boat backward and yelled "Hang on!" Just as I'd guessed, everyone but him listened. A moment later I was reaching into the river, grabbing ol' Steroid by the shoulder straps of his life jacket and yanking him in like a limp fish. He looked pissed.

"I told everyone to hang on," I said in my defence.

Steroid Man clambered back to his seat while the other guys laughed. Usually a few seconds of a person's breathing holes being covered by water while their ass slammed into rocks was all it took to motivate co-operation. Steroid Man, however, wasn't so easily convinced. So, in the second rapid on the Indian he found himself "accidentally" out of the raft for another swim. He wasn't happy but his buddies found it hilarious.

We neared the confluence where the Indian joined the Hudson. The rafts at the front of our company convoy had pulled over to make sure those behind were okay to carry on. As usual I was running sweep, which meant that I was designated to be the last raft and carry the major first-aid kit. If another boat needed help, the sweep could always get downstream to them. I lifted my paddle to signal everyone could continue, but the guide who'd been in front of me waited. When I was within earshot he asked, "Everything all right?"

"Another beautiful day on the river," I replied.

"Just noticing more swims than usual."

I gave an exaggerated shrug. "It's like someone moved the rocks on me or something."

The guide smirked. We both called "All forward" and continued onto the Hudson. Unlike its narrower tributary, this section of river was wide open. The trees at the confluence were mostly cedars and instead of coming right down to the river like on the Indian, they were held neatly off the water by high rock ledges. The guy seated in the back left of my raft looked at me suspiciously. I smiled at him, wondering if he had any idea how cute he looked with his dark curls poking waywardly from the holes in his helmet. He asked, "Have you been throwing him out on purpose?"

"Would I do that?"

He lifted a thick eyebrow. "I'll give you twenty bucks for every time you get him in."

It wasn't always easy to make someone swim, but Steroid Man's choice of seat paired with his top-heavy build made him an easy target. By the time we'd gone through Entrance—the rapid that

27

marks the start of the meaty part of the trip—Dark Curls said, "FYI, our little deal tops out at a hundred bucks." Even Steroid Man laughed. We were growing on each other, and he was listening more, but I still got him to swim a couple more times. "For old times' sake," I explained as I hauled him in.

As we drifted through the flats toward the end of the trip, we talked about relationships, work and dogs, and somewhere in there I told some stories about rivers I'd worked on out west. Dark Curls asked, "How'd you get into rafting anyhow?"

"For the money."

"No, seriously."

"It's kind of true," I said as I steered us around a rock. "I worked for a season as a video kayaker, which was super fun. But the guides were paid twice as much as I was, so I figured I should try rafting. Turns out I kinda like it."

I didn't mention that contrary to what they believed, the money wasn't all that bad if you kept your lifestyle in check. Although I likely earned less than any of them, rafting still paid better than many local jobs like working at the grocery store or serving tables at the diner. One of my closest friends was raising four kids on her own on rafting wages and tips.

"How'd you get into kayaking?" the groom-to-be asked.

"When I was twelve or thirteen, my parents took my sister and me rafting. When they first told us we were going, I was terrified. I honestly thought I might die."

"Because you imagined having a guide just like you?" Steroid Man asked.

"I'd seen the promo video in a mall. Rafts flipping, people swimming, ropes flying everywhere. It looked like a crash course in survival of the fittest and I could barely survive gym class. I spent the whole drive to the river praying our car would break down. But apparently the god of automotive affairs takes weekends off, 'cause we made it to the river no problem."

"And you survived rafting and loved it."

"Actually, it was a little boring," I said. "The video had been shot in spring high water, but we went in late August so the rapids were small compared to what I was expecting."

"This story is like her jokes. It drags on forever," Steroid Man said.

"Not all of them," I said in defence of my jokes.

"The three fingers one was short," one of the guys said.

"But it tied in with the sperm one her mother told her, which wasn't short," added another.

"Anyhow," I continued, "the water was low but a group of kayakers was surfing the holes. It looked like so much fun. I loved canoeing at summer camp, so I figured kayaking was something I could learn. I tried to recruit friends to take lessons with me, but no one was interested. At one point my dad said he'd join me on a weekend course, but he changed his mind when he found out we'd have to stay in a tent. So, then around half my life later, I was finishing up third-year university and going into my last real summer vacation. I figured if I didn't learn to kayak that summer I never would. So, I bought a copy of *Paddler* magazine and mailed my résumé to all the places in there advertising kayak lessons."

"You've been doing this since the pre-internet days," the groom-to-be said.

We all smiled, as though printed classified ads were as dated as cave drawings.

"I figured if I got a job at a kayak school I could learn while also making paddling friends. And I got a job working in the office at this very company, and met lots of paddlers and learned to kayak. But enough about me. That big white foamy mess out in front of us is Bus Stop, so called because it's a hole big enough to stop a bus. Prepare to get wet. All forward!"

The more rivers I worked on and the more comfortable I became as a raft guide, the more frequently guests asked how I got there. But there was no big sexy flash of a moment when timid young woman was bitten by radioactive river otter and transformed into confident raft guide. Like most people's lives, my route had climbs and descents, icy steering-wheel-clenching hairpin turns counter-balanced with windows-down, tunes-cranked, singing-at-the-top-of-my-lungs straightaways.

Perhaps my journey to guiding had begun with our family rafting trip. Perhaps it'd begun on my first summer camp canoe trip where I'd been introduced to how simultaneously full and simple life felt when only two things dictated our days: the distance we had to paddle and the elements of nature, which in my sheltered life had never before been so inescapable. Part of me even wondered if the journey had started way back when I was six months old and I'd experienced swimming on my own for the first time. My parents had taken me to the neighbourhood public pool and started chatting with a man whose young children were good swimmers. "They've been at it since they were a few months old," the proud father had said. "Babies swim naturally. Want me to show you?" My parents had eagerly watched as this stranger set me free in the water to prove his point. Of course I don't remember that moment, at least not in any conscious way. However, I've always been one of those lucky people who feels wholly at home in the water—as if those four hundred million or so years since our ancestors emerged from the sea were barely a tick on the clock.

Occasionally I answered the question of how I became a raft guide with the story of my unintentional first day on the job.

The summer after working at the rafting company office in the Adirondacks, I signed up for guide school on the Ottawa River, thinking Canada's most popular rafting river would be a fun next step. Arriving with my own kayak and a freshly minted film degree, I immediately had guides try to convince me to become a video kayaker—the person who kayaks down the river shooting videos of the rafting trip. Even when I explained that I was really only a Class II paddler, the guides kept telling me I should try it. But I'd come to the Ottawa to learn to be a raft guide, so I kept focused on that goal.

My performance in guide school was solidly mediocre, but my enthusiasm led me to be one of two students chosen to stay on with the company as guide trainees. I soon discovered that training in rafts with paying customers was very different from training with a group of fellow students in guide school. During the course, I'd had opportunities to be in charge on real rapids. But once I started training on actual trips with actual guides, I was relegated to steering rafts through smaller rapids while the guides training me took over on the bigger ones. That was fun enough for a while, but soon it seemed like no matter how well I did on the small stuff, none of the experienced guides were going to give me a chance to be in charge on anything pushier. I wanted to really learn about whitewater. I wanted to read the lines and steer my own way through the rapids. I didn't want to spend the summer as a rafting passenger who traded work around the base for meals and a place to pitch my tent. And so I told my boss I'd take as many video kayaking shifts as he'd give me. Which turned out to be almost every day.

The Ottawa is a deep, pool-drop river. Its depth makes it unlikely that anyone who falls out of a boat will get badly spanked by rocks. And its short rapids followed by large pools mean any accidental swims are brief and the swimmers easy to collect. What makes the Ottawa exciting is its high volume. Its waves and holes are enormous. Sometimes people get pulled down into holes so deep that sharp pain stabs through their inner ear and they begin to believe they'll never resurface. In the end, though, there are very few serious mishaps on this heavily travelled river. So, although the Ottawa rapids were far more intimidating than the beginner runs I'd paddled during my first summer in the Adirondacks, the Ottawa guides easily convinced me that even if I swam I'd be okay. And swim I did. I swam all the big rapids at one point or another— meaning I capsized, didn't successfully "roll" (right myself) and therefore ungracefully exited my kayak mid-rapid. But in terms of doing my job, I always managed to get to my next video-shooting point before the rafts came by, even if that meant temporarily abandoning my kayak and front-crawling like mad to shore (which of course meant that after I finished shooting I had to jump back in and front-crawl like mad over to the eddy my abandoned kayak was still circling in to retrieve it).

Mornings at the rafting base started with all of us staff leaning sleepily into couches and chairs, as our boss read out who was responsible for which tasks. During one of those meetings, the boss announced I was on bathrooms, which was better than it sounded. It was a quick cleaning job that meant I'd have time for breakfast once I was done. Then the boss started to read out which guide would lead which group. I was only half-listening until he assigned a rafting group to me.

"Um, I'm the video boater," I reminded him.

"The office overbooked, so today you're a guide. Congratulations," he said in monotone, barely looking up before continuing on to the next item on his sheet. After the meeting I approached him, concerned. Each company on the Ottawa had hopeful trainees going down the river every day and some never got to captain their own ship. I'd stopped training because I'd felt destined to fall into that category. So, how was I suddenly ready?

"You've run this river for the past, what? Thirty-five days in a row? You know the lines," he said.

"In a kayak," I countered.

My boss looked down at me. His nose twitched, a tic he displayed when he was annoyed or concentrating or both. His eyes silently held mine long enough to make me uncomfortable. Finally he doled out this sage advice: "Tamar, a monkey can guide a raft. Keep it between the banks."

With those inspiring words and a booking error, I officially became a raft guide. But in my heart that was still far from true. I took the easiest lines and gave the family in my boat what may have been the most boring trip ever down the Ottawa. I wasn't proud of the job I'd done, and for the rest of the summer I happily returned to video kayaking.

Summer turned to fall. The maples flamed yellow, orange and red. Workdays on the Ottawa trickled to a halt. Seven of us loaded rafts, kayaks and mountain bikes onto and into an old white school bus named Yoda. Our ultimate destination was Jalcomulco, Mexico, where my boss had teamed up with a Mexican rafting company to run trips for the winter. But before arriving in Jalcomulco, there was much paddling to be done. With The Verve's "Bitter Sweet Symphony" on high rotation, we zig-zagged through the southeastern US, hitting the supposed Class V runs of West Virginia's Upper Gauley, Maryland's Upper Youghiogheny and even a last-minute detour to the Chattooga, which flows along the border of Georgia and South Carolina. The Chattooga holds a special place in the heart of many paddlers for its starring role in the classic whitewater film *Deliverance*. It's also one of the rare whitewater rivers in the Lower 48 that remains undammed for its entire length, and thanks to a night of biblical rains, we got to run the Chattooga while it was filled to the brim with powerful chocolate-milk-coloured rapids.

That road trip was one of the best ever, despite the couple of times I nearly drowned. First I got myself jammed upside down beneath an undercut rock on section 4 of the Chattooga. When the current and some really good luck finally flushed me out, two of the other paddlers were already pulling out rescue gear—although they later admitted they thought there was less of a chance of it being a rescue than a body recovery. My second mishap came in Mexico, on the Alto Filo section of the Bobos River, when instead of boofing (a.k.a. launching) over a hole, I landed in the middle of its frothy mess. The recirculating current put me through the spin cycle, slamming my head against a rock with each rotation. When the hole finally spat me out, I rolled myself upright, feeling proud I'd managed to hang in there. Then a fellow kayaker approached.
"You okay?"

I patted the top of my helmet to signal that I was good to go.
"You sure?"
"What's wrong?"
"There's blood dripping out of your ear."

I touched the ear that had engaged in multiple visits with the underwater rock, then looked at my hand. There was indeed blood, but I happily reported: "Surface wound."

"You're good to keep paddling?"

We had a day and a half of kayaking ahead of us and the biggest rapids yet to come. My head pounded and both my balance and confidence were shot. But there were no roads or obvious trails nearby, just dense jungle that was home to venomous snakes and invertebrates.

Like anyone would in that situation, I said, "Yep, I'm good!"

I flipped several more times over the next day and a half. Each time I went upside down sharp pain cracked through my ear, but the real consequence of the Maytagging I'd received only revealed itself a week later. The bacteria in the river water I'd accidentally swallowed had incubated, resulting in far more extreme gastro-intestinal issues than I'd ever experienced before.

The rest of the crew left on a new adventure while I moved into the bathroom full-time. I wasn't entirely alone though: a colony of biting red ants lived there too. One day an Australian paddler I knew stopped by and found me on the bathroom floor covered in ants that I no longer had the energy to swipe away. He wiped the insects off me, got me to drink some clean water and left to find one of the locals from the rafting base. Neither the Australian nor I spoke much Spanish; however, after playing some rather graphic question-and-answer charades with the local man, he disappeared for a while and then came back with a bag full of powders, liquids and pills. I hoped I understood what he was telling me to do with all of them. I was pretty sure he said that if I took them correctly they would get me through a flight. I didn't want to leave, but while curled up half delirious on the bathroom floor I'd had a moment of clarity. I'd realized I was the sickest I'd ever been in my life and was getting worse. So, with a bagful of unfamiliar medications I bid *adios* to Jalcomulco.

My winter back in Montreal was bleak. Aside from working a soul-sucking desk job, two of my grandparents passed away. To escape from reality, I buried myself in writing a screenplay about a girl who creates an unconventional life for herself building custom motorcycles. Her fictional world helped shelter me from real life, but as winter warmed into spring it was time to face the world again. With the snow melting and rafting season on the horizon, it should have been easy to see my next move. But after months of marinating in the details of my kayaking mishaps, I was afraid.

Then someone from the Ottawa crew emailed to say they were back from Mexico with my kayak and I should come pick it up. Once at the rafting base, I was easily convinced to paddle—after all it was just the Ottawa; I already knew what it was like to swim almost every rapid. I quickly realized our southern road trip had changed me. The big hit on the first rapid that I'd always found intimidating was now just pure fun. By the end of the day I wanted nothing more than to spend another season, or perhaps the rest of my life, on a river. And by the time I'd driven back to Montreal, I'd realized I also wanted to go back to the Adirondacks, where in just one summer I'd begun to build friendships I imagined carrying on for the rest of my life. I didn't know if working in the States would be possible, but I called up my former boss and told him I wanted to guide. He welcomed me back as if I'd never left.

I began guiding on the kid-friendly Sacandaga, a Class II tributary to the Hudson. Our drive to the put-in took us across the bridge over a waterfall at one of the Hudson's narrowest sections. The bus driver would slow to a crawl so that the young families—nervous about what they were taking their six-year-olds on—could have a good look at the white foam spewing off Rockwell Falls as the guide at the front joked, "And this will be our first rapid of the day."

Spring flowed into summer. The tiny green buds that had been poking out from the branches when I'd arrived swelled into leaves. Days became so hot that we guides jumped off our rafts to cool down at every opportunity. Workdays were followed by visits to the ice cream shop. And nights at the bar were followed by skinny dips in the local lakes and rivers. As temperatures climbed and no rain came, river levels fell. One day, as we crossed over Rockwell Falls it looked like it had dropped to a runnable level.

Two summers earlier, when I'd been working in the office, I'd gone with the guides to Rockwell after work. I'd been part of the audience seated on the rocks on the far side of the river. With beers in hand, we'd watched as the good kayakers prepared to run Rockwell. I'd still been so new to whitewater that I'd had no idea where the line was, or even how the falls were different that day than the week before. To my eyes it was the same big scary drop. One by one, boys in kayaks hucked themselves over the falls and disappeared into the bubble bath of aerated water below. Some popped up still upright. Others were upside down. Most of the upside-downers rolled up. One pulled his skirt and swam, but someone threw a rope and pulled him to shore in no time.

When Liz—the best female kayaker I knew—paddled out of the eddy, I was encouraged to see a chick run the falls. She looked strong as she ferried across to where she needed to be, but the last stroke she took before going over the lip of the falls lacked oomph. Her boat barely cleared the edge before pencilling straight down. Then it stopped dead. We all went quiet. Hers was an older-style kayak, long and thin with a pointed bow. And that pointy bow was now wedged into the rocks at the bottom, holding the kayak vertically inside the flow of the falls. Liz was stuck in her cockpit, with the heavy stream of water crashing relentlessly over her. Helplessly far away, we stood as if to support our friends on the closer side as they ran around with throw bags of rope trying to figure out how to unpin Liz before she drowned. One of the guys was wearing a life jacket with a rescue belt, and another started tying him in so that he could jump into the river and try to manually dislodge Liz's boat. But just before that attempt began, Liz somehow managed to fight the strength of the water, release the spray skirt that covered her cockpit, exit her boat and thoroughly amaze us all. Someone tossed her a rope and pulled her to shore. Liz was safe. The relief on both sides of the river was palpable. Then Liz amazed us for a second time: she ran the falls again. This time without getting pinned. She was the coolest woman I could imagine. I wanted to be brave like her. *Who are you kidding? You won't ever have the guts to run those falls. And even if you did have the guts, you will never have the skill.*

Two years after that incident, and two hours after crossing over Rockwell and seeing it was low, I went by myself to scout the falls. Standing just upstream of the drop, it seemed like a different waterfall than the one I'd watch Liz get pinned in. That waterfall had been a messy mass of white where nothing had looked runnable. But here I saw each stroke I'd need to take.

On the Sacandaga, we ran three trips a day. Being a slow day, I'd easily been relieved from trip number two to go on my scouting mission. When the bus pulled in from that trip, I approached a guide I sometimes paddled with. "Rockwell after work?" I asked.

He'd never run it either. He paused just a moment before giving me a big grin. "Let's do it."

By the time the last Sac trip of the day was done, word of us running Rockwell had gotten around. Arriving at the falls, we were joined by some guys from another company who wanted to paddle it as well. Across the river a crowd formed on the rocks—just like the day two years before. The one big difference was that now the only female kayaker was me.

I slid my kayak into the eddy. *Remember when you said there was no way you'd ever run this? Remember Liz? Do you really think you could get yourself out of that situation?*

I snapped my spray skirt tight around the cockpit of my boat while my inner critic grew louder. *Think about Liz. Think about Liz. Get out now. It's not too late to change your mind.* I inhaled, dug my paddle in and propelled myself across the eddy line to where it was indeed too late to change my mind. Like magic, my inner critic shut up and made room for logical thinking: *Ferry across to that eddy behind the rock.* I set my angle, and with my back to the falls took the necessary strokes to get behind the rock. *Turn around and face the falls.* I did. I looked for the spot to aim for and found it. *Paddle hard.* I paddled to the edge, took one final boof stroke over the lip, lifted my paddle overhead so as not to hammer myself in the face when I landed and became consumed by the incomparable sensation of freefall.

The laws of physics say it would have taken just under a second to reach the bottom. It's incomprehensible to me that the human body can feel so much in under a second. Landing at the bottom, aerated water wrapped itself around me. It was the first time I'd ever been upright and fully surrounded by white, the first time I felt embraced by the river. I resurfaced still upright and paddled to shore. It was only then that sounds began to register and I heard the water and the cheering and the car passing over the bridge. It was only then that I realized it was the first time in my life that I'd focused on just one thing while every other thought, and even the outside world, went silent. Screw meditation and yoga. Dropping waterfalls was clearly the real path to enlightenment.

At the time, I still thought I wanted a career in the film industry. But landing that drop may have been the moment of no return when I committed to take my whitewater life as far as it would go, even if I had yet to realize it.

CHAPTER 4

Williams Lake, BC
May 2007

Spring was migration time for raft guides, and I was on the move. I'd made a pattern of starting rafting season in New York's Adirondack Park in early April, when melting snow turned the upper reaches of the Hudson River into a liquid roller coaster. Then, once the snow had mostly disappeared and the Hudson's water level began to drop, I would reinforce the structural duct tape on my beat-up Honda, strap my kayaks to the roof and drive to British Columbia to row rafts on glacier-fed rivers that were just beginning their rise.

I'd seen over five thousand kilometres of North America by the time the familiar landmarks of Williams Lake appeared around me. First came the Husky gas station and the twenty-four-hour Tim Hortons, unifying features of many British Columbian towns. I passed the Save-On-Foods where we shopped for our rafting trips, and then the smaller shops and restaurants of the downtown. In the distance, stacks of freshly cut trees waited to be turned into lumber. Williams Lake, a.k.a. the Puddle, would never be referred to as the Paris of British Columbia, but it had a certain mill-town aesthetic I found strangely welcoming. Glancing at directions jotted on the back of a gas receipt, I turned into the industrial park and found the big blue warehouse at the end of the road.

A pickup truck weighed down with rafting gear sat in the driveway. Beside it stood a hulking man with shaggy blond hair. I pulled up beside him and turned off my car. It let out a wheeze like a sigh of relief.

"Welcome back, T-mar," said Graham, the owner of the rafting company.

Graham stretched his arms out to their full condor-like wing-span. Instead of slouching to accommodate our fifteen and a half inches of height difference, he stood straight, as though greeting another six-foot-six-inch person. I hugged his midriff while he wrapped his arms around the air in front of him.

"You haven't grown," he said.

"I swear I water myself as often as I can."

I'd first met Graham in the spring of 2002, after a single phone conversation with him had inspired me to set off on my inaugural cross-country drive.

"I've been wanting to hire a woman for a few years," he'd told me over the phone. "But none of the other women who've applied have been qualified."

I wasn't sure why he thought I'd bucked that trend. Graham ran multi-day trips on remote rivers in BC, Alberta, Yukon and Alaska. His rafting company was the only one I knew of that was actively explor-ing whitewater rivers not yet being run commercially to see if they could be. I, on the other hand, had worked only on well-established day-tripping rivers. My inner critic had been quick to point out the only reason it thought I might be useful: *He must be really desper-ate to have someone who'll talk to female guests about wilderness tampon etiquette.* I'd tried to ignore that thought and remind myself that the many rivers I'd kayaked for fun counted as experience. But there'd been one practical matter I'd needed to bring up. "I've always worked as a paddle guide. I've never rowed an oar rig."

"No worries. I'm running a guide school in the spring. Why don't you come join it? On me, of course. You'll get time on the oars and maybe help out enough with the course that I can find a reason to pay you. We'll see how things go from there."

It had been far from a concrete job offer and it meant leaving my job on the Hudson and my community in North Creek—a.k.a.

the Crik, a river and town that felt more like home than anywhere I'd lived before. But the draw of adventure was too strong to turn down this chance.

I'd packed up my hatchback and embarked on what would be the first of many cross-country drives. The plan was to meet up with everyone for the guide school in Lake Louise. I'd arrived early and decided to take the time to reorganize my messy car. In a near-empty parking lot, I'd dumped all my stuff onto the asphalt and was figuring out how to better repack it when a pickup with a kayak in the bed pulled into a nearby spot. The driver got out, eyeing the kayak on my roof. Naturally, we started talking about paddling and soon he asked what I was doing in Lake Louise. When I'd told him my plan, he'd physically recoiled.

"Seriously?" he'd asked. When I nodded he'd said, "You don't want to work for Graham. He's a real asshole."

Having quit my job, left my friends and driven clear across the continent, those weren't the encouraging words I wanted to hear. But this random paddler, who seemed like a really nice guy, continued on about how untrustworthy Graham was. Before he left, he'd reached into his truck and grabbed a business card. "If you change your mind after you meet him, I could use another video boater."

Five years later I was still working for Graham as one of his lead guides. The remote and challenging rivers we ran brought me no shortage of stress, but they were fun, plus they helped me in a way I rarely admitted to. Whenever my life slowed to a less stressful pace, thoughts on the meaninglessness of my existence found too much time to loiter in the alleyways of my mind. Those thoughts would pile one on top of the other, gathering what felt like a physical weight. The weight made it a challenge to get out of bed or talk to friends. And if I didn't conjure up the strength to fight that weight, thoughts of how I was wasting my life despite being given so much pushed me down even farther. Graham, as an employer, was my antidote to that. I sometimes referred to him as Charlie, a reference to the '70s TV show *Charlie's Angels*. Each week on the show, the three female detectives known as the Angels got a call from their mysterious boss,

Charlie, that catapulted them into a new adventure. Of course, nothing about my baggy clothes and frizzy-ponytail-under-ballcap look was the least bit reminiscent of the perfectly coiffed Angels, but Graham was my call to adventure.

Not long after I met Graham, I'd told him about my conversation in the Lake Louise parking lot. Graham had said, "I don't even know who that guy is." Then he told me about a similar conversation he'd had with a stranger who—not realizing he was actually speaking to Graham—had unknowingly proceeded to tell Graham what a jerk Graham was.

"But he didn't even know you," I'd said.

Graham had laughed and waved it off. "What other people think of me is none of my business." Years later, we still joked about me not heeding the warning of the parking lot guy.

Aside from rafting, Graham had many other interests, including real estate. The warehouse I'd pulled up to in Williams Lake was his most recent acquisition. He led me inside. The few functioning overhead lights didn't didn't do much to brighten the cavernous space, so Graham cranked open the truck-sized garage door. Daylight illuminated a forest of objects wrapped in moving blankets and dust.

"This front part is used by a moving company that's been renting here forever," Graham said. "But look at all this space we have in the back. We can build shelves to hold our gear. And that Jayco trailer outside is for guides to crash in when we have to spend a night in the Puddle."

An old travel trailer and a dark, dusty warehouse: probably not an exciting combo for most people, but they were just what we needed.

"This is awesome," I said. "Now tell me about the new guides."

Over the years at Graham's company I'd worked with quite a few guides. They'd come from a variety of countries and whitewater backgrounds, but one thing they'd all had in common was a Y chromosome. That was about to change. Graham had hired a male–female couple who'd guided on the Ottawa and in Mexico. He was also bringing on a new female trainee.

Although working with all men had been fun and secretly made me feel kind of tough, I was excited to welcome other women on board. The small contingent of female guides on the Hudson included some of my closest friends. A tight bond held together us women who'd chosen lives off the well-worn path. I pictured forming the same sort of connection with these ladies. Also—perhaps to make up for not planning to have kids—I liked the idea of mentoring younger female guides, who I hoped would in turn inspire more women to follow in our wake.

In the time I'd worked for Graham, our trainees had all been guide school students with no whitewater experience. They'd traded unpaid labour for a fun summer on the river, while both they and we had known they weren't going to gain the necessary skills to guide the Chilko. But Graham believed this new trainee, Megan, could be different.

"She's only guided in Jasper," Graham said. "So basically float trips, but she's very keen on improving her skill set. I called her manager for a reference and he couldn't stop raving about her. It sounds like she's an excellent worker...Either that or she's banging him." He paused before adding, "Speaking of which, I apologize for not hiring any single guys for you to lure into your lair."

"I'll be okay."

"You always are."

"Except for maybe that summer you asked me if my vagina was broken."

"I hadn't heard any rumours about you. I was concerned."

"You're so thoughtful."

"That's what good managerial skills are about."

The company ran rafting trips across BC and beyond, but the river we ran most often was the Chilko. Graham had been staging trips out of a lodge on Chilko Lake for years, and when the lodge recently changed hands he'd convinced the new owners to hire him to manage it. His new title didn't surprise anyone: Graham liked being in charge. His wife gently joked that the position was another small step in his plan to rule the world.

Graham had asked any staff who could to arrive two weeks before our first trip and help get everything set up. We started in the Williams Lake warehouse where we took advantage of the unseasonably hot spring day, cleaning all the gear and spreading it across our driveway. By late afternoon we reached a point where the only thing we had left to do was wait for tents to dry. The beers came out.

Graham had hired a young woman named Nikki to help with miscellaneous chores for the summer. Her hair fell in long tight curls and when she smiled her cheeks turned her eyes into half-moons. Like everyone, she'd worked hard all day. But instead of going right for a cold brew, her first matter of after-work business was sitting on a cooler with her guitar. Nikki's fingerpicking made everyone else go quiet in anticipation. Her cheeks turned pink as she realized she had an audience, but she continued. I didn't recognize the song she sang, but it fit the hot day perfectly. Graham unfolded a camp chair beside her. His legs were so long that his knees bent up high in front of him as he sat down.

When Nikki finished that song, Graham asked if he could use her guitar and play one. Whereas Nikki's style was intricate fingerpicking and newer, alternative folk sung in a beautiful but quiet voice, Graham's style was heavily strummed three-chord camp-fire classics sung with—as he always said—a voice that made up for not being great by being loud. Their musical approach, their size, their age were all noticeably different, but as they passed the guitar back and forth, showing each other tricks and trading songs, the feeling of unity between them somehow encompassed us all. According to the calendar it was still spring, but between the early-season heat, the acoustic guitar and the barefoot guides lazily drinking beers, it felt so much like summer I could almost smell fresh peaches in the air. I pulled up a camp chair to savour the moment, tingling with the joy of looking forward to a summer so full of promise.

The next day we loaded the gear we'd need for our first trip and drove the four hours west to Chilko Lake. What we referred to as "the lodge" was actually a rustic resort made up of cabins of different sizes and styles. The main building, which housed the communal spaces, was a large log cabin whose dining room had two-storey-high windows that perfectly framed the northern end of Chilko Lake. Each season, on my first day back, I'd let out a big sigh of contentment upon seeing that view again. Chilko is one of the largest high-alpine lakes on the continent, and its transparent blue-green waters seemed to disappear over the horizon like an inland ocean lined on both sides by forested mountains. Guest cabins spread out along the shoreline, surrounded by grass, wildflowers and a few horses that roamed wherever they pleased. The property looked like it was straight out of a brochure for "Beautiful British Columbia"—but it needed work.

We scrubbed cabins and organized storage. We drove the four hours to town to buy parts to fix plumbing problems, and then drove into town again the next day to buy parts for unexpected electrical repairs. We assembled barbecues, made beds and learned how to work the generator. I was happy to help downsize the extensive collection of dead wildlife decor the previous owners had been so fond of, but each time I folded yet another hospital corner on a bedsheet—for a guest who was willing to spend the following five nights in a sleeping bag—I wondered why I'd offered to help instead of staying on the Hudson for a while longer. Chris was smarter than me and had put off coming to the lodge until closer to the first trip. He'd only just arrived when Graham said to the two of us and the third senior guide, "I need one of you to do the shop tomorrow."

Buying groceries for our six-day trips wasn't a quick spin to the store. On top of the four-hour drive each way, our shopping list was a five-page spreadsheet requiring multiple hours and shopping carts. Plus, there were always other tasks tacked on once we were going to the Puddle. None of the three of us wanted to go, but Chris had just driven all the way from Nelson—plus I knew it would be good for him to catch up with Graham—and the other senior guide was being whiny, so I reluctantly volunteered.

Graham rounded up two helpers for me. As advertised, Megan, the new trainee, was eager to assist anywhere she could. She was a petite but strong twenty-four-year-old with long blonde hair and big shiny teeth. Mike, the other helper, was a buddy of Graham's who'd been hired to run the bar and dining room. I knew Mike from years past. He was in his early forties and stood out from the guides because he was always clean-shaven and neatly dressed. He sometimes referred to me as Bossypants because years before on a training trip I'd forced him to paddle more than he'd wanted to, but we got along well.

In the morning, while checking that our trailer was properly secured to the truck, I was body-slammed by a feeling that something was about to go terribly wrong. The sensation was so strong that I looked around for a tangible cause. There was nothing. The lodge looked like a serene rural tableau: gently rolling lawn, glassy lake and two of the old horses sleeping comfortably on their sides (a habit that often led guests to think the horses were dead). I told myself what I felt was just nervousness about the beginning of the season. Even so, I hurried into the driver's seat before Mike claimed it.

I didn't consider myself a great driver. Even with all my experience driving from the Atlantic to the Pacific, down to Mexico and up to Yukon, I was still insecure about my vehicle-handling skills, especially on unpaved roads. The summer I'd worked on the Ottawa, I'd flipped an SUV on a gravel road while trying to avoid a head-on collision with a school bus. The vehicle had been totalled, but thankfully no one had been hurt and even the kayaks had escaped from the roof rack unscathed. For the rest of that summer I'd been known as the girl who could roll three kayaks at once...plus an SUV. I'd laughed each time someone repeated the joke—I appreciated cheesy kayaking humour—but each retelling also reminded me of my incompetence. There hadn't been a day I'd driven since when I didn't imagine flipping the vehicle. So, it wasn't confidence in my own driving that made me get into the driver's seat ahead of Mike that morning at Chilko Lake. It was fear. Mike drove too fast for my comfort. If something were to happen, at least we'd be going slower if I was at the wheel.

Mike climbed into the passenger seat, clearly not caring who drove. Megan showed up with her pillow and sleeping bag, stretched out in the back seat and promptly fell asleep. The truck and trailer clattered through the wooden gate and onto the gravel road. An ominous feeling hung over me like a low-lying cloud. I knew there was no logical way to predict the future, but emotions don't always embrace logic. My senses were on high alert.

An hour later, we passed from gravel onto paved highway. The joints of the old truck stopped creaking. My shoulders relaxed and migrated back down away from my ears. Mike fell asleep. The Chilcotin Plateau sprawled out before us. Wooden fences made of criss-crossed horizontal beams snaked down the highway, separating the road from ranchlands and farmer's fields. Despite the fencing, cattle still roamed the highway; some moved in groups swiftly along the edge, while others roadblocked the middle. In some areas the edges of the highway were densely forested with dead and dying lodgepole pine trees. With our warming winters, pine-beetle infestation was getting worse all over the west. Rays of morning sun burst through rust-coloured needles, rendering the dead trees strangely beautiful. I wondered if the beetles would eventually kill every lodgepole pine in the province or if something would stop them first—like a change in weather, human intervention, or perhaps the beetles themselves would instinctively know when to stop, since destroying all the trees meant destroying their own species. I wished for the latter, it gave me hope that we humans might also stop annihilating everything we needed before it was too late.

The tires hummed along. The sun rose above the ailing forest. We approached some turns in the road. Megan and Mike were both asleep when the truck began pulling to the right. Having driven many old vehicles with personality quirks, I barely thought about the pull as I gave the steering wheel a slight turn. The truck surprised me: my gentle adjustment didn't take. The truck continued moving right, just where the highway twisted left. The tires rolled off the smooth asphalt onto the gravel shoulder. The truck rumbled and shook. My hands tightened on the wheel. I steered harder toward the left. This time the vehicle responded. We were back in our lane. Then the truck kept going—right over the yellow line and into the oncoming lane. I cranked the wheel back toward my lane. It was too much. The wheels skidded out. I tried to steer into the skid, but I didn't get it right and the truck fishtailed down the road. Hitting the brakes would have made things worse but the truck was going too quickly for me to control, so I removed my foot from the gas pedal to slow down. Without the accelerator, I lacked steering power and the back end kept fishtailing. Gravel ricocheted off the door panels like machine-gun fire.

Mike woke up. "Stop! Stop! Stop!"

"I can't. I'm sorry," I said, probably too quietly for Mike to hear.

Being at the wheel yet not in control was a feeling I'd been anticipating. Not just that morning but for the nine years since my accident near the Ottawa. The tires lifted from the ground. The world slowed. My mind revisited a former roommate talking about the night he'd fallen asleep at the wheel. His car had crashed through a barrier and rolled down a hill. The vehicle had been mangled. His rescuers had told him that being asleep had got him into trouble but had also saved him. His body hadn't tensed in response to the situation.

Stay calm, I instructed myself. *You'll be fine as long as you stay calm.*

My mind narrowed to focus on just one thing: remaining calm. And just like when running a rapid, that focus left no room for fear. As the rolling gained momentum, it became hard to tell what was up and what was down. Earth and sky swirled together. The rainstorm of shattering glass and the sharp squeals of bending metal rang in my ears. *Stay calm. You'll be fine as long as you stay calm.*

The seat belt held me tight as we spun over and over. Sharp stings of crumbled safety glass and gravel burrowed into my skin. I heard the metallic crumpling sound of the roof crushing in deeper each

48

time it hit the ground. With each crush there was less room for me. For a while I truly believed that as long as I stayed loose and calm I would be okay. Then the roof pushed down almost to the level of the steering wheel. I was pressed into my seat as far as I could go. It occurred to me that I might die if the truck didn't stop rolling soon. That thought didn't knock me out of my focus on remaining calm. But it made me think of all that I would miss. I thought of my parents and my sister and how lucky I'd been to have such a fun and caring family. I thought of my oldest friends, Karen and Liane, and the three decades worth of inside jokes we shared. I thought of paddling friends across the continent and beyond. I thought of the many rivers I'd gotten to know. I was happy to find in that moment I wasn't consumed with thoughts of what I wished I'd said or done, just of what I was sad to leave behind.

Almost as soon as that thought was complete, the revolutions slowed. The truck came to a stop on its roof. I was strapped into my seat, upside down. My hand searched for the key and turned off the ignition. Because of how the roof had folded in, I couldn't see into the passenger side or the back seat.

"Mike, Megan, are you okay?" I asked.

No one answered. My mouth went dry and my throat constricted. *You only think of yourself. Why didn't you tell Mike and Megan to stay calm? Why did you stay quiet instead of coaching them through it? Why didn't you let Mike drive?* Seconds before I'd been without regrets. Now they piled on so heavily they immobilized me. Then I pushed them aside. I had to find out if my passengers needed help. "Mike, Megan, are you okay?"

"I think I am." Mike's voice was weak and slow.

I felt an odd sensation, like my lungs had stopped exchanging air without me noticing, but the sound of Mike's voice allowed them to resume.

The smashing glass and bending metal during the rollover had sounded just like in the movies, which led me to picture how many of those movie scenes ended: the vehicle in flames.

"Find a way out of the truck," I told Mike.

49

"I don't know if I can."

"Find a way."

An older man I didn't know appeared at my window. He bent his head awkwardly to accommodate talking to me while I was inverted. He looked frightened.

"Are you okay?" he asked.

"Do you see a girl in the back seat?"

"No, there's just the two of you. Are you all right?"

Just the two of us. Megan had been asleep in the back. She hadn't been wearing a seat belt. She must have been thrown from the truck. I needed to find her. I unbuckled my own seat belt and started to wriggle around trying to get out of the tight space.

"You should stay still," the man said.

That was solid first-aid advice. I ignored it. I also ignored the throbbing in my back.

"Please help me look for Megan," I said.

If she could still be helped, I needed to find her fast.

"Stay still." The man held his palms up for emphasis. "There are only two of you."

I didn't have time to argue. The window frame had been compressed to something much smaller than its original shape. I put my arms through it, placed my hands on the grass and pulled my head and torso out. In the worst Winnie-the-Pooh moment, my butt stuck in the frame. I tightened my glutes and twisted and pulled and finally made it through, while mentally cursing the lodge chef for her never-ending supply of banana bread. The man stared down at me. He looked even more scared than before.

"I'll go find a phone to call for help," he said, his voice uncertain.

"That would be great. Thank you."

The truck and trailer resembled crushed beer cans, but no smoke came from beneath the mangled hood, nor were there any other signs the truck might burst into flames with Mike still inside. I didn't want to abandon Mike before he was out, but I decided to trust that his ability to speak—and therefore breathe—wouldn't be short-lived. I went in search of Megan.

The truck had rolled off the highway, caught air over a wooden fence and come to rest in a large grassy field. I walked quickly in the direction we had come from, scanning for a sign of Megan. I saw only the green of the field for what seemed like forever. Then finally a glimpse of orange—Megan's down jacket. I hurried closer. Megan lay on her back. Her head rested on a rock as though it were a pillow. She would have looked peaceful if not for her usually blonde hair being completely red with blood. My brain began to cloud over, wanting to switch off and not have to face the truth. *This isn't real. Megan can't be dead.* Everything in my body seemed to slow to a standstill. Like I was ready to go into hibernation. Ready to shut down and wake up months later after all this had been dealt with by someone else. But there was no one else. If Megan could still be helped, I had to do it. I ran to her and forced myself to think of Megan as a living victim, not a dead body.

"Megan!" I dropped to my knees beside her. "Megan, can you hear me?"

She moaned. My heart jumped.

"Megan, can you hear me?" I asked again.

Megan's eyes opened. She looked at me. I wouldn't have been more surprised to be spoken to by a burning bush. It was a miracle.

"Megan, do you know where you are?"

"Umm?"

After a few questions, it was clear she didn't know what had happened, but she knew her name and who I was. A quick assessment showed the bleeding from her head had stopped and no blood was seeping through her clothing from additional wounds.

Mike approached. Blood oozed from a laceration over his eyebrow, creating a thick red stripe over his eye, down his cheek and off his jawline from where it then dripped onto his shirt. Mike and Megan looked like extras in a horror flick. But they were alive.

The accident had occurred only minutes from Alexis Creek, home to the only RCMP detachment between the lodge and Williams Lake. A police officer arrived quickly. With someone else there to take charge, I allowed myself to notice the pain in my back. Even though I'd been walking around, it was still possible I had a spinal injury. In first-aid courses we're told about people walking away from accidents only to turn their head later and find themselves paralyzed.

"Lie still," I reminded Megan. "I'll do the same."

I lay down and breathed in the fresh smell of the field. Inhaling a full breath sent sharp pain through my back. I didn't care. We were all lucky to be alive, to be able to feel the sun on our faces and the itch of stiff grass on our necks.

The RCMP officer knelt beside me and asked questions about what had happened and how fast I'd been going. Then he asked, "Do you want us to contact anyone for you?"

"My boss. He'll need someone else to shop for the rafting trip."

"Anyone else? Husband? Boyfriend?"

"Just my boss. Thank you."

"Are you sure?"

The officer seemed more concerned about this than about my driving speed. It took a few tries, but I eventually convinced him only Graham needed to know immediately.

The paramedics arrived. I lay still and didn't turn my head to look at Megan. I listened to them talking to her. They wanted to cut open her jacket to remove it.

"Please don't," Megan said. "It's brand new."

I pictured her orange down-filled jacket. It was nice but not worth risking spinal health for, so it seemed like a positive indication of Megan's condition that she asked and that the paramedics obliged by carefully removing her jacket without cutting it. They explained to Megan what they were doing as they fit her with a neck brace and strapped her to a spine board. When they were done, they came over to me and slowly lifted my arms to remove my jacket. Pain ripped through my back. Every muscle in my body, including in my face, tightened in response.

"Sorry, but we're going to have to cut your jacket off."

I didn't care what they did, as long as they stopped trying to move my arms.

The paramedics strapped me to a spine board and loaded me into the ambulance. Mike, who insisted he was fine, was directed to a seat beside my gurney. A helicopter took Megan away. I'd taken it as a positive sign when the paramedics hadn't cut open her jacket, yet as the sound of spinning rotors faded into the distance, I was overcome by fear Megan would never walk again. *It's all your fault.*

As the ambulance drove down a hill, I slid forward slightly on the backboard and the pressure from the neck brace increased. The paramedic noticed me wince. "I can't give painkillers until a doctor checks your spine," she said. "But I can give you laughing gas."

"No, thanks."

"You sure? It'll make you feel better."

I'd just totalled someone else's vehicle for the second time in my life. The accident had nearly killed two co-workers. I had no idea how bad Megan's injuries were, but being medevacked was never the best sign. I wasn't in a laughing mood.

"I'm sure," I replied.

"I'll take some," Mike said.

The paramedic shook her head. Mike leaned his face down to me and whispered, "Tell her you changed your mind and hand it to me."

My eyes filled with tears that quickly flooded across my cheeks. Snot oozed from my nose. It was a stellar time to be strapped to a backboard with no way to wipe my face.

"I'm sorry," I said through the soggy mess.

"About the nitrous?" Mike asked.

"I'm sorry for what I did."

Even with his *Return of the Living Dead* look I could see the kindness in Mike's face as he said, "Hey, it was an accident, Bossypants. No one's blaming you."

He leaned closer and kissed my salty wet cheek. I cried even harder.

CHAPTER 5

Williams Lake, BC
June 2007

"So aside from the stitches, you're really okay?" I asked Megan, not quite believing I'd understood her.

The truck and trailer had spun through the air with enough height that we hadn't damaged the fence we'd passed over. Megan had woken and grabbed the front seat, but the force of the revolutions had wrenched her hands away and launched her out the window, sending her soaring through the air, then crashing into the ground, head colliding with a rock. Yet, I was the one morphined-up on a hospital bed while she stood over me—her toothy smile as sparkly as ever.

"They said I'll be sore for a few days," she answered, like it was no big deal.

This person I'd thought dead only hours before now looked ready to star in a toothpaste commercial—well, maybe after she washed the blood out of her hair. As a test to see if I was dreaming, I bit the inside of my lip. The sharpness of teeth against skin made me believe Megan really was alive and well. I wanted to jump up and hug her. Tell her how happy I was. Tell her I hoped she'd live forever. Instead I said, "I guess there's something to be said for being twenty-four and doing yoga every day."

Soon, Mike joined Megan by my bedside.

"What did the doctors say?" I asked, worried Mike was more injured than he claimed.

"I'm fine, just like I told you. They sewed me up and kicked my ass out."

I wondered if I could get myself to start believing in God. I wanted someone to thank.

Chris was driving in from the lodge to pick up Mike, Megan and perhaps me—the verdict was still out. The two of them settled in for their wait while I was wheeled around for X-rays and scans. Eventually a male doctor with wavy hair and a French-Canadian accent told me, "You have wedge fractures in four vertebrae. T3 through 6."

He explained the vertebrae had been compressed by the collapsed truck roof and were now permanently misshapen. No surgery would plump my bones back up. The only thing to do was rest and hope the soft tissue healed enough to make up for deformed bones.

"We'll keep you here for a few days to monitor you for spinal damage," he said. He added in a reassuring voice, "You walked away from the truck, you must have a strong back. You should be fine. And you didn't lose too much height."

"What?" I said, trying to lighten the mood. "I'm even shorter than I was this morning?"

He looked upset I'd asked. "Many people with the same injury never walk again."

The curtain around my bed parted and Chris came in.

"You'd better heal up soon. Who am I going to debate with on long drives?"

My brain wanted to tell Chris he need not worry, he couldn't get rid of me that easily. But my mouth didn't get the memo and blurted, "I'm sorry for fucking everything up."

"You haven't heard what's on the police report, have you?"

My stomach fluttered. Megan and Mike were okay and that was what mattered most, but the words "police report" don't generally lead to good news.

"They determined the truck pulled to the side because one of the trailer tires blew. It was just bad luck having it happen in a winding section. It could have happened to anyone. The report states it's not your fault."

Megan pulled back the curtain and looked at Chris. "Can we go to Tim Hortons?" she asked like a kid anxious to get to Disneyland. "I'm starving."

"You're going to scare the customers," I said. "Your hair's covered in blood."

"Don't care. Need food."

Once again, I felt amazed and relieved at how okay she seemed. After they left, I mentally repeated what Chris had said. *It could have happened to anyone. It could have happened to anyone.* But tires go flat before they blow. Even though it was on the trailer not the truck, I should have realized something was wrong before we started pulling to the side. Barring that, I should have been able to stay in control once the tire did blow. Tires fail all the time without resulting in demolished vehicles and injured passengers. If I hadn't been so fast to jump behind the wheel, Mike would have driven. I no longer understood why I hadn't wanted that. He surely would have done a better job and none of this would have happened.

A nurse wheeled me into a room with six beds and parked my gurney beside the only empty one. "Oh, good," she said. "You got one with a trapeze."

A metal triangle hung from the ceiling.

"You'll be able to use it to help pull yourself up to get out of bed. But not yet. The doctor says you have to stay put for a few days. I'm not even giving you slippers."

She placed a bedpan within easy reach and instructed me to use it when nature called. On many a cold rainy night camping, I'd fantasized about being able to relieve my bladder without leaving the warmth of my sleeping bag. In my hospital bed I discovered that peeing while lying in bed wasn't the treat I'd imagined it to be. The next time I needed the toilet, I ignored the doctor's orders and slowly pulled myself up with the help of the trapeze and walked barefoot to the bathroom. Once done, I was surprised to not see a sink. I wandered into the hallway and came across two teenage boys.

"Excuse me, do you know where I could find a sink?" I asked.

They looked at me and then back to each other. They fidgeted and stared at the floor like they were scared to reply. I assumed the problem was my lack of slippers. They knew I wasn't supposed to be out of my bed and didn't want to be accomplices to my crime. I continued down the hall, eventually settling for hand sanitizer.

Returning to my room, I realized the sink had been hiding in plain sight on the other side of the door. The reflection in the mirror above it shocked me. It hadn't been my bare feet that made those teens uncomfortable. After the crash, Mike and Megan had looked like horror movie extras, yet it hadn't occurred to me that I might not look my best either. In the mirror was a face swollen round like a pumpkin. Eyes surrounded by dark-purple circles. Hair teased up like a 1985 prom queen, only instead of being held in place by Dep gel and Final Net hairspray, copious amounts of dried blood did the trick.

"That's nice," I said aloud, even though no one was listening. "My giant head makes my ass look smaller."

"I'll take time off work and come out there," my sister said, when I called from the hospital.

My mom also said she'd come out.

"Thanks, but there's no reason to," I told them both. "With all the painkillers, I mostly just sleep." I didn't want them to come to some out-of-the-way town to be bored out of their minds sitting in the hospital while I slept.

I did get a few visitors when people I knew passed through town. And as word of the accident spread among my friends, phone calls became more frequent. I could see there were people who cared about me, yet when a nurse surprised me with a fresh spinach salad from the cafeteria, I choked up. It meant so much that she'd noticed and cared I wasn't eating my meals. After taking so much pride in my independence, it was difficult to admit I felt alone. The RCMP officer at the accident scene had asked multiple times if there wasn't someone other than Graham I wanted him to contact. At the time I'd found it almost funny that he'd been so convinced an adult woman should have a husband or boyfriend who needed to know where she was. I'd always been proud to surprise people by escaping those expectations. But lying in a hospital bed in a town full of strangers, my certainty in the decision to remain single began to waver and my mind had time for an extended wander.

It was no secret I'd taken advantage of being a woman in the predominantly male world of whitewater. At the end of my first season working for Graham he'd said, "I like the way you handle the guys. Sleep with them all and put them in their place." It was an exaggeration. I'd only slept with two of them and I wouldn't say I'd put anyone in their place. But it did seem that treating sex as the fun activity I saw it as—as opposed to a doorway into a commitment I wasn't looking for—made it easier for many men to relate to me as a friend. Some people thought I was too free and easy with my sex life, but it didn't matter to me what they thought. The combination of fresh air, physical activity and feeling confident in my body's strength made me horny as hell. And I enjoyed the challenge of initiating flings. It was fun to be the hunter, not the prey as women are often portrayed. I felt none of the antiquated need to protect myself from being labelled a slut.

My mind cruised back to sitting at the bar in North Creek with a couple of friends. One of them is twirling a blonde dreadlock with her finger and talking about miniature golf.

"I was going to invite you," she says, "but I realized I don't have your number."

Our male friend chimes in, "Next time, check the men's room. Tamar's number is listed on the wall under 'for a good time call.'"

My dreadlocked friend wrinkles her nose and snorts in a way she somehow makes cute. "It's funny because it's true," she says through her snorts. I laugh too. Not only do I find his comment funny, but I even feel a little proud.

From the Crik, my mind doesn't even stop back into the hospital before continuing its wander through time and space, landing at a truck stop in Utah.

Chris and I are driving a couple of company vehicles back to BC after a springtime rafting trip through Cataract Canyon. The trip was the first time we'd met, and Chris, who is both a dedicated coffee drinker and a keen observer of those around him, quickly noticed I didn't partake in his morning java ritual. However, as we start into our seventeen-hour drive I'm thoroughly hungover and sleep-deprived—farewell drinks in Moab had turned into an all-night celebration for me and a couple of the guides we'd met there—and so I treat myself to an extra-large black coffee when we stop for fuel.

"I thought you didn't like coffee," Chris says.

"I love it. I just don't let myself drink it often. It's too easy to get addicted."

Chris looks at me like I've accused him of starting his days by drinking deep-fryer oil.

"Coffee," he says, "has many health benefits."

"I'm not saying it's unhealthy. I just don't like the idea of being addicted to anything. It's too much of a commitment."

That one comment leads to years of Chris attempting to lure me into being a dedicated coffee drinker. "It's a good gateway drug for you. It could lead to you being able to handle a real relationship. Who knows, you might even decide to have kids."

"I'll stick to water, thanks."

Back in my hospital bed I thought about how other people seemed increasingly concerned with the ticking of my biological clock. Far more than I was. It wasn't that I hadn't considered that I might at some point want kids. I'd given it lots of thought. In my teens and twenties I'd assumed I'd eventually feel ready to reproduce, but as the window grew smaller I didn't feel any closer to wanting to be a mom. And with 6.6 billion people in the world and no shortage of problems from our overconsuming ways, I saw no need to produce another mouth to feed. Without the procreation factor, changing my lifestyle to settle down didn't sound like fun. In the mental novel of my life, I imagined I was still in the earlier chapters, with many exciting plot twists yet to come. A year-round job, marriage and children were all boring epilogue material. But even though singlehood felt right for me, two men in my life had been harder to walk away from than the rest. From the stark hospital room in Williams Lake, my mind eagerly wandered back to meet them again for the first time.

It's October 2000. Nighttime at the Moose River Festival, New York. Inside the pavilion, music plays, people dance and talk, and vendors show off the latest gear. I head outside to where I've stashed a few beers. It's cooler and quieter outside. The soft glow of the moon is a nice change from the pavilion's fluorescent lighting. I spot Trace, a Hudson guide, so I go over to say hi. He's surprised I haven't met his buddy Drifter before and introduces us: "Drifter's the other yurt-bag."

During the winter, Trace and Drifter live in a yurt at Jay Peak, a ski area in Vermont where Trace drives a snowcat.

"Are you a groomer too?" I ask Drifter.

"Patrol," he answers. "What do you do in the winter?"

"Still trying to figure that out."

Our conversation meanders to what sections of the Moose we'd kayaked that day. I tell him I'd kayaked the Lower with my neighbour and a group of his religious friends I'd never met before.

"Nice people, but I don't think I'd paddle with them again. They said a prayer at the put-in, which was cool, but as soon as they got on the river it was clear they weren't ready for Class IV. They dropped into holes sideways, swam all over the place and generally scared the shit out of me. My neighbour says they always paddle out of their league because they trust God will save them, and if He doesn't, they're going to a better place anyway."

"A better place," Drifter repeats. He smirks and his almond eyes turn up a bit at the edges.

I wonder if I've rambled on too long. Drifter puts an empty bottle to his mouth and spits dark liquid into it. I'm surprised to realize he dips. His beard has done a good job of hiding the lump of tobacco under his lip. It's not an attractive habit but neither is drinking to the fall-down-drunk stage, which I do more often than I should. We all have our faults.

Drifter interrupts my thoughts. "You should try a winter at Jay."

It's only a casual suggestion, one I won't follow up on. But that winter—which I spend in Quebec snowboarding, working four jobs and having a seasonal fling with a non-paddler who's still a teenager—I think about Drifter's suggestion often. I think about Drifter often. The Zen-like calm about him. How genuine he seems. His almond-shaped eyes that seem mysteriously inconsistent with his British heritage. The fact that he lives without electricity in a yurt, which tells me that not only is he self-sufficient and not a major consumer, but he also can't be wasting away his life sitting on the couch watching TV.

In the spring, Drifter starts guiding for one of the other rafting companies on the Hudson. Not long into the season we're all at our favourite roadhouse when I invite Drifter home. A co-worker is my staff-house designated driver and a group of us cram into his old minivan.

"We should all get naked," Drifter suggests.

Everyone but the DD complies. And so begins many years of friendship, paddling and random acts of nudity.

Back in the hospital I considered how I loved the river for its ability to make me focus on the present, but I also loved that it gave me so many memories to dive into. What would I have done in the hospital without them? I supposed that was what the unused TV over my bed was for.

From that first conversation with Drifter, I'd been smitten. And my instincts hadn't been wrong. He was a thoughtful friend and an excellent paddling partner. He was also fun in the sack—or on the riverbank for that matter. But I hadn't been looking for commitment. Even his using my toothbrush our first night together had made me uncomfortable. I had no issue swapping bodily fluids with him, but sharing a toothbrush felt like something people only did in a committed relationship. Of course, my own commitment fears weren't the only issue. No one gets a nickname like Drifter for being the one to insist on staying in one place with one person for an extended time. And although I did occasionally feel jealous of his relations with other women, I felt a connection with Drifter that for many years firmly withstood our habit of sleeping with other people—including each other's friends. Such behaviour wouldn't have made sense to everyone, but in those golden days of North Creek life it was the norm. Things became more confusing when Kevin entered the picture. My mind happily turned back time to meeting him.

I've just driven down to Vermont from Montreal to visit Drifter, Trace and another friend. Like many January nights in Vermont, it's Arctic-level cold and stepping into a toasty bar feels particularly inviting. The Belfry was once a church but now it feels like a ski cabin with its warm lighting, wood-plank ceiling and windows webbed with frost.

"Kevin's here," Trace says, pointing his chin across the crowded room. He leads our small crew in that direction.

The guy he speaks to has long reddish hair and huge blue eyes. He wears a flannel shirt and overalls. Even seated it's obvious he's tall and strong—not the kind of strong that comes from bench pressing but the kind that comes from a lifetime of working outside. I'm taken aback. Years earlier, as a teenager, I'd been in a small New Hampshire town when a tall redheaded teenager in overalls had walked by and triggered a thought that I don't remember ever having about a stranger before or since: *I could marry that guy one day*. I hadn't thought about that moment in years, but seeing Kevin sitting there I think, *Holy shit, that's the same guy*.

"Kevin," Drifter says, "this is Tamar."

Kevin glances at me and makes a sound that's somewhere between "Hi" and a grunt. Then he resumes talking to someone else. Our crew turns and goes to find seats at the bar.

It's not the same guy, I unconvincingly tell myself. *This is New England. There are lots of big, strong redheads who dress like*

JUNE 2007

farmhands. Not to mention you're staying at the yurt tonight— home of the hottie sitting beside you right now.

I don't see Kevin again until the spring when Trace convinces me to go to my first Dead show. I catch a ride with our mutual friend Palka, whose short hair and clean-shaven face make him look like the square amongst his hippieish buddies. Only the look in his dark eyes gives a hint that Palka is wilder than any of the others. We stop to pick up Kevin on the way. This time Kevin immediately strikes up conversation with me, and within minutes he's removing his shirt to back up his claim of having the world's ugliest tattoo: on the lower half of his back are three large skulls smoking joints, the smoke swirling all the way up to his shoulders.

"At least the quality of the artwork isn't that bad," I say.

Palka shakes his head. "C'mon, look at that big old tramp stamp. It's like a goddamn public-service announcement for why not to get tattooed when you're fifteen and drunk."

A huge gang of friends has turned up for the show, and at one point we're all trying to get from one location to another. Someone suggests holding hands so that we don't lose each other in the crowd. When we get through and everyone else lets go, Kevin keeps a firm grip on my hand.

Kevin starts commuting on weekends from Vermont to the Crik to train as a guide. One night there's a big birthday party by the lake. It's a typical North Creek bacchanalian affair. Bottles of tequila polished off. Clothes discarded. Everyone kissing everyone else. More tequila.

I wake early, curled up in the back of my hatchback, naked except for my bra. Strange, since in my last memory of the night two people were simultaneously sucking my nipples. I wonder why I'd put my bra back on. In any case, I need to get to work. Luckily, I'm not new to the Crik's party scene and I've brought extra clothes. I reach into the front seat for my backup wardrobe and am surprised to find Kevin's dog asleep on the seat. *Well, this is something new. You've never woken up naked with a dog before.* I notice Kevin's hat and T-shirt on the floor, so I'm guessing the dog

63

didn't show up on his own. I should probably find Kevin and give him his stuff back, but I don't know where he is and I'm scheduled as the only guide on an overnight trip I have yet to start preparing for. I scratch the dog between the ears, then scoot him out the door and drive away.

A few hours later, I'm at the Hudson put-in, hungover as a teenager the morning after prom, reeking of tequila and not yet realizing that I've accidentally packed multiple coffee pots of different sizes but nothing to cook in.

"Where'd you sleep last night?" one friend asks with a smirk.

"You must be feeling great," another says.

My guests are a nice suburban family, which makes me really wish my friends would all just shut up. Then I see Kevin. I'm embarrassed because:

A) I don't remember what happened when the evidence is strong that something did.

B) I probably initiated it so I really should remember, but I have a bad habit of blacking out when I drink, especially when tequila is involved.

C) Even though I've been trying not to, I've somehow developed a huge crush on this very good friend of Drifter's.

I feel like an asshole, but I also feel like I need to get my guests away from anyone talking about last night.

"Hey," Kevin says in his super-deep sexy voice.

"Your shit's in my car," I say. Then I turn away to lead my guests down to the river.

Back in the Williams Lake hospital I smiled at the memory. "Your shit's in my car" was still a line Kevin teased me about. The beginning of our relationship would never inspire a great romance novel, but the memory still made me all giddy.

I was often confused by my strong feelings for both Drifter and Kevin. I liked being single, yet I occasionally had thoughts of a future with each of them that sometimes even included children. It confused me even further that it wasn't just one man I felt that way toward, but two, and they happened to be good friends. Luckily, the itinerant seasonal lifestyle was on my side. Whenever I leaned toward becoming too attached, I conveniently had to move across the continent.

My relationships with Drifter and Kevin were similar in many ways. We enjoyed river running, road tripping, whiskey drinking and dancing naked around campfires. I respected them both for never shying away from physical labour. I was amazed by their array of practical skills, and turned on by the feel of their rough, workingman's hands. My relationships with the two of them had differences as well. There were times Kevin made me feel like he understood me in a way no one else did. Like the frosty November day he, Drifter, Trace and I were working together at Drifter and Trace's Christmas tree farm near Glover, Vermont.

The guys are all dressed in the business suit of northern Vermont: Carhartt pants and jackets, plaid flannel shirts and bright-orange chainsaw chaps and helmets. I wonder at what point in this Montreal girl's life men in chainsaw wear became super hot to me. In any case, we're taking turns with different jobs and currently Kevin is cutting down trees. Drifter is running them through the baler, the machine that ties down the branches for easier transportation. I'm standing atop the pile of tied trees on the flatbed while Trace hands more up to me to position on the load. When we get all the trees they've tagged for this area, Trace climbs into the truck to move us to the next zone. I stay on top of the trees, looking down at Drifter and Kevin as the truck drives slowly through rows of small conifers. The balsam firs smell sweet like cotton candy, which may be what influences my thoughts. I picture myself as a parade queen on a tree-themed float. I giggle at the image.

Kevin looks up at me and says, "Wave to the crowd. You look like the Glover Parade Queen riding your float."

Another time I feel Kevin gets me is at a house in Maine. A whole crew of us is staying there while paddling rivers in the area. I'm climbing the stairs when I pass a square hole cut out of the wall. I have no idea what it's there for, but it looks into the kitchen where Kevin and several other friends are hanging out. I drop my pants and stick my bare ass through the hole—imagining that on the other side it will have a similar effect to the dead animal heads people mount on walls. My butt goes unnoticed for a few moments. Then the chatter stops.

"She's mooning us!" one friend says.

I hear Kevin's chuckle. Then his deep voice: "Looks like someone's been trophy hunting women's asses."

Spending time with Kevin was exciting. I never knew when he might show up, but that also meant that when he told me he'd be somewhere he often wasn't. Also, Kevin and I fought. Not small tiffs. Big blowout screaming fights like trashy reality-TV couples. Accusations of trying to make the other jealous were often thrown around.

On the other hand, Drifter was dependable and he and I never once raised our voices at one another. The two times I could remember being upset with him had been trivial. Once I'd loaned him my new kayak while I was guiding the Hudson. After I'd finished my workday, I'd heard through the grapevine that he and Conway planned to run another creek that evening. They hadn't invited me. When I'd knocked on Drifter's door all pissed off, he'd asked, "Are you really mad at me?"

"I can't believe you're taking my boat but not me."

"You don't have to get mad. Just come with us. I'll use my own boat."

And that was it. Problem solved. The other time had also been a case of me overreacting, although Drifter hadn't said that. When he'd realized how upset I was, he'd wrapped his arms around me. It was on a Grand Canyon trip, and for a moment the only noise had been the scratchy sound of our Gore-Tex dry suits rubbing together and the hum of water flowing by. Then he'd said, "You know you mean the world to me."

Drifter made me laugh with impressions of our friends that

hit on their funniest mannerisms without being mean. He acted respectfully toward others even if they were jerks. And whatever was going on in our lives, I knew if I needed him, he would be there. I was confident he knew that went both ways. I could talk to Drifter about anything. Except how I felt about him. The day he'd said I meant the world to him, all I'd responded with was, "There's room for you in my tent, if you want."

I loved both those men. But more than ever before as I lay in the hospital, Drifter's dependability seemed like a crucial trait.

The RCMP officer's words looped through my mind: "Are you sure there's no one you want me to contact? Husband? Boyfriend?"

With each pass of that loop, an idea forming inside me gained substance: it was time to tell Drifter how I felt. There was, however, the issue of his girlfriend, Sage. Drifter had introduced us a few months earlier, on our fourth paddling trip together through the Grand Canyon. Despite my initial wariness, I'd really enjoyed getting to know Sage. She was intelligent and lots of fun and had great stories from her world travels. I totally understood Drifter's attraction to her. The thing was, Drifter and I had both dated people we were well suited to before. And still we circled back to each other. I recalled an evening in North Creek shortly before I left to guide out west for the first time.

I'm on the front porch of the bar being quizzed by a friend about the girl Drifter's been hanging out with. "Palka says she's Drifter's girlfriend, but does Drifter think that too?" my friend asks.

I don't know the answer, so I shrug and take a sip of beer. This maybe-girlfriend is a very young, very cute, very in-the-know-about-all-the-jam-bands-Drifter-listens-to girl he's been hanging out with. She seems perfect for him. So I kind of hate her.

"Why don't you just ask Drifter what the deal is?" my friend presses.

"What's the difference? I'm leaving soon anyway." I try to take another sip from my glass, but it's empty. "I'm going to get another."

It's Friday night and crowded inside. I take a few steps toward the bar, but suddenly Drifter is standing in front of me. "Don't go," he says.

I'm confused. I just walked into the bar, not out. And when did I ever leave early? He's looking at me intently. I want to tell him how much I'll miss him, but instead I say: "Just going for a refill." Then I add, "Wanna do a shot?"

"Don't go out west." He says it calmly, but I feel like I've unexpectedly intercepted a fifty-pound medicine ball with my stomach.

As much as I enjoy the company of men, until meeting Drifter I'd never been able to picture a future with any of them—or at least a future that doesn't involve drunken brawls and screaming children. But with Drifter I sometimes picture us years from now, going on family canoe trips, teaching kids to make wreaths at his Christmas tree stand, growing old and still wanting to hold one another. Despite these feelings, when I realize what he is asking of me, these words rush out: "I need to. It's a once-in-a-lifetime opportunity. Wouldn't you go if you were me?"

His intensity drains. "Yeah, I guess so."

A few nights later a group of us are out at a different bar to see a local band. It's the last time I'll see Drifter before I leave. The band finishes and Drifter comes over to me: "What time do you start work in the morning?"

"7:30."

"So, if I set my alarm for 6:30, you should be okay?"

It's a pretty forward question, considering he's supposedly seeing that other girl and what little conversation we've had hasn't even hinted at our spending the night together.

"6:30 is perfect," I answer.

Like many old Adirondack houses, the place Drifter lives in with Palka and Trace was built before the widespread use of indoor plumbing. When bathrooms were eventually added to these homes, the lack of good insulation meant the easiest way to prevent frozen pipes was to build the bathroom near the middle of the house—so we need to walk through the bathroom to get to Drifter's bedroom. Even passing through a bathroom shared by three male river

68

rats doesn't dampen our enthusiasm. The door to his tiny room is barely closed and already we've managed to manoeuvre most of each other's clothes off. It feels like we've just found each other for the first time, not like we're headed for an indefinite goodbye. At the end, I hold him tightly as I shudder and keep on holding for a while afterward.

Eventually we readjust, trying to get comfortable in his single bed. My mind tries to record the warmth of his skin on mine and the weight of his arm across my chest. And then I pretend to sleep, not wanting to risk saying words that sometimes want to come out at times like this. At 6:30 a.m., the alarm goes off. We don't have much time, and someone is using the bathroom outside. We try to be quick and quiet, but the bedsprings are loud. We hear Palka chuckle as he pees. When we're done, Drifter looks into my eyes.

"Thank you for your hospitality," I say with a grin.

"That should hold you over till you get to BC," he says in return.

We get dressed and wait for Palka to finish up in the bathroom so that we can leave. Outside, we hug and say goodbye. I'm still leaving with no plan to return, but somehow it feels like we've folded down the corner on this page so that down the road we'll be able to easily find our way back here again.

In the Williams Lake hospital my mind nestled me back into Drifter's arms. I felt their strength and inhaled his scent: a blend of chainsaw fuel, balsam fir and the natural odour of his skin, which somehow always smelled sweet to me, even when he hadn't showered in over a week. I needed to call Drifter and finally tell him I loved him. But all that reminiscing had made me tired, so first I just needed to shut my eyes for a little while. And then maybe take another day or two to psych myself up for the task.

CHAPTER 6

Williams Lake, BC
June 2007

"Call for you." The nurse's words woke me. I groggily took the phone from her hand. "Hello?"

"We got her!" I heard my friend Lori say to someone else. Then she turned her attention to me. "Oh, honey, I'm so happy to hear your cute little Canadian accent. You had us all scared back in the Crik. I told you, you shouldn't leave."

Lori was a raft guide who'd been born and bred alongside the Hudson River. That spring I'd paid her and two other friends a few bucks' rent to sleep on a worn-out sofa bed on their porch in North Creek. Lori was a tough Adirondacker who could spend all day splitting firewood and afterward, instead of passing out on the couch, she'd bake up a batch of homemade pizzas and throw a dinner party. Her voice carried the richness of the Adirondack woods. It transported me from the hospital to the Hudson River surrounded by people I loved. Of course, being Lori she'd gathered a few of those friends to talk to me on the phone. After speaking to me for a few minutes, she passed me on to our friend Josh, who eventually passed me to Dorrie, who then passed me to Palka. The warm joy of friendship wrapped itself around me like a cocoon.

"Hey Tamars." Palka had a habit of adding *s*'s onto nouns for no apparent reason. A habit I, and many of his friends, found inexplicably endearing.

"Hey, Palkas, how's things at the shop?" I asked.

"Have you heard about Drifter?"

My already-tight muscles tightened even more. Palka was often the one to tell people news no one else was brave enough to bring up.

"What happened?"

"He knocked up his girlfriend." Then, in case I somehow hadn't understood, he added: "Drifter and Sage are having a kid."

After seven years of starts and stops, my relationship with Drifter was truly over. *He's better off without you. I bet Sage has never come close to killing anyone.*

A nurse arrived rolling the trolley filled with all the gizmos to check my vitals. She gave me a little plastic cup of pills and a glass of water. I was happy to know I'd soon be fast asleep.

A few days into my hospital stay I finally convinced a nurse I was strong enough to shower and wash away my crusty helmet of hair. She gave me my very own pair of paper slippers for the walk to the shower room. I felt like Cinderella ready for my big transformation.

Walking to the far end of the corridor tired me out enough that I wanted to lie on the shower floor and nap upon arrival, but once the nurse left I turned the faucet handle until I was under a stream of water so hot I could barely stand still below it. The near-scalding water streamed down my body, stripping away the physical mementos carried since the accident. Grass, dirt, gravel, glass and chunks of hair swirled around my feet in the dark reddish-brown water— like a river in flood showing off how its liquid strength overpowered solid debris.

Once the water ran clear, I turned the shower off and sat on the foldout seat. I was shrouded in steam and cleansed of the physical remnants of the accident, but that hot water had done nothing to wash away the image of Megan lying on the rock with her eyes closed and her hair covered in blood. Why had I taken on the responsibility of driving people if I couldn't protect them when things went wrong? Why had I built a career—a life—on doing things that pushed the limits of my capabilities?

Graham was already in the hospital solarium when I walked in. As usual, he reached his arms out like he was going to hug someone his own size while I hugged him around the waist.

"Can you tell I'm even shorter now?" I asked.

We talked about the lodge and my co-workers and the insurance claim on the truck.

"I'm sorry." I'd already said it to him on the phone, but that feeling hadn't changed.

Graham asked how I was feeling and about my hospital stay and then, finally, about the accident. "Did you keep your foot on the gas?"

My face heated up. I shook my head. "I needed to slow down." I forced myself to keep looking him in the eye, even though I wanted to stare at my paper slippers.

"You should have kept your foot on the gas and steered out of it." He demonstrated turning an imaginary steering wheel while pushing forward with his sizable right foot. He didn't say it like he was angry, more like advice in case the same thing should happen again. His words still hit hard. After my experience on the Ottawa, I should have known better. People say your first accident makes you a better driver. But how many good drivers flip two vehicles?

"We're lucky it was you driving. If it had been someone tall, they probably wouldn't have survived."

I assumed he said that to make me feel better. I didn't believe him, but it did make me feel better to know he cared enough to make that shit up.

"Are you planning on going to Whistler when you leave here?" he asked.

"I guess."

"You should come back to the lodge. I'll figure out some way to make you useful. It would be a good place for you to heal."

"Really?"

I tried to sound grateful without going overboard, but I couldn't have been happier if legendary paddler Bill Mason had risen from the dead and asked me to go on a canoe trip with him. It wasn't just having somewhere to go—I was welcome at my sister's house in Whistler or at my parents' apartment in Montreal or even on Lori's porch in North Creek—Graham's invitation meant he thought I was still worth having around. When I'd first come to work for Graham, he had believed I could guide rivers that most people in the industry would never have given a small woman a chance on. He had been right to believe in me then. I wanted to believe he would be right about this as well. That I wasn't a lost cause.

"Maybe that guy in the Lake Louise parking lot was wrong after all," I said to Graham. "You're not really that much of an asshole."

After five days with no signs of numbness, Dr. Briggs, a thin, pale, serious-looking man, decided it was time to free up my hospital bed. I wasn't yet strong enough to travel, so he arranged for me to stay at the hostel next door, which was set up for visitors of out-of-town patients. I walked every day—a little longer each time. I stopped taking the oxycodone prescribed to me, so I ached more and barely slept but my mind felt clearer. And I thought a lot about Drifter and Sage. That pain hadn't decreased either, but I wanted to call him. There was something I needed to say. Finally I got up the courage. I lay down in the sun outside the hostel and pulled out my phone. Sharp, dry grass poked at my bare arms.

"Ya Mar," he answered, using a nickname derived from a Phish song. "I heard about your accident. Sorry. I'm a jerk for not calling."

I hadn't even considered that, but he was right. He should have called.

"No worries. I hear you have a lot going on. Congratulations!"

"Thanks." He sounded more worried than excited. "I'm still trying to wrap my head around it."

"Well, I assume you've still got a few months?"

"We aren't prepared for a kid."

"If everyone waited till they were ready," I said, "humans would be an endangered species. You and Sage will make it work. And you know you'll love being a dad."

I'd often watched Drifter interact with kids at his Christmas tree stand. He'd had so much fun that when I'd imagined having kids with him it was so I could share in that joy. I had no doubt Drifter would be a fantastic father. My certainty of that had given me the strength to dial his number.

"Thanks," he said. "I appreciate that." He sounded like he meant it.

I finished the call confident that Drifter would be happy, and as someone who cared about him, that would make me happy. Even if it took a long time to stop feeling the accompanying pain.

After a week at the hostel, I went for an appointment with Dr. Briggs in his office.

"What are you going to do for work?" he asked.

"What do you mean?"

"Well, you won't be able to work as a raft guide ever again."

I felt a giant wave slam me down against a rocky riverbed.

"McDonald's is hiring," the doctor added.

I was used to people thinking raft guiding required no more skill than loading people onto an amusement park ride. I was fine with people saying how nice it must be to have a job with no responsibilities. I didn't expect anyone else to see my job as an achievement. But still, having the doctor imply I only had enough skills to work at a place known for giving inexperienced teens their first job made me want to tell him to fuck himself. Instead I said, "Maybe I can become prime minister. It doesn't require sitting at a desk all day or heavy lifting."

The doctor handed me a business card. "A friend of mine. He might be able to help."

The card was for a lawyer. Dr. Briggs read the confusion on my face.

"Perhaps your boss shouldn't have made you drive with faulty tires."

What I wanted from Graham was nothing a lawyer could help me with. I wanted him to believe what so many other people said:

that the accident wasn't my fault. If he believed that, maybe I could too. Then perhaps I would think it was okay that I was already dreaming of taking responsibility for people's lives again and getting back on the river.

CHAPTER 7

Chilko Lake Lodge, BC
July 2007

Megan insisted on carrying my bag from the lodge airstrip to the staff cabin. Seeing her so healthy gave me a rush similar to running a river.

I helped at the lodge as much as I could: peeling vegetables, answering phones and taking on any other tasks that required neither strength nor sitting. I also spent hours walking with Koots, Graham's black Lab cross who had a dignified greying muzzle and a tail like a whip when he was happy.

One afternoon I lay on my back on a banquette in the empty dining room, looking through the windows at the intense turquoise of Chilko Lake. I'd been helping Graham in the office, but I'd maxed out my sitting and standing tolerance. Graham passed through the dining room and stopped to scrutinize me for a moment.

"You know, you should become a prostitute so you can earn a living while lying on your back all day."

"Yeah, I'll keep that in mind. Thanks for the advice."

"I'm always thinking."

Graham laughed and I joined him. I didn't find it particularly funny, but I liked that Graham still seemed to enjoy having me around, even if it was to act as fodder for his punchlines. Besides, I had my own plan that didn't involve being horizontal: early each morning before the wind began to blow, I'd carefully pull one of the kayaks across the sand to the water. It hurt, but I paddled every day. I was determined to rebuild the strength needed to row a raft, because even though the idea of rowing guests through Lava Canyon terrified me, the one thing that scared me even more was the idea of never doing that again.

A month after I flew into the lodge, Graham said I could use one of his vehicles for a doctor's appointment in the Puddle. I hadn't driven since the accident and was far from excited about the prospect.

"Just remember it's a truck, not a raft; it's not made to bounce off obstacles," Graham said.

I drove even slower than usual. I shifted around trying to get less uncomfortable, but the muscles in my back grew tighter by the kilometre. As I approached the area where I'd rolled the vehicle, my back grew tighter still. I held my breath rounding the corners. I had to pull over in Alexis Creek to unhook my bra. My trapezius muscles had formed a knot so large it was stretching the bra straps to capacity, forcing them to cut into my skin. The straps had drawn blood. Still two hours to go.

The good news was that when I asked Dr. Briggs about higher-impact activities, he said, "Try anything you like. You may find it too painful and have to stop, but you don't need to worry about making your injuries worse." The bad news appeared in his next sentence: "You're done healing."

I assumed I'd misunderstood. It had been only five weeks since the accident. I'd broken an ankle and wrist in the past, and both of those less-serious injuries had taken more than five weeks to fully heal. I still wasn't strong enough to lift the glass water jugs at the lodge. My mid-back was so sensitive it hurt to inhale all the way. In an amazing example of the body's ability to protect itself, I couldn't even sneeze.

"There must be room for improvement," I said. "Shouldn't I go to physio or something?"

"Physio won't do anything for you."

"It helped a lot with other injuries I've had."

The doctor sighed and realigned the papers on his desk. "Fracturing four vertebrae is different from breaking a wrist. But I'll write a referral for a local physiotherapist if that's what you would like."

I didn't want a referral to a physiotherapist he didn't believe in, in a town I didn't live in. I wanted hope. I left his office with neither.

Outside, with the warmth of summer on my face, my tears flowed like a glacier melting in the sun. I cried as I walked past strangers on the street. I cried as I fiddled around under the truck's hood, trying to get the battery to reattach properly so that I could leave town. I cried as I unlatched my bra in preparation for my tense muscles. I cried sporadically as I drove the four hours, picturing flipping over at every bend in the road. But I forced myself to stop crying before I got back to the lodge. I needed to look strong. That facade was all I was sure I had left.

Before my appointment, I'd picked up the milk Graham had asked for. I'd carefully placed it in the cart and wheeled it to the truck. But back at the lodge, I forced myself to pick up two jugs and attempted to carry them inside. Graham hurried out, reaching his hands toward the milk. "Don't strain yourself."

"It doesn't matter. This is as good as I'm going to get. The doctor said so."

My back screamed in protest, but I hung onto the jugs and kept going toward the kitchen door, which suddenly seemed impossibly far away. Graham blocked my route. Koots the dog tilted his head like he was trying to figure out what was happening.

"Give me the jugs, T-mar."

"Dr. Briggs said all my healing is done. I can't make myself any worse."

"Don't believe that bullshit."

"He's a doctor."

"Look, I know that's not what you wanted to hear, so if you need to take a few days to feel sorry for yourself, have at it, but don't hurt yourself in the meantime."

I nearly argued, but I wanted him to be right. Besides, I was pretty sure I couldn't carry the milk more than a few steps farther. I let Graham take the jugs.

Koots sprawled out on my saggy queen-sized mattress. I lay on the more back-friendly floor, alternating between trying to learn to play the harmonica that Soren, one of the guides, had given me and trying to picture life minus the river. Neither was going well.

Koots stayed by me for my day-and-a-half self-pity fest. He seemed prepared to continue, but there were only so many times I could butcher "Blowing in the Wind" on the harmonica. Morning paddles were back on the menu. I helped as much as I could in the kitchen and office. I tried running, but pain shot up my spine, so I put that on hold. On walks with Koots I memorized details of wildflowers and looked them up later in my field guide, which was too heavy for me to carry along. One morning while trying to recall the difference between asters and fleabanes, I wondered if I would have found it easier to retain which petal pattern belonged to which flower the previous summer. Since the accident there were lots of things I found difficult to remember. I often forgot words mid-sentence. A day earlier while Mike was talking, I'd stopped paying attention to his words when I became preoccupied with the fact that I couldn't remember his name. It hadn't been an isolated incident.

I put my face closer to the purple daisy-like flower and tried to picture images in the book. "Fleabane. Definitely. I think. What do you think, Koots?"

Upon hearing his name, Koots wagged his tail.

"I knew you'd agree."

Charlotte, one of the lodge staff, caught up to us. She pulled her giant over-the-ear headphones down to her neck so that we could talk.

Charlotte had been experiencing back pain intermittently for a few years, and in the previous week her back had started spasming badly again.

"How's your back today?" I asked her.

"Oh, you know. How's yours?"

"Getting better, maybe? But I keep having dreams about piggy-backing a grand piano."

"Back pain sucks," she said, still smiling like she usually did.

"Yeah, it does."

We laughed for a moment, just because.

"But really," I said. "I'm just lucky to be alive."

Charlotte probably agreed; however, I didn't register anything she might have said. I was distracted by a sudden thought: *But everything would be so much easier if you had died.*

Like the ominous feeling before the accident, this new thought hit with an almost physical force. I didn't understand why I would think that way. Weren't near-death experiences supposed to wake us up to the fragility of life and make us want to experience everything we could?

Graham kept telling me to invoice him for the days I worked before the accident. I didn't want to. I was far more indebted to him than he was to me. Some of the things I felt I owed him for had a numerical value: the replacement truck and trailer, Megan's airlift bill, my meals at the lodge. But there were also two important things that didn't have a price tag: making me feel valued by inviting me back to the lodge and, of course, giving me so many years of unwavering encouragement and friendship. For some reason I couldn't bring myself to tell him how I felt, so I put it off, hoping the topic would fade away. But he kept asking. After being told enough times, I finally invoiced him. I soon wished I'd forced myself to explain why I hadn't wanted to. He didn't pay the invoice. Instead, it lingered on his desk like a symbol of my ingratitude. It may as well have been a memo saying, "All that you've done for me isn't enough."

Despite everything, Drifter's voice made my stomach flutter. "Back healing up well?" he asked.

I weighed his question as I watched horses nibbling grass outside the lodge window. I was standing, not lying on the floor in pain, so it seemed safe to say, "I'm getting better."

"This feels like an awkward time to ask, but I'm making tree-season plans. Will you come back?"

I'd been thinking a lot about Drifter and Trace's Christmas tree operation, which had been my fall employment for the past few years.

"I don't think I can this year," I said. I hoped he didn't hear the catch in my throat.

"Not harvesting at the farm," Drifter said. "Just making wreaths at the yurt and selling and decorating at the stand? You won't even have to load trees onto the customers' roofs."

Making wreaths had never before seemed physically demanding. Now just thinking of lifting piles of boughs and clipping them into usable sizes made my back muscles tense up. "I want to, but I don't think I can. Besides, the stand is probably better off without me. Like Palka said: a Jew at a tree stand isn't all that Christmassy." I was trying to make light of the situation, but I could almost hear the click as one more door in my life closed.

I stayed at the lodge until August. I was amazed by how much Graham continued to make me feel welcome. He even invited my parents and sister to stay for free. I'd taken my family rafting in the Adirondacks, but they'd only had a few glimpses into my river life. It meant a lot to have them at the lodge even if I wasn't guiding. I wasn't able to do much with them, but one of the guides took them for a float down the upper part of the river, and my dad came out for a morning paddle with me, and we all went for walks together with Koots.

On their last night at the lodge, I was particularly achy, so they came to hang out with me in my room. Nikki poked her head in to say hi. Within minutes, she was seated on the floor fingerpicking her guitar and singing. Soren heard the guitar and came in to jam along with his harmonica. Koots thumped his tail like he was on percussion. I couldn't share the river with my family this time, but it felt good to share a moment of the river life.

CHAPTER 8

Whistler, BC
September 2007

"You're progressing. I can tell you actually do your exercises at home," the physiotherapist said.

I didn't know why anyone in my situation wouldn't do the exercises, but I appreciated her encouragement and was thankful the workers' compensation board (WCB) was paying for me to see her three times a week.

My sister, Mara, had invited me to stay with her in Whistler. Mara is only two and a half years older than me but infinitely wiser and more grounded. She'd recently bought a small townhouse through Whistler's affordable housing program. She'd been on the waiting list for years. I couldn't imagine buying a house, never mind having thought about it a decade earlier. It's true I'd spent seven years on the waiting list for a permit to paddle the Grand Canyon. But the Canyon was three weeks of fun, not a long-term financial commitment. Despite our differences, Mara and I got along well. We looked a fair bit alike too: short stature with near-black hair and a Jewish nose. But Mara was thinner, better dressed and better looking.

Mara had recommended this physio, and I liked her. Aside from giving me lots of exercises, the physio was a real force of positive energy. My improvements felt slow, but any improvement was better than what Dr. Briggs had forecast, so I figured what I was experiencing was the most I could hope for. Then Erin—my WCB case manager—told me about a ten-week intensive occupational rehab program at the Whistler rec centre, where a team of occupational therapists and physical trainers helped WCB clients get in return-to-work shape.

"Sounds better than winning the lottery," I said.

"Don't get too excited," Erin warned. "Your physio isn't sure you're ready for it. But I can arrange for you to get tested and see what the people in the program decide."

It was discouraging to hear the ultra-optimistic physio doubted my ability. But her positivity had been centred on how hard I tried. An "A" for effort only gets a person so far.

"I would really, really like to try," I told Erin.

"Okay, I just need to ask: Are you experiencing any negative emotional repercussions from the accident, like anxiety, depression or guilt?"

The question caught me off guard. I'd never spoken to Erin about my mental state and I was concerned about how any deficiencies in that area might affect this opportunity, but I'd always been honest with her and I didn't want to change that. I closed my eyes and took a deep breath. "Yes."

"Oh," she said, with a slight change in her voice. "You never told me that before."

I stayed quiet, scared the program accepted only those who were mentally tough enough.

"Do you have nightmares?" Erin sounded like she was reading from a list.

"Yes," I answered.

"Fears while driving?"

"Yes."

"Feelings of hopelessness?"

"Yes."

After each answer, I heard Erin's fingers tapping on her keyboard—more than three letters each time. I wondered what she was writing in my file.

"Hmm," she said.

I held my breath.

"Sounds like you could benefit from the full-day program that has counselling as well."

Relief lifted me sky-high.

"The program is in Vancouver."

My mind fell from the fluffy cloud it had briefly floated upon. Vancouver was two hours away. At my healthiest, doing that drive twice a day for ten weeks would suck. But at the speeds I was driving, the commute wouldn't even be possible and my back would never tolerate that much sitting. The only alternative I could see to driving would be to stay in Vancouver, and I couldn't afford to rent a place in such an expensive city.

Erin read my silence. "WCB will put you up in a hotel Monday to Friday and pay for your transportation and a per diem for your meals."

It sounded too good to be true. Maybe it was. Erin had said she wasn't sure I'd get in. This program I hadn't even known about half an hour earlier now felt like my one big chance to get my life back on track. I just needed to figure out how to convince the rehab people I was strong enough to join.

CHAPTER 9

Vancouver, BC
September 2007

Wayne and Mathieu, the occupational therapist and the kinesiologist, asked lots of questions about my injury and the types of movement needed for my job. Then they led me into a large open fitness room with stark white walls and fluorescent lighting. About a dozen people were spread across the room. Some trained on gym equipment. A few stretched on mats. Others simply hung around chatting. It was like a commercial gym except most of the clients wore old T-shirts and shorts instead of brand-name spandex. Mathieu went off to work with someone else while Wayne led me to a corner with a few empty milk crates and a shelf of beanbags arranged by weight.

"Do this ten times."

Wayne lifted a crate straight out in front of himself so that his arms were parallel to the floor. "Start with an empty crate, and we'll see how much weight we can add. Stop if it hurts."

An empty milk crate couldn't weigh more than two or three pounds. It frustrated me that lifting it caused so much pain. Maybe I really wasn't ready. Although maybe what I'd said to Drifter applied here too: if we always waited until we were ready, a lot of good things would never happen. I smiled at Wayne to hide the pain and lifted the crate a second time and then a third. I managed four lifts before my fake smile lost its fight to the grimace waiting to take over. I tried for a fifth lift but Wayne took the crate.

"Stop if it hurts," he reminded me.

Wayne demonstrated lifting to the side. Once again I didn't get halfway to ten before Wayne took the crate away. We continued through a whole series. Wayne never added any weighted bean-bags. I never made it to ten.

Wayne scribbled some notes and then looked at me. "The team will go over your results later to decide if you're an appropriate candidate. Can you come back tomorrow morning at nine?"

"I can probably squeeze that into my busy schedule," I said, while thinking how kind it was of him to pretend I still had a chance of getting into the program.

I'd expected a clean-but-bland hotel room, tucked away on a side-street. And so, I'd been surprised to check into a suite with floor-to-ceiling windows and a view of downtown. Looking at all those other buildings with floor-to-ceiling windows made me feel like a tiny fish in a giant glass reef. I often found anonymity liberating—we all carry baggage, yet somehow the contents can feel lighter when no one around knows what's inside—however, that day I didn't feel like going out and taking advantage of that freedom. I wanted so badly to be accepted into the program, but I was still so weak it seemed hopeless. What if Dr. Briggs was right? What if I never recovered? I lay on the bed watching the glass reef reflect changes of light as afternoon melted into evening, then night, and finally to morning.

With the bags under my eyes refusing to keep the secret of my sleepless night, I stood in the waiting room flipping the pages of a magazine without absorbing words or pictures. Wayne and Mathieu came through the door. After polite greetings, Wayne sucked in his lower lip and nodded slightly. He looked me in the eye and for a long moment said nothing, like he was giving me time to prepare for bad news. Finally he spoke: "The team discussed it, and unfortunately we don't think you're right for the program."

I'd spent all night trying to ready myself for that verdict, but hearing the words still made me feel a bit like that day one of my rafting guests had lost control of his paddle's T-grip and slammed me in the mouth with it. "Oh. Okay. Will I be able to try again if I get stronger?"

They both looked at me silently for another moment, and then Mathieu laughed.

"He's playing with you," Mathieu said.

"Most of our clients don't even want to be here," Wayne explained. "They come because they have to or they won't get their WCB cheques. You're so enthusiastic, you'll do great."

It took a moment to process what they were saying. "You jerks!" I said. The muscle movement in my face felt unfamiliar. I'd almost forgotten what it was like to smile that wide. I was on my way back to the river.

The word *multifidus* meant nothing to me before meeting Mathieu, but by the end of the first day in rehab it was embedded in my daily jargon. Mathieu pressed two fingers to my middle back while patiently explaining how to activate the multifidus muscle, which helped control my spine.

"Are you sure everyone can do this?" I asked. "Or is it one of those weird things that only some people can do, like wiggling your ears?" Concentrating on finding a muscle I'd spent my life unaware of felt like trying to bend a spoon with my mind.

"Keep trying," he said. "You'll get it."

I kept at it for several days, each day doubting more that I'd ever figure it out. Then it happened. I didn't even know what I'd done differently, but after thirty-four years of my conscious mind and my multifidus muscle living under the same roof without speaking, they suddenly became chatty pals, allowing me to contract my multifidus at will. The motion was so subtle that someone looking at my back wouldn't have been able to see it. Yet, that tiny movement repeated multiple times a day created huge results. For the first time since the accident, it was possible to sit for more than a couple of minutes without excruciating pain.

"You're a miracle worker," I told Mathieu.

"You're the one doing all the work."

"I was working hard before this; it's you that's making all the difference."

The rehab group was so supportive that they reminded me of the Adirondack paddling community. It took almost no time to feel like part of the club: laughing, telling stories, getting to know people's quirks and finding out the answer to every rehabber's favourite question, "What are you in for?"

My initial assessment with Bruce, the mental health counsellor, took place at the end of the first week. Bruce led the daily walks I'd gone on all week. He told lots of jokes and funny stories. He was easy to like. I walked into his office confident he would do for my mind what Mathieu was doing for my back. Bruce handed me a questionnaire and told me to take as much time as I needed. I carefully read each question and considered the multiple-choice answers.

Bruce tallied my score. Fluorescent lights hummed overhead and reflected off his shiny bald head. Beneath his moustache, his usual smile faded.

"I wasn't expecting this," he said, looking me in the eye. "According to your answers, you're suffering from major depression."

I was taken aback by his words. I'd been so wrapped up in post-accident feelings of guilt, shame and fear, the word *depression* hadn't even crossed my mind. I had no right to be depressed. I was lucky not to have killed anyone. Lucky to be alive and mobile.

Although those ideas rang true, I knew depression didn't always show up where it made sense. I also knew the reason Bruce's words hit so hard was because they were true. I reminded myself that Bruce was part of my rehab team and, just like Mathieu and Wayne had done, he'd create a plan for me and I would follow it and get better. I took a deep breath to prepare myself for the work that lay ahead. "Okay. What do I do to change that?"

Bruce pushed his palms into his desk while keeping eye contact with me. "Unfortunately, because of your score WCB won't allow me to work with you."

"But that's why they sent me here instead of keeping me in Whistler."

Bruce smiled gently. He looked apologetic. "I'm only certified as a counsellor, so WCB doesn't deem me qualified enough to deal with major depression. But don't worry. I'll set up an appointment for you to meet with Derrick, the psychologist in the pain management program."

The pain management program shared our classroom space but hardly anyone in their program was able to work out in the gym. Because of that, my first thought was that Bruce was writing me off as part of the hopeless group. I quickly realized that was a sweeping generalization of people I knew next to nothing about, and being offered more highly qualified psychological counselling was something I should consider a bonus—like an unexpected seat upgrade on an airplane.

"Well," I said to Bruce. "WCB clearly doesn't know you well, because there's nothing about you that falls into the category of 'only.'"

At the entrance to the gym was a bookcase filled with binders, each with the first name of a program participant printed on the spine. The pages inside mine had stick men Mathieu had drawn to illustrate the exercise plan he'd devised for me. There were also little boxes in which I recorded repetitions and weights. Each number stood as visual proof that I was one step closer to my goal. When I put my binder back on the shelf at the end of that day, I thought about the mental challenges that lay ahead. It was inspiring to know that soon I'd have a psychologist on my team—another coach to help me get down that road.

"Let your mind wander as your eyes follow my fingers," Derrick said in a tone I assumed was meant to be calming. He waved his index and middle finger slowly back and forth in front of my face, using a technique called eye movement desensitization and reprocessing. EMDR was recommended by the World Health Organization, but the process reminded me of hypnotism in the cartoons

I used to watch as a kid. I half expected Derrick to say, "You are getting sleepy" and then command me to bark like a dog.

My eyes followed his fingers. But while wandering was normally what my mind did best, when told to do so it rebelled by refusing to leave the scene of the accident, replaying the same images in perpetuity. Derrick's fingers stopped. "What are you thinking about?"

"Megan's hair red with blood."

Derrick was uninterested. "Follow my fingers."

The next time he stopped, I'd been remembering the sounds of the truck windows shattering. Derrick's nostrils flared. "You need to let your mind wander away from the accident."

Derrick had met Bruce's verdict of major depression and then upped the ante with post-traumatic stress disorder. According to him, the best way to cure PTSD was with EMDR. I'd heard a soldier on the radio talking about being diagnosed with PTSD. He'd experienced extreme relief when a doctor told him there was a name for what he was going through. I felt no such relief. Derrick might as well have told me I had QRST and we would try to resolve it with LMNOP. The letters held as much meaning to me as reading a bowl of alphabet soup. But that wasn't the real difference between that soldier and me. The soldier had witnessed friends being killed and children having their limbs blown off. I'd rolled a truck and caused two people to need stitches. That didn't seem like enough trauma to cause PTSD.

The next time Derrick stopped the finger movement and asked what I was thinking about, I said, "I took my foot off the gas pedal when I should have kept it on."

He put his hand down. "The accident wasn't your fault. The police report clearly states that." Derrick sounded like a parent trying to stay calm while telling his five-year-old, for the third time in a row, that she couldn't have a treat.

I regretted my words. I should have simply said I was thinking of the moment I took my foot off the gas pedal. Derrick always got frustrated when I mentioned anything being my fault.

"You have driven many more kilometres than the average

person," he continued. "Statistically you're doing very well. It was normal to lose control of your vehicle in that situation. It could have happened to anyone."

"Yes, I have driven more than the average person. So, I should be better at it than them."

"Surely you know you're being unreasonable?"

"I don't think I am."

"No one else thinks the accident was your fault."

"Graham does. That's why he asked me to invoice him but never paid me."

"Or he forgot. Have you asked him about it?"

"No. I don't want him to pay me. I totalled his truck and trailer and he had to pay for Megan's helivac."

"Let's return to the EMDR."

"Stop seeing that hack. You're always happy except the days you talk to him," one of my fellow rehabbers—a barrel-chested logger— said one day after my appointment with Derrick.

"Ask Wayne to let you see Bruce instead. You and Bruce are always joking around together on the walks," the rough-voiced female Greyhound driver suggested after another appointment.

"That guy is an asshole," said the construction worker whose fall from scaffolding had required surgeons to temporarily remove the top of his skull to relieve swelling in his brain. The resulting red scar wound its way around his pale bald scalp in a pattern and colour scheme that made his head look remarkably like a baseball. The two of us were out on the sidewalk getting a breath of fresh air—his accompanied by a cigarette.

"They made me speak to Derrick too," he said with his strong Eastern European accent. "He told me I might feel better about myself if I wore a hat." The construction worker threw up his arms. "What kind of bullshit advice is that?"

The suggestion didn't sound so ridiculous to me; I'd noticed people cross the street to avoid walking past him, but his vehement reaction made me laugh.

He slapped me lightly on the shoulder. "See you don't need to talk to that idiot. When you feel bad just talk to me."

No one encouraged me to keep seeing Derrick. Even Wayne asked if I wanted to stop the appointments. But they saw me only during program hours when I was generally happy and getting physically stronger. They weren't with me behind the wheel of my car where each curve brought images of losing control and fishtailing. They didn't know I was scared to have passengers and that I saw all the people in other cars as potential victims of my next mistake. No one else knew that each time a semi approached in the oncoming lane, I had to use every ounce of focus I had to fight my mind's goading: *Swerve in front of it. Your rusty old Civic would be a speedbump to that truck. The driver would be fine and you could relax. Forever.*

EMDR was frustrating, but learning to contract my multifidus muscle had also been frustrating. I kept telling myself that if I stuck with EMDR, surely something would click.

Derrick and I didn't have a regularly scheduled meeting time; he'd just find me early in the week and let me know when to be at his office. But then a whole week passed when he didn't come to find me, and whenever I'd spot him, he seemed to rush off to avoid me. I felt like I was in high school being ignored by a boyfriend who didn't have the guts to officially dump me. I tried to convince myself I was imagining the problem and he was just busy. But eventually I couldn't stand it. I cornered him and asked, "Are you mad at me?"

"No," he said, without looking at me.

"Are we going to meet this week?"

Derrick was quiet. He looked like a kid caught throwing a ball through a windowpane.

"I'm sorry," he said after a moment. "I haven't responded appropriately to the situation. I just don't know how to help you."

My inner critic lapped up his words. *Everyone in this program is injured. Everyone has needed to stop working. Everyone's had to make life changes. Yet, you're the only one too messed up for the mental health workers in both programs. Why can't you get your shit together like everyone else?*

"I'll suggest WCB finds you a psychologist in Whistler when you're done here," Derrick said, like a sales clerk offering to call another location for my size.

Instead of going directly back to my hotel that day, I walked along the seawall and watched the late-afternoon sun reflect off the water. Water weaves its way around and through Vancouver. The Strait of Georgia. English Bay, False Creek, Vancouver Harbour. Creating the city's southern border is the Fraser River. I couldn't see the river from where I walked downtown, but some of the water I was looking at had flowed up from there.

I thought about all the changes the rivers went through on their journeys and all the obstacles that water had overcome. I pictured where the clear turquoise waters flowed out of Chilko Lake and into the Chilko River. My mind followed that water as it dropped into the beautiful chaos of Lava Canyon, then on to where the milky-green waters of the Taseko River merged in, turning the Chilko opaque. Continuing downstream I saw where the Chilko was joined by the Chilcotin, an insignificant stream compared with the high-volume Chilko, but from that point forward the maps declared the river as the Chilcotin. On our trips, we spent several days rowing the Chilcotin. There were stretches of turbulent waves where I needed to push so hard on my oars I'd be pouring with sweat inside my dry suit, and other stretches so calm I tucked my oars beneath my knees, leaned back and watched the scenery go by.

The Chilcotin waters travelled through canyons and rangelands, past where the forests waned and into where the desert took over. The same water that had taken us by fir, spruce and aspen, and allowed us glimpses of grizzly bears and moose, also immersed us in a land of barren sand dunes, towering hoodoos, tiny cacti and bighorn sheep. At the end of its 240-kilometre run, the Chilcotin treated us to one last fun stretch of roller-coaster waves before its milky-green waters disappeared into the muddy-brown Fraser. There, giant whirlpools grabbed at our boats and spun us around helplessly before letting us go unscathed. I thought about where we took out at Churn Creek. The sun beating down on the desert canyon. I pictured jumping into the Fraser to cool off and hearing an underwater noise I'd only ever heard the Fraser make—an endless grinding sound as the billions of sand particles it carried rubbed against one another. Our trips ended there, but the water continued on, eventually coming out by Vancouver and into the sea beside which I now stood.

Rivers. Time. Life. Everything kept changing and moving on. I wanted life to pause while I got better, physically and mentally. I wanted things to go back to where they were before the accident. Unchanged. But that couldn't happen. At nearly thirty-five, I was already old on the river. They say time heals all wounds, but I didn't have time to spare. I had to stop thinking so much about the past and embrace going forward instead.

I focused on pushing myself at the gym. I started looking for a winter job. I answered an ad for cross-country ski instructors. I'd never taught cross-country skiing, but the ad said they offered an instructor course for the right applicants. Applying was intimidating, but I was confident the job would be easier on my back than sitting at a desk or serving tables.

One of the company owners was in Vancouver, so we arranged to meet at a coffee shop "after work." My cover letter conveniently left out the fact that my current full-time job was as a client in occupational rehab. We drank hot chocolate and talked about cross-country skiing. When he asked why I was in the city, I told him about my back.

"And you'll be able to ski?"

"My kinesiologist set up resistance bands to mimic the muscle movements used in cross-country. It felt great."

My potential boss stood up. "Can you do this?" He reached his arms above his head.

A few weeks before, that movement would have sent pain shooting down my back, but now I copied the motion easily.

"We store some skis in the ceiling beams," he explained.

I looked up at him. He was about a foot taller than me.

"We've got milk crates for people like you to stand on."

"Are you calling me short?"

He smiled and said, "I'll talk to my partner and get back to you soon."

The following day he called and said, "We'd like to hire you, but our insurance company requires a letter saying you're capable, signed by your doctor, your physio and your occupational therapist. I'll email you the letter outlining specific movements required for the job."

"Great," I said, while wondering if my therapy team would actually sign the letter. They had always been very supportive of my progress, but saying positive things was simply sending sound waves into the open air. Signing a document meant taking responsibility for your opinion.

"So, I kind of got offered that job as a cross-country ski instructor," I said to Wayne.

"Kind of?"

"They're worried about me getting reinjured on the job." I held the printed letter out to him.

He read it over. "I'll bring it up at the team meeting."

The team doctor had me do a series of movements. My range of motion had improved greatly since the start of the program, but my mobility was still only a fraction of what it had once been. Under her scrutiny, I felt like the *Wizard of Oz*'s Tin Man before Dorothy oiled him.

"We'll have a decision for you tomorrow," the doctor said.

After rehab, I walked downtown listening to snippets of conversations and arguments and noticing the various styles people wore. Smells of different takes on sandwiches from around the world danced and mingled in the air: shawarmas, gyros, burritos, rotis, crepes. How lucky was I to live in a time and place where so much variation was readily available? Why was I wasting so much time hiding from this world? *Get your shit together and move forward.*

"Your graduation certificate," Wayne said.

I eagerly took the signed letter from his hand. I was excited to gain the independence of having a job, although it came with a side order of sadness, knowing my bond with the rehabbers would soon dissolve.

To see how I'd progressed, Wayne needed to give me the same test that he'd given me the first day. This time, instead of starting with an empty milk crate, he placed a ten-pound beanbag inside to start. When I lifted the crate easily, he added another ten pounds. I lifted the crate again.

"Just so you know, fifty is the max I'll put in," Wayne said, adding a third beanbag.

I completed each exercise with fifty pounds.

"What a change," Wayne said. "You should be very proud of yourself."

"So should you. I'd still be struggling to wash my hair if it wasn't for you and Mathieu."

I felt like I did after running a rapid, like the heaviness of worry had lifted from my body and I'd become so light I was only a small step away from learning to fly.

CHAPTER 10

Whistler, BC
December 2007

Whistler was gearing up for the 2010 Winter Olympics, and I was employed at the newly opened cross-country ski area built for the games. The trails wound around towering old-growth conifers and over creeks that could still be heard running under the ice and snow. On clear days, the views looked out at a seemingly endless supply of jagged, snow-covered mountains and made sense of trail names like "Top of the World."

I was still stiff and skied with all the grace of Frankenstein, but outdoor activity felt great. When I wasn't working, I trained at the gym, spent time with Mara and occasionally went out with my co-workers. Yet, back at my apartment I still hid in my room, not wanting to hear about my roommate's epic ski day or meet his friends who came over to hang out. Even when I was home alone, I spent most of my time in bed staring at the ceiling, feeling like a giant weight had pinned me there. True to his word, Derrick had suggested to WCB that they find me a psychologist in Whistler. Just like Derrick, the new psychologist believed that EMDR was the key to helping me with my PTSD. And just like with Derrick, I felt worse every time I saw him. I'd been so excited to graduate from rehab and get my life back in gear. But without the support of the rehab group celebrating each small achievement, I found myself struggling with all the things I still couldn't do.

I suspected Mara had told my parents she was worried about me, because in a last-minute decision they flew out from Montreal for my thirty-fifth birthday.

Most years, my birthday was a low-key affair. I was born December 30. Not many people want to party hard the night before New Year's Eve. But the previous winter I'd turned thirty-four in North Creek, a place where no matter the date, friends won't stand for not celebrating a birthday. It had been one of my most fun birthdays ever. Among other events, my friend Lori had organized my first experience with a birthday spanking machine. She'd had everyone at the bar—even the visiting skiers I didn't know—form a line, with their feet spread wide to create a tunnel. Then she'd sent me crawling through the tunnel and each person spanked my butt as I passed through their legs. It was completely juvenile, in the best way. Later, a whole crew of us had ended up naked and laughing uproariously in a newly befriended weekender's hot tub. And sometime in the wee hours, a charming twenty-six-year-old guy with gorgeous green eyes had come home to Lori's couch with me.

At the time, thirty-four had sounded old. Birthdays were always like that. According to my mom, I'd had a tantrum when I turned six because I wanted to stay five. But despite how old thirty-four had sounded, it hadn't felt much different from being fourteen—other than being legally allowed to drink, having no curfew and being able to bring boys home. On my thirty-fourth birthday I'd felt young. Better than young. I was in better shape at thirty-four than I had been through my teens or the pre-paddling years of my early twenties.

Now, only a year later, I was turning thirty-five and feeling ninety. The highlight of my day was a gift from my parents: an extra-large heating pad.

"Thanks. This is exactly what I need." I immediately plugged the pad in. As advertised, it relaxed the stiff muscles of my back. "This is awesome!"

Although the heating pad helped relieve some pain, and spending time with my parents was a nice change, my struggles to deal with the guilt and fear and constant reliving of the accident just weren't going away. On an evening shortly after my birthday, Mara and our parents read by the fire while I cooked dinner. It was a simple meal—black bean burgers—that I'd made countless times before. But this time, the patties weren't sticking together properly and the edges were practically burnt while the insides stayed almost raw. Like internal fireworks, explosions of anger lit up my brain. It didn't matter that it was just dinner. Or maybe that made it matter even more. I'd been cooking for decades. I was often paid to do it. If I couldn't be trusted to get a simple dinner right, what could I be trusted to do? The fireworks came faster and brighter. When they reached the splendour of the grand finale, I grabbed the frying pan by the handle, swinging it with everything I had. "Fucking burgers!"

The crumbling patties flew out of the pan, arced through the air, hit the floor and skidded down the laminate boards toward the fireplace where my family sat.

"Calm down," my dad said. "It's just dinner."

"I can't fucking do this!"

"The burgers are fine. Calm down."

I didn't want to calm down. I wanted someone to acknowledge that my problem wasn't dinner. I wanted someone to recognize that I was descending into a deep hole. I wanted someone to help me out into the light. I knew that my family understood that, and I knew that it was unreasonable to expect them to know the right way to react when I didn't even know if there was a right way. But none of that knowledge helped contain the explosions in my head and my frenzied emotions. It was terrifying not knowing how to control myself or what I'd do next. I was back to being a toddler with no ability to reason, having a temper tantrum in hopes that my parents would make all the pain go away—like they had so often when I was young.

My dad asked, not for the first time, if I'd speak to his friend who was a psychiatrist. I'd been wary about talking to him in the past, but now I nodded in agreement. He had to know a thing or two about helping crazy people.

My dad called and spoke with him for a few minutes, then handed me the phone. I went upstairs to talk. Maybe it was because he knew me that he became so exasperated. Maybe it was because I knew him that his exasperation hurt even more than Derrick's or the psychologist's in Whistler.

"You must see that you're being ridiculous. That the accident was not your fault."

I didn't see that at all. I was terrified I would never get better because everyone who tried to help me expected me to believe the accident wasn't my fault. It was like they were trying to help me by saying I had to believe in God. I couldn't just suddenly believe because someone told me to. I went back downstairs and handed the phone to my dad. By then I was crying so hard I couldn't even say goodbye.

After the accident I'd lost weight. For the first time ever, I could borrow pants from Mara, who'd always been much thinner. But instead of feeling good about trimming excess fat, I mourned the muscle I'd lost along with it. I hadn't felt so uncomfortable in my body since before I started paddling, and as a result my sex drive had disappeared. I mentioned my lost libido to a friend who I had some sexual history with. He drove up to Whistler to help me cure the problem. Initially it sounded like a fun challenge, but when it didn't work, the failure made us both feel a little worse about ourselves.

I was also still forgetting words all the time, and my discomfort in sitting made my limited attempts at socializing awkward. When I tried talking about it, I was told, "It's normal, we're getting older." I understood that many people had back pain. I'd had lower back pain from my early teens into my late twenties, which I eventually dealt with by doing Pilates almost every day. I found the routine as boring as watching someone else read, but it worked. I'd started doing Pilates again as soon as I could toward the end of rehab.

I knew that in time—even with daily Pilates—age-related aches and pain would appear. But wasn't fracturing four vertebrae different from that? And wasn't a sudden loss of memory different from a gradual one? Shouldn't I try to recover from these obstacles instead of learning to endure them? Maybe I was being vain, but I hated having people constantly telling me I was old. Whistler had an abundance of retirees showing off how fit a person could be past seventy. I didn't see why at thirty-five I couldn't look forward to getting better. I wished I could be with my Adirondack paddling friends, who I imagined would be more encouraging. But reaching out by phone had become immeasurably hard. The rehabbers would also have said I was suffering from injury, not age—which meant there was still hope of improving—but I no longer had that group. We'd all returned to our old lives. I wondered how many of them felt as alone as I did. Welcome back to the real world.

The psychologist in Whistler used a different method of EMDR than Derrick had. Instead of asking me to follow his fingers, he had me close my eyes while listening to pinging noises on headphones. One day, when I felt like I just couldn't stand that sound any longer, I yanked off the headphones and asked, "Can we just talk for a while?"

"What would you like to talk about?"

"How do other people get over guilt?"

"Accept that it wasn't their fault."

I put the headphones back on and concentrated on not screaming in frustration. Megan and Mike were okay and I wanted to forgive myself for nearly killing them. I didn't understand why I had to deny responsibility to do that. I didn't understand why I was being judged more harshly for admitting I had made a mistake than for the mistake itself. Sometimes we screw up. I just wanted help getting beyond that. But after each session with the psychologist I came out feeling worse about myself. Eventually I realized I had to stop seeing him—I didn't think I had space to get any lower. It felt like the truck roof was crushing down on me again.

I focused on work, improving my cross-country ski technique and going to the gym. I mentally revisited every waterfall and big rapid I'd ever paddled, picturing sequences of waves, rocks and holes. I was trying to relive the feeling of being so connected with the river that I felt its energy inside my heart, but it didn't work. All I felt was fear of everything that could go wrong. Fear that I would follow in the footsteps of Ron Thompson.

Despite that, I kept working toward getting back to the river. Growing up I'd been scared of so many things: fire, roller coasters, spiders, elevators, horses, playing any sport where I could let my teammates down. But then my parents had taken Mara and me on that rafting trip down Quebec's Rouge River, where once I'd realized I wasn't going to die, I'd actually had fun. By the end of that trip something inside me had changed. I'd continued to have many fears, but I'd stopped allowing them to always hold me back. I believed if I could return to the river, it would have the power to change me once again.

CHAPTER 11

Chilko River, BC
May 2008

I didn't make it to North Creek in April, but by late May I was in the Puddle preparing to guide the first trip of the season. Chris and I packed frames, oars and dry boxes into the trailer. When it was time to load rafts, which weighed around 240 pounds apiece, Chris said, "I'll get Kyle."

Kyle was new to our company but not to the river. He'd been guiding for a company that ran a trip or two down the Chilko each year, and he'd migrated over to us now that he'd started dating Charlotte. Kyle was young and strong with flawlessly messy blond hair that made him look like the picture-perfect raft guide. He was everything I wasn't.

"I'll load the boats with you," I said to Chris.

Chris paused for a moment, unsure, but then agreed. I assumed he was thinking the same thing I was: if I couldn't carry a raft, I likely wasn't strong enough to row it through big rapids. And here on dry land was the better place to find out.

The rafts were deflated and rolled into tight cylindrical shapes secured with straps. Squatting down on either side of the rolled raft, we got into position to use a technique called an oil-can carry.

Chris counted, "One. Two. Three."

In unison, we stood.

"You okay?" Chris asked.

"All good."

We walked to the trailer and placed the raft inside. Lifting the raft with Chris felt like it had in years past; I wouldn't want to walk a kilometre with it, but the oil-can carry made 240 pounds manageable for short periods. Chris eyed me for signs that it had been a bad idea.

"Ready for the next one?" he asked tentatively.

"Let's get it in."

The boats were packed and floating at the launch, and I was just making some final adjustments when Graham came by.

"Make sure Megan gets time on the oars," he said to me. "I need her guiding Lava soon."

"I need practice too. It's been a while."

"You know the river."

Graham began every season by getting as many staff on the river as possible. So, even though our first Chilko trip of the year had only four paying guests, the roster also included all the guides except Graham, some lodge staff and one new trainee, Emma. She was a vivacious Australian in her early twenties with a pronounced difficulty in keeping her pants over her butt crack.

After breakfast we launched our three rafts. Gusting headwinds tested our strength and will to get through the long flat stretch of the lake before entering the river. The weight of the oars in my hands felt familiar—like being reunited with a part of myself I'd been missing. I spun the stern into the wind and pulled my oars as hard as I could. Rowing backward is normally a guide's strongest stroke, but now my backward stroke didn't feel any more powerful than my forward one. *You're still too weak to row this raft.* I disregarded my inner critic. The only way to build those muscles was to work them. Besides, the most important factor to getting down the river wasn't power. It was the ability to read water and understand how to use the currents to help you instead of fighting against them. On the other hand, when it came to wind on the lake, the only thing to do was fight. A tingling numbness crept across my back. It was a welcome change from the usual pains. It motivated me to pull even harder.

Eventually we got to the river and the pull of the current took over. There were no real rapids on the first day, but the water flowed swiftly and required lots of manoeuvring to avoid getting tangled in the roots and branches of the many dead trees lying in the current's path. With oars in hand I felt a confidence I hadn't felt in a long time.

When I'd had my fix, I let Emma try steering for the first time. She practised turning the boat and rowing forward and back. She was strong and doing well powering around obstacles, but if she was going to run rapids, she'd need to understand boat angles.

"See how the main current is moving toward that fallen tree?" I asked. "If you angle your stern at about forty-five degrees away from the line of the current, the water will work with you to help you get away from the tree."

Emma pivoted the boat and tried it, immediately feeling how much easier it was to work with the river rather than against it. I leaned into the squishy comfort of the dry bags and took in the breeze on my face, the splashing sound of oars entering water, the laughter drifting over from the next boat. For the moment, I let go of all my mistakes and simply enjoyed being home.

In terms of scenic value, Camp One was the least memorable of the trip. Yet, as I led Emma down a well-treed path to the clearing where we'd set up the groover (a.k.a. the portable toilet), I was taken aback at how much more beautiful it was than I remembered. The trees were alive with tiny songbirds fluttering around, building nests and crooning about their lives. And although the water flowing past was simply a wide-open section of medium current, it was still a wild river we could watch while emptying our bowels. That in itself seemed pretty amazing. I demonstrated how to take the locking lid off the groover, and explained how we used a stick to mix down the contents and create more room before lidding it back up when we broke camp. "The glamorous side of guiding," I said.

The sun lingered so late after dinner that everyone was in bed before the sky was truly dark. I spread my sleeping bag under the same old Douglas fir I'd slept beneath many times before. Every muscle in my body was exhausted, and yet my brain had no interest in sleep. I watched the needles on the tree move with the light breeze and supervised the sky to make sure it eventually went dark.

I felt like I'd only just fallen asleep when I was woken by the jarring cries of a Steller's jay. I wondered if it was the same bird that had woken me under this tree so many times before. I undid the valve on my self-inflating pad, as was my habit from years past. Once the valve was open, the barrier between my body and the cold—often rocky—ground quickly disappeared, persuading me to get up. Even though my mind enjoyed being first up and having time for Pilates before I started preparing breakfast, most mornings my body resisted leaving the warm cocoon of my sleeping bag. But of all the hours in a day, the quiet early morning ones carried the strongest promise of hope. And on days when the wants of my tired body won out and I slept late, I always woke feeling like I'd already missed my chance of making the most of the day ahead.

As I started into my Pilates routine, mindfulness was notably absent. Aside from feeling like I was going to puke, my inner critic fretted even more than usual. *If you want to run whitewater, just go kayaking. Stop taking responsibility for other people's lives.* But it wasn't only whitewater pulling me back here. I craved helping others experience the joys of the river. I fought against my inner monologue of negativity by reminding myself Graham believed I was ready. I trotted out a memory of one of the many times he'd proven himself right to believe.

Steam rises from the aluminum wash buckets. Soapy water warms my sandaled toes as it drips off the dinner dishes I'm scrubbing alongside Graham.

"I think Farwell's going to be big tomorrow," I say. "What do you think?"

It's my second season guiding on the Chilko, but I'm still finding levels at Farwell Canyon harder to predict than upstream sections like Lava Canyon.

"It'll be big," Graham says. His smile is big too. Graham loves whitewater.

I haven't yet run Farwell at high water with Graham. The guides I have run it with favour a line skirting two big waves at the top to avoid a hole below them. The process involves more moves than seem necessary to me. I feel like we could bash right through those top waves and still miss the hole. But the scouting point is from a bridge so high above Farwell it's difficult to know for sure how much impact those top two waves will have on a raft.

"What's your line?" I ask. Graham often chooses different routes from everyone else.

"I'll plow right through those top waves. All that farting around you guys do to miss them screws with your momentum."

Exactly what I'd hoped to hear. "Is it a strength move?"

"You can do it, T-mar. Just follow me."

The next morning the river leads us through a world of changing vegetation, from coniferous trees to grasslands to sagebrush. We enter into a desert landscape of hoodoos and giant sand dunes. The river here is wide, fast and an opaque green that stands out brightly against the beiges and browns that dominate the terrain. We pass an abandoned cabin teetering on the edge of the bank high above us. High-water days over the years have eroded the bank to the point where part of the cabin no longer has any ground to support it, and it now sticks out above the water like a diving board. Not far past the doomed cabin, we pull into an eddy barely large enough for our three rafts. We've decided not to scout but we'll still regroup and run the rapid close together.

The first raft to exit the eddy is captained by a tough Scotsman who has guided all over the planet. He starts into the customary wave-skirting line. Graham rows out next, aiming straight for the waves the Scotsman worked so hard to miss. Graham glances back to make sure I'm following. As predicted, the water level is high and the waves look menacing, which means the hole just downstream of them will be even more so. *Do you have some sort of stupid Napoleon complex? Get over it and just stick to the usual line.*

I push hard into my oars. Graham is well aware of the size and strength difference between us. He trusts I can run this line, and I trust him.

"All forward!"

We hammer into the first wave.

"Get down!"

Everyone holds on tight. The guests in front rise above me as the boat starts to ascend the wave and the force of the water bends the bow back. The bow straightens again as we crest. I throw in an oar stroke and we hit the next wave with a very similar effect.

We come off the second wave exactly where we need to be to avoid the nasty hole. My guests and I hoot with excitement, and we still have most of the rapid left to go.

Years had passed since that day, along with many more instances of Graham encouraging me when I'd doubted myself. As I started breakfast preparations at Camp One, I cycled these words through my head like a mantra: *Graham thinks you can do this. Trust him.*

A few hours later, the other guides and I stood side by side on the ridge looking down at Bidwell—all of us silent as though in reverence to a great deity. It was earlier in spring than we normally began, and the river was lower than we'd run it. To people who don't know rivers, high water always sounds exciting and low water boring. But sometimes high water buries rocks so deeply that the river features become easier to navigate whereas low water can expose new hazards that render the river more dangerous—which looked to be the case that day. Near the top, a triangle of rock jutted out like the snaggletooth of an underwater monster. The potentially raft-ripping rock could easily be in the way of a boat that was just a tad off line.

If Graham had been on the river that day, he would have complained about stopping to scout. "I don't know why you guys bother. I've run Bidwell over a hundred times and the line is always the same." I could see once again his words held true. Even with new rocks exposed, the line I wanted to run hadn't changed. I was scared, and my mind flooded with images of everything that could go wrong on the river, peppered with flashes of Megan unconscious and bloody in the field. But Megan was standing right near me, healthy as ever, and I knew from years of experience where the water would be pushing me and what I needed to do to stay on my line. There was no reason to continue standing there staring at exposed rocks. On the river, as in life, nothing good comes from focusing too long on where we don't want to go. I turned toward the trail that would take me down to the rafts, where we'd left Emma in charge of the guests.

"Tamar," Chris called. He signalled me to come back.

Once I was standing beside him, Chris asked, "What do you think?"

"It's low, but same line as always."

"And that rock?"

"It doesn't look friendly," I said, stating the obvious.

Chris launched into his worst-case scenario. The other guides joined in. Although I was nervous about rowing Bidwell, to me it still looked runnable. Listening to the other guides' doubts made me wonder if it was my river-reading skills I should be questioning more than my strength. Chris suggested we stay put and set up camp, in hopes that the water level came up overnight. So we hauled all our gear up the steep trail. It was challenging, but it was also exciting to camp somewhere new and not know exactly what we'd be facing in the morning.

When we woke, the sharp rocks stood out just like they had the day before, but all the guides agreed to run it. Perhaps the unplanned hard work of the day before had whetted the group's appetite for adventure. Chris suggested reducing our risks by running the top of the rapid with only guides in the boat, then reuniting with the guests in an eddy not far below the Three Sisters. Everyone agreed.

"I think the top is going to be more of a power move than usual," Chris said. "And Soren is the strongest." Chris looked up at Soren, "So, if you're in, I'd like you to row."

"I'm in," Soren said, his eyes glinting with enthusiasm.

Chris began organizing who would be the onshore rescue team and who would paddle the rafts. He asked Kyle and Megan if they wanted to paddle. My eyes likely sparkled with the same excitement I'd seen in Soren's when I realized the reason Chris hadn't asked me was because he'd already assumed I would be part of the rafting crew.

We led the guests over rocks and roots, to the edge of an eddy we'd be able to squeeze the rafts into. There we set up safety precautions in case anyone swam. Aside from being ready with throw bags, we also set up for live-bait rescue—where a rescuer was tethered to a rope, ready to jump in and grab a victim unable to grab the rope themselves due to injury or loss of consciousness.

Once those of us on the rafting crew had hiked upstream to the boats, Chris and Megan sat in front of Soren while Kyle and I took the spots in the stern. Sometimes when a raft was loaded with guides everyone had their own idea of how things needed to go. To avoid that chaos, we all agreed Soren was in charge.

"All forward," Soren shouted.

In unison we pulled our paddle blades through the water.

"Take a break!"

We stopped paddling. Soren pivoted his oars, manoeuvring us around the first rock we had to avoid. Then he turned the bow to face the right side of the river.

"All forward, dig it in!"

Soren pushed forward on the oars while the rest of us dug deep with our paddles. The pins-and-needles sensation spread across my back. I didn't care. It felt so good to paddle hard. With five guides working in unison, our raft glided more quickly across the water than any of us was used to. Within seconds we were clear of the snaggletooth we'd worried over.

"Break," Soren yelled.

We approached the section of lava rock I used as a landmark to turn downstream. I expected Soren to do the same, but he allowed the raft to continue riding its momentum toward the right shore. The canyon wall grew closer. I saw Chris and Megan drop to the floor preparing for impact, but I was sure Soren would call for us to back paddle. Kyle and I continued to sit up high, our paddles ready for action.

The bow hit the canyon wall. The raft recoiled, and Kyle and I both tumbled into the churning cold water.

Just like every other time I'd been through Lava, my world narrowed to focus only on what I needed to do. When my head bobbed to the surface, I looked for the bright yellow of the raft. It was upstream. Current moves slower at the surface than it does deeper down. Because my body dangled down into that faster current while the raft sat on the slower surface, I would naturally move downstream faster than the raft. As this wasn't the kind of river where I would soon be dumped into a calm pool where the raft could easily pick me up, I needed to be proactive. I rolled onto my stomach and did the head-up front crawl as hard as I could toward that yellow. There was no chance my swimming would propel me upstream, but I swam my hardest in hopes of slowing my downstream momentum and closing the gap between me and the raft. One after another, waves lifted me up, then held me down. Each time I came up I took a breath, unsure how long it would be until my next inhale. As I swam, Soren, Megan and Chris continued to row and paddle. We slowly closed the gap between us. Chris put down his paddle, leaned over the bow, grabbed the shoulders of my life jacket and pulled me in.

"Thanks," I said, while gulping air.

"Are you okay?" Chris, Soren and Megan all asked.

"I'm good," I said between panted breaths. "Where's Kyle?"

"We don't know," Chris said.

We were still hurtling downstream. The river doesn't stop for drama. Through the bucking waves, we scanned for a flash of colour from Kyle's helmet or life jacket. Nothing. Soren steered us into the eddy where the rest of the crew waited. My mind flashed images of Kyle tangled in underwater branches.

Finally we saw him scrambling along the rocky shoreline on the opposite bank. We signalled for him to jump in and we'd throw him a rope. He swam only a few strokes before a rope reached him. He grabbed it and was pulled to shore. The whole ordeal lasted seconds. Everyone was pumped. Except Kyle. He barely spoke. Some of the others thought he was being a jerk, but I silently empathized. To repeatedly lead people down rapids that could possibly kill them, you needed to see yourself as a hero. Right then, everyone was treating Kyle like a victim. That clearly hurt his self-image. I was a little ashamed of how well I could relate.

On our way to get the next raft, Soren said, "Sorry, guys. My brain just froze for a second."

"No worries," I said. "I should have back paddled. Or at least hung on."

I hadn't considered being upset with Soren. He'd just had a little brain fart; everyone does now and then. Plus I was a guide; I should have known to get down. I still trusted him as much as before, and from what I could tell everyone else felt the same. It struck me, though, that if I'd been the one guiding when we'd hit the wall and two people went for a swim, I'd be furious at myself and assume that everyone was angry and had lost all confidence in me. I wondered over the dichotomy, but my wonderings didn't have time to go far. Chris's words cut them off: "I have to say, Soren, that was perfectly timed. If everything had gone smoothly, the guests would have questioned our decision not to take them. But having Kyle and Tamar swim instills confidence that we weren't overreacting."

Chris was right. Which of course highlighted how ridiculous our profession was. But I loved everything about it. I quietly reflected on the fact that maybe it was okay I was still guiding. The day before I'd worried that I'd dangerously misread the river as runnable when it wasn't, but overnight the level hadn't noticeably changed. And although Soren had been recruited for his power, we all realized that hadn't been necessary. I had read the river correctly after all.

CHAPTER 12

The Road to Inuvik, NT
June 2008

The cessation of movement woke me. Chris turned off the ignition in the truck. We were at a gas station somewhere in northern BC. According to my watch it was a little after 3 a.m.

"Are you ready to drive or should I grab myself some caffeine?" Chris asked.

"Good to go as soon as I pee."

"Want me to get you a coffee?" Chris asked with a smirk.

"No, thanks."

"Still not ready for that commitment, eh?"

I smiled and shook my head.

With the tank full and our bladders empty, I steered us out of town. I'd thought my co-workers would be at least as apprehensive as I was when it was my turn to drive, but Kyle fell asleep in the back before we were even out of the gas station and Chris drifted off in the passenger seat shortly after.

We were en route to Inuvik, Northwest Territories, the most northerly place we could drive to in Canada without using an ice road. From Inuvik we'd fly the final 185 kilometres to Ivvavik National Park, on the farthest tip of Yukon, where we'd put in on the Firth River. Our trip was taking us deeper into the wilderness than I'd ever been. Even through my tightly clenched jaw I could practically taste the adventure.

The sun peaked over the horizon by 4 a.m. About an hour later

I caught a quick glimpse of movement in my peripheral vision before a huge bull moose swaggered onto the road. I pressed my foot down on the brake. Our rental truck stopped far more easily than anything I'd ever towed a trailer with before. The moose also stopped—right on the yellow line, as though making a statement about who the highway belonged to. Chris opened his eyes partway, not wanting to fully give up his much-needed sleep.

"What's up?" he mumbled.

I pointed my chin toward the moose.

Chris's eyes opened all the way.

The moose stood his ground for a few moments before swaggering off. I resumed driving. Chris watched me. I assumed he was looking for clues that I didn't want to drive anymore, or that he shouldn't want me to drive anymore.

"Awesome brakes. Can't say I miss the old truck at all," I said.

"And how nice is it to also have a trailer with working brakes?" Chris replied.

I nodded in agreement. Chris fell back asleep. I scanned the sides of the road ahead of us while imagining what could have happened if a moose had come out to the road two hours earlier. Our rig was the best we'd ever had, but could I have reacted fast enough if I hadn't seen the moose until it was lit by my headlights? I pictured a moose hoof sticking through the windshield, shattered glass, Chris covered in blood. *You shouldn't be driving.* I kept going. If I wanted to be on the river, I had to take my turn at the wheel.

Our guests were a diverse group of ten: a jovial birder, a professional photographer, a concert violinist and her husband, Chris's parents and a family of four who we referred to as the Tall Family. The father, Cal, measured six-foot-six. His three twenty-something offspring were tall as well. Stephanie, the eldest, stood six-two; Brandon was six-seven; and Beth, the youngest, referred to herself as "a petite five-foot-ten."

The Tall Family saw the whitewater aspect of the trip as an unfortunate and somewhat daunting obstacle they'd grin and bear in hopes of seeing caribou. Ivvavik Park's coastal plain is the calving ground of the Porcupine caribou herd—*Ivvavik* is an Inuvialuktun term meaning birthplace. Calves are born in early June. Soon after, great swarms of mosquitos and flies become active in the area. The insects pester the caribou so much that the ungulates cut down on their feeding and concentrate most of their time on getting away from the bugs, effectively launching the world's longest land migration. Each member of the Porcupine caribou herd usually walks between two and three thousand kilometres a year between their calving grounds near the Beaufort Sea and their winter range in the Alaska-Yukon boreal forests. I wondered what the caribou would do with their time if only they had access to bug spray. Instead, they use a community-minded method of bug repellent. They reduce the harassment of the bugs on any individual by clustering together into enormous groups—sometimes numbering in the tens of thousands—as they migrate.

Their timing and exact route vary year to year; therefore, the chances of us being in the right place at the right time within the park's ten-thousand-plus square kilometres aren't great. But still, we were all excited by the prospect that it could happen. The Tall Family was even prepared to run rapids they were wary of.

Early in the morning, while our guests were still cozy in their hotel rooms, Chris, Kyle and I unloaded our trailer onto the Inuvik airport tarmac. The plan was to load the gear into a Twin Otter—the classic Canadian bush plane—and fly Kyle and me in to inflate and pack the rafts while the plane flew back for Chris and the guests. The ground crew weighed our load. Chris and I both swore under our breath when we saw it was significantly over the limit. We'd already whittled down as much as we could while still claiming to be a high-end trip. Now we'd have to book a third flight, which meant the trip would lose money. Before we could get too concerned about that, Bob, the pilot, started telling us which pieces of gear to bring him. Bob was in his fifties and had an air of confidence like he'd come out of the womb knowing how to fly, yet he displayed none of the cockiness often associated with pilots. His speech was monotone, but not in a boring way, more like a dead-panning comedian.

Bob stood inside the plane with his co-pilot while the rest of us carried stuff over in the order he asked for it. Eventually there was a lull as Bob eyed the pile on the tarmac and the space left in the plane. We expected him to say that load was complete, but instead he explained, "I like to make it aesthetically pleasing."

He looked again at the pile of remaining gear and said, "Bring over those frame pieces."

He kept asking for more until the tarmac was empty and the plane was as stuffed as a Thanksgiving turkey. Bob read our unspoken surprise. "Other people want to fly today," he said with a shrug.

All but two of the passenger seats had been removed from the plane to make room for our load. In the far back, behind a moun-tain of cargo, Kyle and I wedged ourselves into those two seats. Bob's safety talk began with the usual fare about seat belts and life vests, but then he concluded with, "We will be travelling at a cruis-ing height of about...ten feet."

Kyle and I laughed.

"How long is the flight?" I asked.

"About an hour and a half as the crow flies. Two hours as I fly. Once I'm up there I like to look around."

I loved meeting people who loved how they made a living.

Our trip down the runway was longer than usual for a short takeoff-and-landing aircraft. We wore ear protection to shield us from engine noise, but eye contact made it clear Kyle and I both wondered if Bob's decision to cram in all that extra weight was really such a stroke of luck after all. Then the wheels lifted from the ground and our concerns were forgotten as the Mackenzie Delta spread out beneath us: a great maze of watery highways winding through flat, muddy ground. It looked like somewhere a person could go out in a boat and never find their way home. We veered from the delta toward the treeless mountains. We passed over one jagged ridge so closely it appeared to be only centimetres away from rubbing the belly of the plane. When the landscape flattened again, Bob dropped down lower. Not quite as low as the ten feet he had joked about, but low enough to scare one poor moose into a run.

Bob brought us down gently onto grassy flatland beside the calm-looking river. When he opened our door, he immediately referenced the takeoff: "Sometimes I have to keep driving and trust that eventually the curve of the Earth will take over."

We unloaded the plane, then watched the Otter lift off the ground much faster than it had leaving Inuvik. Once the plane was gone, the only remaining sounds were the river calmly flowing by and the calls of ravens in the distance.

Previously, my most northerly experience had been on the Tatshenshini and Alsek Rivers, which flow through the corner of the world where the borders of Yukon, British Columbia and Alaska intersect. On those rivers we'd looked up at jagged glacier-topped mountains and rowed rafts around glistening pale-blue icebergs. The Firth put-in had none of that visual drama; instead, grassy meadows led to softly rounded hills in the distance. If someone were to take a picture and edit in a few cows, it could pass for farmland in southern Canada. Yet, there was an amazing vastness that was impossible to capture within the frame of a camera.

The first time I'd kayaked through the depths of the Grand Canyon was also the first time I'd become physically aware of what insignificant specks humans are. On my first trip down the Tatshenshini—the summer before the truck accident—I'd felt that smallness even more intensely standing atop a Yukon peak. With endless chains of rugged mountains and silty green waters winding through wide valleys, the landscape had seemed to stretch out forever. Yet, in all that distance there'd been no signs of any other humans.

"What do you think?" Graham had asked.

My mouth had opened but my brain hadn't found the words to describe how big the world seemed, and how minuscule I felt. Although not in a bad way. I'd felt honoured to experience true wilderness, and to see how little my own mistakes mattered.

"I'm glad you're suitably impressed," Graham had said. "If you want, next season you can do all the northern trips with Chris."

I'd wanted it very much. Unfortunately, breaking my back had delayed those plans.

At the Firth put-in, the vastness was almost tangible; it was as though we could feel those thousands of hectares between us and the closest human settlement. The sensation was both exciting and overwhelming. Like how I imagined I'd feel in a sailboat in the middle of the Pacific Ocean.

The first day of the trip had no significant rapids, but the swift current tried to push the rafts into the banks at each corner. Graham had purchased three sets of lightweight oars for the trip. We'd each eagerly clipped a pair into our frames. But I couldn't keep mine from slipping inside the clamps meant to hold the angle of the blades, and I kept taking strokes that didn't pull water. I pulled into an eddy and changed them out for the older-model oars we'd brought as backup.

After the next set of riffles, Chris asked, "Better?"

"Awesome," I said.

"What were you doing wrong with the new oars?" Kyle asked. "Mine work great."

Kyle had been taking digs at me during the whole journey north. I knew he was saying the problem was me, not my oars. I also knew he was probably right, but it wasn't the time to discuss my shortcomings.

"I'm just an old-school kind of girl," I said with a smile. Then I tuned Kyle out and concentrated on doing my job.

As the Firth carried us northward, we left behind the wide, flat stretches of the put-in and were soon surrounded by the British Mountains, whose sharp edges had been sanded down by time. The valleys up here were V-shaped as opposed to the wide U-shaped ones in the more southerly Coast Mountains or the Rockies. The area encompassing Ivvavik Park had escaped glaciation in the last ice age, so the erosion of its mountains was the work of wind and water. The softly rounded mountains of northern Yukon stood in startling contrast to the rough-edged mountains of southern Yukon. Down there glaciers still existed as mementos of the ice age and the wide valleys and jagged mountains stood as evidence of the moving highways of ice and rock that once slowly carved through them.

It wasn't only the landscape that was different. On the Firth, we also lived beneath a midnight sun. Although I knew there'd be twenty-four-hour daylight, I'd imagined the sun dropping closer to the horizon at night. I'd been wrong. Day and night, the sun circled at the same distance from the horizon, never once dipping down for a rest. On top of that, the sky was almost completely devoid of clouds. The sun burned down with far more intensity than I'd expected in the Arctic. Tarps we normally used to protect us from rain, we now set up to provide shade. Before cooking dinner, I jumped fully dressed into the river so that my wet clothing would cool me while standing over the stove.

One evening the discussion turned to how some of our group were having trouble sleeping. Brandon, the tall son, proudly showed off his eye mask. It was basic black—not at all interesting like the one Audrey Hepburn wore in *Breakfast at Tiffany's*—but even in its plainness, about half our group was jealous of it. I wasn't one of them. Falling asleep in full sunlight was a longer version of one of my guilty pleasures: summertime naps under the noonday sun. I felt like unending daylight made every aspect of life shine brighter and reminded me how to enjoy being alive.

We hiked up to an area where, for hundreds or perhaps thousands of years, the Inuvialuit people—and perhaps their ancestors the Thule—hunted by corralling herds of caribou over a cliff with the help of a stone caribou fence. Not much of the fence remained, but a powerful feeling of the past lingered, demanding we stop to imagine how resourceful the Inuvialuit had been. I wondered what they would think of our lives: how we'd flown in by air with thousands of pounds of gear to keep us comfortable, including meat that someone else had raised, butchered and packaged. I wondered what they'd think of us coming to their hunting grounds for no greater reason than to relieve the boredom of everyday life. I supposed they wouldn't understand. And why should they? It was my life and I didn't really understand.

My raft was in the lead as we came around a corner and saw the wave of fur and antlers moving across the river. I signalled Chris and Kyle to eddy out. We'd beat the odds and met up with the caribou migration.

Once on shore we watched hundreds of caribou trotting down the hillside toward the river. Caribou are the only members of the deer family whose females have antlers. Alongside the antlered adults were hundreds of young that would have been born within the past two weeks. Their little legs worked overtime keeping up with the herd. Seeing hundreds of animals in one place and hearing the sound of all those hooves hitting the ground was astounding. But what amazed me most was the smell. The musky aroma of so many wild animals was unlike anything I had known before. "No one ever mentioned the scent to me," I said.

Chris took a deep breath. "It smells like life."

Graham had once said that the caribou he'd encountered on the Firth "ran around like they were on acid when they saw us." I'd assumed he was exaggerating, as many good storytellers were apt to do, but in this case he was pretty accurate. When the caribou coming down the mountain toward us caught sight of our group, they dug their hooves into the dirt and skidded to a stop, miraculously avoiding a twenty-caribou pileup as they did so. Then they ran off in every direction to avoid us. That was totally understandable behaviour for any wild animal, even more so considering we were likely the first humans many of those caribou had ever seen. But what made me question their survival instincts—and agree that they did indeed seem like they were tripping—was that after a couple of hundred metres they'd stop to graze, chewing calmly until they casually looked around, were reminded of our presence and began running again. The ones in the river were equally bewildered.

In their panic, caribou that had already left our side of the river turned around and came back toward us again. Others attempted new routes downstream. But the river flowed faster there, and some calves were pushed around the corner by the current. I'd always imagined the caribou migration as a beautiful ballet of Mother Nature. From where we stood it looked more like drunken square dancing. And we were clearly the root of the problem.

"I think we should go," the birdwatching guest said.

It was a huge relief for a guest to suggest it first. A chance of seeing the caribou migration was a selling point of the trip. We all knew how lucky and rare it was to be in the midst of it. Yet, everyone quickly agreed to get back in the rafts and carry on. We'd felt the wonder of being there, but we didn't want to keep causing problems for the herd.

Our three rafts cruised with the currents, leaving behind the chaos of caribou. Because Ivvavik had escaped glaciation, species of flora and fauna that had perished elsewhere during the ice age continued to thrive and evolve near the Firth. Not long after leaving the caribou, we rounded a corner and saw a small herd of muskoxen grazing by the river's edge. Shaggy brown heads hung low to the ground while their horns formed shields across their foreheads, making them look armed for battle. The males make use of the shields when they fight each other, running full steam into one another's heads. But when it comes to outside threats, they mostly rely on safety in numbers instead of aggression. They stand side by side creating a defensive wall while the young tuck in close to their mothers.

I considered what I knew about these animals: short legs, dark untameable hair, more proficient at staring contests than physical fighting. I felt solidarity with them. Unfortunately, they didn't see it the same way. They saw us as a threat and acted accordingly, lining up shoulder to shoulder while hiding their young and giving us the stink eye.

"Hey, muskoxen, how's it going?" I hoped that hearing a calm voice would placate them, a method that often worked with dogs or bears.

My voice didn't have the desired effect. The herd broke formation and ran up the hillside, their long shiny fur flowing in the wind.

Stephanie, channelling the silky-haired models of old Pantene shampoo commercials, said: "Don't hate me because I'm beautiful."

We all laughed. Then we talked about how lucky we were and what amazing things the river brought. That day about a year earlier, the day Dr. Briggs had told me I'd never guide again, began to fade.

One morning, about halfway through the trip, Chris, Kyle and I packed the kitchen while discussing the day's plan.

"We'll pull out in the eddy on river left above Sheep Slot," Chris said.

Sheep Slot was the Firth's largest rapid, but the anticipation hadn't made me wake up nauseous with fear like Bidwell. Chris, the only one of us who'd run the river before, had described Sheep Slot as straightforward Class IV: something we should look at, but less pushy and technical than many rapids we'd run together. Photos on the Parks Canada website backed up Chris's description.

We pulled away from camp with Chris's boat in the lead. In my boat, the Tall Family took in the scenery as the river moved us into a canyon. Walls of sedimentary rock slowly stretched upward around us and closed in tighter. The current reacted to the squeeze by creating more riffles and small rapids. The Talls were strong paddlers but uneasy about the upcoming whitewater. I tried convincing them it would be fun, but they insisted on seeing rapids as unfortunate obstacles in an otherwise excellent experience.

We heard the low rumble of water cascading over rocks. Chris signalled to eddy out. Ahead of him I saw the horizon line where the river dropped steeply out of sight. Splashes of white flickered up from beyond the horizon line, hinting at excitement waiting below. We pulled out on the left shore, secured our rafts and walked downstream to see what lay in store. After a quick discussion with our guests, we left them on an open part of the shoreline while Kyle, Chris and I scrambled downstream along the rocks, looking for a better vantage point. When we stopped, we were all silent for a moment. Sheep Slot looked much more powerful than Chris's description or any pictures had led me to expect.

Chris confirmed my thoughts by saying, "Water's higher than I've seen it."

At the top of the rapid, most of the water flowed over a steep ridge into a giant wave-hole that built and crashed and then built again. The waves downstream broke on diagonals in a mess of directions. Along the edges of the rapid, where the river met the canyon walls, powerful whirlpools swirled chaotically. Despite the mayhem of the rapid, the line I wanted to take was almost instantly apparent to me.

"Those whirlpools could slam a raft into the wall," Chris said.

Pointing out worst-case scenarios was something I both expected from and respected about Chris, but it surprised me when Kyle joined him in pointing out everywhere something might go wrong. I didn't know Kyle well, but he usually gave the impression that nothing fazed him. I listened carefully to their opinions; however, all the features they spoke about were far from my planned route. The line I saw cut straight through the meatiest section in the middle. All the manoeuvring they were discussing sounded very technical, and to my mind it increased the chances of sending a paddler overboard.

"What do you think, T-mar?" Chris asked.

"I'm running guts."

I didn't want to influence anyone's decision, but to me that looked like the safest option.

"It's pushy," Chris said.

"Pushier than Bidwell?"

"Your paddlers are scared. They'll probably hide on the floor instead of helping."

"I have a plan for that."

"We don't know what's around the corner."

From where we stood, we could see Sheep Slot emptied into a short calm stretch followed quickly by a slightly smaller rapid. That rapid led around an almost ninety-degree bend. Not knowing what was there didn't change my route plan. I wasn't trying to be a cowboy, I was choosing the line that looked safest. It was just happenstance that it also looked like the most fun.

"I'll run guts," Kyle said.

Chris looked at the line one more time. "We'll keep the rafts tight together."

The Tall Family stared at the rapid like it might be the last thing they ever saw. I said to them, "So, this is how it's going to work. Throughout the entire rapid, you're going to kneel on the floor of the raft where you'll be nice and secure." I stopped to let that sink in. Then I smiled and added, "And you're going to paddle like hell from down there."

Usually when people paddled from the floor instead of up on the side tube, they were fairly useless as paddlers. But with such long torsos I was convinced the Tall Family could still be effective, and their low centre of gravity would minimize the falling-out risk.

Cal and Brandon kneeled down in front while the sisters positioned themselves in the stern. My mind filled with doubt. I wondered if I should have let the guys talk me into a different line. That negative thought was joined by many others until my head was so full of noise I could barely hear the thundering rapid. Then we crossed out of the eddy and all that clatter went silent.

"All forward!"

The family paddled in unison with more power than I usually felt from sitting passengers. Within seconds we were looking into the crashing wave-hole.

"Hang on!"

The raft bent up in both bow and stern like a rubber taco. The aluminum oar frame creaked as it fought to hold its form against the folding raft. The wave broke around us, holding us still for a moment before releasing us to the current once again. The raft regained its intended shape. We'd made it through the most intimidating feature but a field of chaotic whitewater still lay ahead. "All forward!"

They dug in hard.

"You guys are like a well-oiled machine!" I'd used that line many times before, but that didn't make it any less true.

The raft continued crashing through the waves, the bow lifting up and slamming down, sending water splashing up over our heads. Then we hit the short flat section.

"Take a break! Awesome job, guys!"

All three rafts came through unscathed. We had a moment to breathe and then we continued into the next rapid. The second rapid was smaller but still exhilarating. We hurtled through its waves, rocked side to side and front to back. Then we rounded the ninety-degree corner. I scanned the water in front of us. A few more waves but no raft-flipping holes. We'd made it safely through.

"Yeehaw!" I couldn't imagine any better feeling. The excited din coming from the other boats made it clear I wasn't the only one.

"Can we do that again?" Brandon asked.

"Yeehaw," I yelled even louder.

One of the few things that rivals the excitement of running rapids is the thrill of converting a reluctant river runner into a whitewater fan. Soon the excited chatter in the boat revealed that Brandon wasn't the only convert. The warm ball of energy I felt in my chest doubled in size.

We came to a tributary named Sheep Creek. Just uphill from the confluence stood a log cabin with a Canadian flag billowing above: the park ranger station. The human-built structure looked out of place so deep in the wilderness. The flag even more so. It represented ideas of borders and ownership that early European settlers had brought with them, a symbol that seemed meaningless in this place that had managed to stay wild despite colonialism. This place where we could almost feel the ghosts of centuries of Inuvialuit hunters around us.

I wondered what it would be like to be a ranger in Ivvavik, to wake up in that cabin and look out at Dall sheep climbing canyon walls and at the green-grey river flowing by. I tried to imagine spending a whole summer so far from civilization, always exposed to the midnight sun. I wondered what the inside of the cabin looked like and if the ranger worked alone or if other people were there as well. I didn't think at the time that I would ever have a reason to see the inside of the cabin or find out anything about who worked there. But, just like when paddling a new river, in life we never quite know what's around the next bend.

Over the next five days we moved deeper into the canyon and then slowly the walls began to recede again, eventually giving way to the wide-open coastal plain. Unharnessed by the canyon, the river spread out and divided into channels. Those channels divided some more, creating the watery labyrinth of the delta. We knew some of the channels would split enough times they'd become too shallow to float a raft. Unfortunately, there was no map to direct us. Kyle and I acted like jerks, insisting Chris stay in the lead. The wind blew fiercely and teamed up with the swift-moving current to play a game against me. Each time the river braided, the forces of nature would try to cajole me down a branch where I didn't want to be. With such shallow water, I couldn't even dig my oars in deep to fight against the wind. The tingling numbness in my back spread and made it harder to access the muscles. My strokes grew weaker. The fact that neither Chris nor Kyle was having anywhere near as much difficulty made the situation that much more of a struggle for me. I tried to keep my cursing inside my head, but a few words slipped out. The Tall Family was once again in my boat. They remained uncharacteristically quiet.

Forcing Chris to make the decisions may not have been kind, but it worked. Following his lead, we made it through without having to unpack and carry our boats. In the distance I could make out the waves of the Beaufort Sea breaking against the shore. Along the beach, mysterious ghost-white structures spiked the landscape. It looked like a mirage. Chris explained that campers constructed shelters from bleached driftwood to protect themselves from the winds. It was a logical explanation, yet the structures looked otherworldly and it was hard to imagine other humans being there recently.

To get to the sea we needed to cross a shallow lagoon against a fierce headwind. My back was losing the fight. When I had nothing more to put into my oars, I jumped into the water and began pulling the raft. We could see the northern edge of the continent and I was waist-deep in water, wearing only shorts and a cotton T-shirt, yet I was warm. Unlike the river that was only a few degrees above freezing, the still, shallow lagoon had been heated by the relentless sun. Soon the family joined me in the water. With everyone working together, the wind didn't have a chance against us. Beth began singing a sea shanty about the North Sea. The other three joined in. They taught me the words to the chorus and I sang along, gradually going from a whisper to a full singing voice, forgetting to be embarrassed that I was permanently off-key. Also forgetting much of what normally haunted me. I was pulling my raft through murky water toward the tip of Yukon, singing with people who only days ago had been strangers. I didn't think about Megan's hair soaked in blood, or the sound of shattering glass, or whether or not people trusted me, or whether or not they should. I just felt alive. "I'm the pirate of the North Sea, I'm brawny and bold..."

Ice floated not far off from the beach where we set up camp, and wind blowing in from the sea carried the chill of that ice. Even though the sun remained uncovered by clouds, we finally put on the warm layers that had sat at the bottom of bags for ten days.

"You should all jump in," Chris said. "How many chances will you have to swim in the Arctic Ocean?"

I hoped to have a few. But that wasn't the point. I unzipped my down jacket. About half the group was willing. Chris counted down and we ran into the water, diving headfirst below the surface of the most northerly ocean. Then we ran out. It was so fast that only once I was back on shore did I realize the water wasn't quite as cold as I'd expected. I felt a lingering pang of regret for not staying in longer. Perhaps the regret came from having been so fixated on getting in and out that I'd forgotten to enjoy the moment. Or perhaps it came from the fact that even though Graham intended to send me back to the Firth, I knew well that the compass course we think our lives are on can change direction at any moment.

CHAPTER 13

Chilko River, BC
July 2008

After the Firth, Kyle and I were scheduled on a two-raft Chilko trip along with Emma, the new trainee. We had only six guests: a fifty-something couple from New York and a family of four from Southern California. The Andersen family consisted of a teen sister and brother and their parents, who would be celebrating their twenty-fifth wedding anniversary on the trip.

The first day, I had Emma and the couple in my raft and Kyle took the family. On Day Two—Lava Canyon day—we swapped. Floating down the calmer section in the morning, I quickly learned one of the Andersens' preferred pastimes was recounting stories of how Ryan, the youngest, found trouble everywhere he went. One story involved him being charged by a rhinoceros in Botswana. They had feared for his life at the time, but in retrospect they found the incident hilarious. Their funny stories were a welcome distraction from my pre-Lava nausea.

"He'll probably fall out of the boat," Ryan's mother, Michelle, warned me. "But don't worry," she continued, "he's good at getting himself into trouble, but he's even better at getting himself out." She meant well, but she was barking up the wrong tree if she thought I wouldn't worry.

We pulled out to scout at Bidwell. The water had risen significantly since the day Kyle and I had fallen out. The exposed snaggletooth rock was back to being buried beneath the waves. Unfortunately, that didn't make me feel any less like throwing up. While still on shore, I gave the six guests the talk about our responsibility as well as theirs, and then had them close their eyes to give us the thumbs-up or down. Everyone was in.

You're not ready. You swam and paddled Bidwell, but you haven't guided it since breaking your back. Do you really think taking a family down is a good idea? According to my inner critic, all the other rapids I'd rowed since coming back from rehab meant nothing if I hadn't rowed Bidwell. We walked back down toward the rafts.

"Truck and trailer," I said to Kyle.

He nodded. The term meant we'd run close together in case one raft needed help. I had no doubt we both presumed that if that were the case, the raft in trouble would be mine.

You're not ready. You shouldn't be running this river.

I pulled out of the eddy with Kyle close behind.

"All forward!" "Get down!" "Get back up! All forward!"

The boat crashed through the rapids. I kept looking to my stern, relieved each time to see Ryan still there.

"What a ride!" Michelle said when we reached the bottom of Bidwell.

"And we've still got over thirteen miles of whitewater to go," I replied. With everyone still in the boat, I felt as excited as she was.

Both rafts ran clean lines through all of Lava Canyon, hitting the big fun waves and avoiding nasty rocks and holes. Everyone was soaked and stoked.

After Lava we often camped in a big clearing sometimes used for celebrations and ceremonies by the local Tsilhqot'in people. Anyone was allowed to camp there, but whenever we heard it was going to be used for a gathering—as we had that week—we respected the fact that the Tsilhqot'in had been on this land since long before Christopher Columbus was a twinkle in his mother's eye. Clearly they got first dibs and we'd camp downstream. No one was at the site yet as we floated by. The wood skeleton of their sweat lodge stood uncovered. I'd never seen it with the walls on, but I liked to imagine it in use. I pictured an Elder pouring water onto the hot

rocks inside. Steam building. People pushing themselves to their limits to endure the heat, wanting to be part of a tradition carried down
for generations. I tried to imagine life for the Tsilhqot'in before all
us outsiders showed up. Back then they had obtained everything
they needed from the river and surrounding land without damaging
either. I wondered if there was any way humanity as a whole could
someday progress back to living in harmony with nature.

Our plan that day was to camp just after the Siwash Bridge.
Passing beneath that bridge was normally a fun little challenge:
the abutments created whirlpools that could grab a raft and hold
it for several minutes. I'd experienced it once and seen it happen to
other guides a few times. The raft would get locked into a whirl-
pool, rocking back and forth out of the guide's control, but the ride
had never been rough enough to eject anyone and the whirlpools
had always eventually let the raft go without any outside rescue
required. We always made a big deal when a boat got stuck—not
because it was dangerous but because of our rule that any guide
who got stuck had to buy post-trip pitchers of margaritas.

We rounded the last corner before the Siwash Bridge and saw a
dead tree wedged in one of the abutments. Part of the tree stuck out
of the water displaying its impressive girth, while the rest remained
submerged—leaving us to guess how much tree was under there.
Kyle and I pulled up next to one another as we floated slowly toward
the bridge. The tree was a new obstacle but it looked passable.

"Should be fine, don't you think?" I asked.

"There's enough room if we angle our boats right," Kyle said.

I took another look at it.

"All forward," I said to the family.

I put in a few steering strokes while my crew supplied the forward momentum. At first everything felt right, but as the bow
passed under the bridge I saw my angle was off and we were on
target to hit the submerged tree.

"All back."

The family paddled backward, but we couldn't counteract our
speed enough. The raft continued its glide toward the tree. I changed

the angle of the raft so that we would hit it bow first. I still wasn't worried. With some backward momentum from the paddling, I figured we would lightly bounce off from the hit without rebounding all the way into the whirlpools on the other side.

"Keep going all back."

My crew kept paddling backward, but as we approached the tree I realized we were going to hit harder than I'd hoped.

"Get down!" I yelled too late. We hit the tree before Ryan could get down, and he was underwater before anyone could grab him. We all looked around. Michelle quickly went from "Oh, there goes Ryan again" to being truly concerned. Seconds felt like minutes while we waited for him to pop up. If he was tangled in underwater branches and the current didn't push him out, it was unlikely we'd be organizing a rescue. The words *body recovery* hung heavily in my mind.

After what seemed like far too long to go without a breath, something stirred beside our stern. Ryan's hand reached up. Michelle threw both her arms in the water and hauled her son in with such fluidity it was like he was back to being a toddler and not a long-limbed teenager who clearly outweighed his petite mom.

Ryan's eyes were open wide like he'd been prepared to take in his final sights of this life. But before the rafts were even unloaded at camp, the Andersens were telling their newest Ryan-in-trouble story with delight. Everyone laughed and talked about the adventures of the day while we set up camp and cooked. Then we all stayed around the fire until day faded into night, energized by our experience on the river.

I crawled into my sleeping bag, which I'd placed a little distance from anyone else. I stared up at the first stars of the night and felt the wet warmth of tears on my face. I had made the wrong call. We all make mistakes, I knew that. But we didn't all make mistakes that could kill someone. If it had been my first close call, I probably could have talked myself out of the feelings I was having. But first there'd been the accident near the Ottawa River, then the one with Megan and Mike, and now Ryan.

I had somehow managed to build the life I'd dreamt of, and had worked as hard as I could over the past year to get back to that life. But working my hardest hadn't been enough. I had to quit guiding. As was the case over the past year, I was once again trying but failing to picture life without the river. Was there room for real happiness in another plan? I lay there listening to a river I didn't think I would ever hear again. Like the current, my tears kept flowing.

In the morning I was the first one up. I did Pilates and put on coffee, just like any other day. When the guests got up, I blamed my puffy eyes on allergies. It was Day Three of the trip. The day with no whitewater. The day to lean back and enjoy passing below the towering bluffs of Bull Canyon, cruising through ranchlands and stopping to hike up to a large cave occupied by hundreds of bats. It was normally a relaxing day (well, perhaps not for those who were afraid of bats), but without the distraction of whitewater my brain occupied itself listing every reason I shouldn't be guiding. By the time we got into some rapids again at the end of Day Four, I'd managed to rip down any shred of confidence that my clean run through Lava had helped build up.

We always said Graham would fire a guide for missing the eddy at the Big Creek campsite. I'd never seen anyone actually miss it, but I'd witnessed close calls where ropes were thrown to pull rafts in. It was a long eddy, and the problem occurred when the guide pulled in just a little too early, hitting the mostly submerged Fuck-You Rock—so called because just when a guide thought they were comfortably inside the eddy, they'd hit that rock and it would slingshot the raft back into the current, like a big fuck you.

I had always managed to avoid the rock. But a significant part of whitewater is staying on top of the mind game and, in the wake of the incident with Ryan, I'd dealt myself a crappy hand. I began to worry early on that I was too far out in the current and I was going to miss the eddy. I started to pull in near the top. I even got my guests to help with momentum. I had passed by that rock so many times. I knew where it was, yet that day I fell for the rock's camouflage trick. I didn't see it until we were almost on top of it.

"Get down!"

Emma and the couple hunkered down as we crashed into the rock and it gave us its standard reply, ricocheting our raft back out into the current. I quickly turned the boat to point where we needed to go.

"Get up! All forward!"

Emma dug her paddle deep into the current and pulled with all her force. The guests paddled hard as well, trying to match Emma's strength. I pushed my oars with all the power I could muster, but it didn't feel like nearly enough.

"All forward!"

My paddlers dug in a little harder. Just before it was too late, we drove the bow of the boat into the upstream current of the eddy. Everyone cheered.

"Damn, you guys are awesome!" I was so impressed with them. And so unimpressed with myself.

We celebrated the Andersens' anniversary that night. Kyle and I baked a thick chocolate cake in the Dutch oven. Then we sliced it in half horizontally and spread icing in the middle so that it looked like a real layer cake. We decorated it with sprinkles and cherries and wrote *Happy 25th* with more icing. Of course, we put in candles and sparklers as well. There was so much joy in the air I forgot about wallowing in my sorrows.

The last days of the trip went smoothly. We ran good lines through the rapids at Bidwell and Big John Canyon. The guests retold the stories of Ryan falling out, and of my raft almost missing the Big Creek eddy. They sounded like typical rafting stories of close calls—the kind of stories people looked for in an adventure, not the kind that spell the end of a much-loved career. We took out at Gang Ranch with the usual mix of sadness (that the trip was over) and enthusiasm (for being one step closer to a hot shower). We drove the guests to the airport and everyone hugged goodbye. Emma, Kyle and I continued to our warehouse in Williams Lake. We unpacked and cleaned gear. Everything seemed so normal I almost felt like I was lying to people. But I wasn't. No one asked me if I was thinking of quitting and I didn't want to tell anyone before Graham.

The sun beat down and heat from the asphalt radiated back up. It was a typical summer day in the Puddle. Sweat dripped down my back while Graham and I stood in the warehouse driveway.

"You're being ridiculous," he said, pushing back his shaggy hair. "Everyone says you're doing great. I've already received emails from the guests saying what a fantastic trip they had."

"I would have missed the Big Creek eddy if Emma wasn't so strong."

"It's you guides who started the rumour that I'd fire someone for missing the eddy. Plenty of people have missed it. Do you know of anyone I've fired for that?"

"I made a bad call and hit the tree under Siwash and Ryan fell out."

"The kid's fine. Why do you have to be so melodramatic?"

"I'm not strong enough to guide safely. I can't do this anymore."

But as much as I believed I meant those words when I said them, I didn't do a good job of sticking to them. In addition to the message Michelle sent Graham, she emailed Emma, Kyle and me. Among other nice things, she wrote: *Tamar, you inspire me to be better. When things get tough you never complain and take care of the situation at hand. You are so thoughtful and loving! I have the utmost respect for you. Thanks for being such a great role model for my daughter and me.* I had failed to be a role model for Megan, but Michelle's letter encouraged me to think other women out there could be inspired by a female raft guide. Less than twenty-four hours after I quit, Graham and I came to an agreement: I would take some time off and return toward the end of August to guide our three Tatshenshini trips. The Tat, especially late in the season, was more of a scenic float than a whitewater trip. It would provide a good chance to be on the river and rebuild my strength without putting anyone at risk.

CHAPTER 14

Tatshenshini River, YT
August 2008

Surrounded by soaring ice-capped peaks and boreal forests, the Tatshenshini immersed us in a landscape where even when we didn't spot any moose or bear, we were always aware of being trespassers in their 'hood. On a clear day, I was almost certain I could close my eyes, point a camera in any direction on that river and come out with a beautiful picture. Of course, not all days at the intersection of Alaska, British Columbia and Yukon are clear days. On my very first trip up there it had rained so hard that we could rarely see the raft in front of us, never mind the scenery. But unlike that first time, we lucked out with mostly clear weather on all three of my "post-retirement" trips.

We hiked glaciers slashed through with crevasses, climbed trails surrounded by wildflowers so tall I couldn't see over top of them, rowed beside glowing-blue icebergs and even chipped off pieces to enjoy margaritas on ten-thousand-year-old ice. One evening, while camping on the shores of Alsek Lake—the only lake I've ever seen dotted with gigantic icebergs—the ground began to shake. Behind us a mountain rumbled. We turned to see a cascade of rocks and dust tumbling down its side. Across the lake, the massive glacier boomed and calved huge chunks of ice into the water, sending waves splashing to the shore of our camp.

"What's happening?" one of the guests asked me.

"Earthquake or end of the world," I replied. Either way, it was mesmerizing. And if we had to say our goodbyes to our world, I couldn't think of a better place to do it.

We only knew for certain it had been an earthquake when the pilot who picked us up a few days later confirmed it. The quake had made us feel like our fate truly rested in Mother Nature's hands, but there were also many less intense moments on the Tat when I felt on the verge of being consumed by the immensity of the land. In those moments it felt so right to be part of the river life that I couldn't imagine ever wanting to leave.

I'd thought that rowing more trips would strengthen my back. Instead, those muscles wore down. I was used to pain, but I couldn't get used to not doing my fair share. I worked as hard as I could when it came to cooking, washing up, organizing and entertaining, but that didn't make up for lagging behind each time we loaded and unloaded the rafts. Over the years there'd been many trips when I hadn't wanted to arrive at the take-out because I'd been enjoying the river so much. On the Tat, I dreaded the end for a another reason as well: the strain of rolling rafts and transferring gear to the plane had become so challenging for me that I felt ineffectual. On our third and final trip of the season, I told my co-workers that once the season was done I was going to stop rafting for good.

"Whatever you say, Brett," Chris said. He and Graham had started referring to me as Brett Favre, the star quarterback who had announced his retirement from the NFL in March that year and then returned to the game that summer.

Soren was shooting a promotional video for the trip, and while hiking up to a lookout point above Alsek Lake he turned his camera on me and said, "You have the biggest smile right now and you've had it all trip. You'll be back. You love this shit too much to quit."

"I do love it," I agreed. "But sometimes that's not enough."

CHAPTER 15

Grand Canyon, AZ
January 2009

River trips through the Grand Canyon begin at a place called Lees Ferry. Our rafting group arranged to meet in Flagstaff, Arizona, the closest city to Lees. It also happened to be where Drifter and Sage had settled.

"I want you to meet my boy," Drifter said on the phone, sounding like a proud father. "How about the Walmart parking lot at noon?"

"Sounds good."

I wondered when the yurt-living hippie I'd been in love with had turned into a Walmart shopper. In fairness, we'd be doing some shopping for my trip there too. Times change. And beer at Walmart was cheap.

Beside their minivan, Sage held their son while Drifter stood with his arm draped comfortably over Sage's shoulder. It struck me that Drifter had never looked that at ease with me, and I'd probably never been that at ease with him. I felt silly for ever comparing his relationship with Sage to any of his flings in the past, or thinking he might choose me over her. These three were clearly a family. A happy family.

"I wish you were all coming on the river," I said.

"Give the kid a few years and we'll be ready to go," Sage replied.

"I'm looking forward to it."

I'd had to let go of Drifter as a lover. But I still wanted him and Sage as friends. It made sense to me that we should all run rivers together—that's what friends did.

Back in the winter of 2001–2, still riding the high of our first Grand Canyon trip, Drifter and I had both eagerly added our names to the Grand Canyon river permit waiting list. In 2006, when that list hit over eight thousand names, it was transitioned to a weighted lottery, and we were both able to pick up permit dates. Drifter's name was a few ahead of mine on the list. Once he'd secured a date for spring 2007, we'd decided that our group of friends shouldn't be so greedy as to go every year, and so I'd picked a trip date two years after his. My date had arrived. Being the permit holder meant I'd been able to invite whoever I'd wanted, but in those two years there'd been a lot of growing up. Some of the people I'd always assumed would be on my trip, like Drifter, no longer had the freedom to drop out of society for weeks at a time.

Drifter helped with our trip by shuttling one of the vehicles to the put-in. Driving down the mountain from Flagstaff, we soon left the coniferous trees behind. The highway took us through a wide swath of dusty landscape dotted with ground-hugging shrubs. When the red walls of the Vermilion Cliffs rose in the distance, I knew we were getting close. But whereas approaching the Canyon in the past had always lightened the load of my invisible weight, this time the weight felt like it was pushing me down even more. The movie theatre in my head replayed a moment from a couple of months earlier in my sister's house.

I'm sitting on the floor crying uncontrollably.

"Just don't go," Mara says.

"Everyone's made their winter plans around the trip," I say. "If the permit holder doesn't show up, National Park Service cancels the trip."

One of the things I'd always relished about Canyon trips has turned into one of my biggest fears: being deeply tied to a small group of humans for twenty-five days. In the past that situation created close friendships, but I'm ashamed of the emotional train wreck I've become and twenty-five days feels like an impossibly long time to hide that.

Mara is trying to think of a way to get me out of this commitment. My sister isn't a brooder. She's a problem solver.

"What if you're too sick to go?" she asks.

"I need to go."

"Not if it's going to do this to you."

"I'll be better once I'm there."

I have reason to believe that could be true. I've kayaked through the Grand Canyon four times before. And each time it felt like some kind of crazy spiritual renewal.

Crumpled on the floor in my sister's house, I try to convince myself the Canyon will perform that same magic if I can just get myself back there. Besides, amid all my failures in life, the only thing I feel I can do right is not back out and screw up everyone else's plans.

Drifter parked the vehicle by the launch area and we all stepped out onto the fine Canyon sand that would soon find its way into every crevice of our gear and our bodies and remain there for the next three weeks. The chatter that had been going on in the vehicle quieted down as everyone looked around. Some of our group of fourteen were seeing the reddish-brown canyon walls and wide jade-coloured river for the first time, while others gazed at the surroundings with a look of pleasure reserved for greeting old friends.

"I should get going," Drifter said once we'd unloaded all the gear from the trailer.

"You're not spending the night?" our friend Joe asked.

"It'll only get harder not to come with you guys."

"There's still a free slot if you want to join us," Palka said.

Drifter, Joe, Palka and I had paddled so many Grand Canyon miles together it was hard for any of us to believe Drifter wasn't coming. Another friend who'd been part of every previous Canyon trip I'd been on also hadn't come due to other obligations. And then there was Kevin. He'd done only one Canyon trip, but we'd paddled other rivers together. I hadn't seen him since just before my truck accident and I missed him. A lot. Since I'd last seen him, I'd spent far too much time reminiscing about the fun places we'd hooked up, like riverbanks and tents and vehicles and a raft on top of the bus roof—it had seemed strange to both of us the first time we'd been together in an actual bed.

I'd also thought a bit too much about that tall redheaded stranger I'd seen when I was a teenager who looked like Kevin and who'd had me thinking, *I could marry that guy one day*. That memory sometimes led me to another: a night at the bar when a drunken Kevin had asked me to marry him. I'd laughed at him for having had too much whiskey and joked about meeting up in Vegas after the next Canyon trip, but more recently I found myself wondering what would have happened if I'd said something different instead.

Seeing so many other friends from the Crik made me miss Kevin even more. I'd invited him, of course. Not surprisingly he'd taken longer than anyone else to reply. I'd held out hope that no news was good news, but eventually he'd declined. He'd invested all his money into buying a skidder to start his own logging business. I'd heard from another friend that money probably wasn't the only reason: Kevin had settled into a serious relationship with a woman I hadn't invited since he hadn't told me she existed. Everything was changing.

Drifter hugged me goodbye. "Stay safe," he said.

I considered saying how weird it would be without him and how much he would be missed, not just by me but by everyone on the trip.

"Don't forget to pick us up at the take-out," I said.

Joe removed his baseball cap and ran his fingers through his floppy hair, making it stand on end for a moment before it surrendered to gravity. He looked again at the giant pile of celery that still needed to be packed. I'd been trying not to ask, but finally I couldn't help myself: "So, why do we have fifty bunches of celery?"

"Guess the girls thought it was fifty bunches, not fifty sticks."

"Here's an empty ammo can we can put more in," Palka said.

My friendships with both Joe and Palka had begun in the Crik and been cemented in the Canyon. I'd met Joe for the first time just a few days into working as the rafting company "office girl" in the spring of 1997. That clear memory surfaced again now.

The office is on the main floor of an old Adirondack lodge whose creaky wood floors hint at stories of the generations of feet that have passed over them. My job is repetitive: answering phones, mopping said floors and occasionally lucking out by getting to leave the office to drive a rafting shuttle. Still, I have no regrets about turning down work on a film set. I hear my boss in the hallway speaking to someone who, depite being in the land-locked Adirondacks, sounds like a quintessential laid-back surfer. A few minutes later the oceanless surfer pokes his head through the office doorway. Tall and thin with gleaming eyes and a bit of a mullet sticking out beneath his faded fishing cap, he introduces himself as one of the guides. Stepping into the office, he casually stretches his arms above his head and the bottom of his T-shirt lifts, leaving a sizable gap between his shirt and very low-slung pants. I feel like the room is getting warmer and tell myself to look away from the skin between this attractive young man's hipbones. He asks to use the office phone, saying: "I wanna find out if I passed my math exam or if I hafta do summer school to graduate."

Nice one, Tamar, checking out the high-school kids. Getting a little desperate?

After his short call, he shakes his head: "Summer school."

"I'm sorry. That sucks."

He waves it off. "My dad took me out of school for a month to paddle the Grand Canyon. It was totally worth it."

I haven't yet learned to paddle a kayak or row a raft, yet I know from the look on this kid's face that a Grand Canyon trip is something I need to do.

It was another four years before Joe pulled his raft up to mine on a long flat section of the Hudson and asked about my post-rafting-season plans. By then Joe was no longer a skinny teen and my crush on him had been replaced by a friendship.

"Whatcha doing in December?" Joe asked.

"Not sure," I replied. "Depends on if you finally get around to inviting me on your trip."

"Guess you're spending December in the Canyon then."

I felt like I might explode with happiness.

My expectations were sky-high. Still, the trip exceeded them. Aside from kayaking through rapids bigger than anything I'd seen before, I'd spent my life in areas lush with trees and grass, and that trip was my first time in a stark desert landscape. The Canyon walls were so much more intricate than pictures had led me to expect; each stratum had its own shades and textures, and each so different from the granite of the Hudson. We hiked through the various layers and came across ancient Puebloan structures as well as rusted-out tools and supplies left by hopeful miners years ago. We tried to imagine what it would have been like to live in this harsh land.

Over millions of years, the Colorado River has eroded the land it flows through. If not for the river, all those layers we see in the rock would have remained hidden forever. The river eroded the outer layers of everyone in our group as well. Within the Canyon walls, the river allowed us to be naked in more ways than one.

Two months before launching that trip, the world experienced the devastation of September 11, 2001. There was an unspoken feeling in our group that we were trying to shed the malevolence manifested downstream of our home on the Hudson, and just live, even for a little while, in a community that was all about loving each other and the world. The magic of the river allowed us to make that happen.

Though eight years had passed since that initial Canyon trip—plus four more since the day he asked to use the office phone—Joe was still one of the mellowest people and best paddlers I knew. He continued to speak with the cadence of a laid-back surfer and rowed a raft with a similar tempo. There'd been many times over the years when I'd stressed about some river feature or other and Joe had calmed me down with his go-to saying, spoken in the tone of a Zen master: "It's just water over rocks, Tamar. Just water over rocks."

I didn't have a clear memory of my first time meeting Palka. Mostly I remembered that I'd originally thought of him as Drifter and Trace's surprisingly square friend. Not long into my first Canyon trip with Palka, I'd realized how wrong that first impression was. Despite dressing like the salesman he was, Palka was far from square. He loved to drink and get high, laughed like a maniac and made everyone else laugh too, had no qualms about frying bacon naked and was unapologetically off the wall. But as much as Palka had a talent to turn any event into a party, he had a mellow side as well. My mind goes back to an afternoon one early spring. I'm sitting on the porch of the staff house watching the Hudson River. I see a lone kayaker in the distance and long before I can make out his face I recognize from the boat, PFD and helmet that it's Palka. When he gets closer we both wave and he continues on to where he's parked his truck nearby. Soon, I hear the old porch stairs creaking as he makes his way up them carrying a beer in each hand.

"Tamars," he says, handing me a bottle.

He sits down beside me, leaning against the old wood siding that will leave a trail of faded red paint flakes on our backs. I thank him and ask how his paddle was, but mostly we quietly sip our beer while watching the water. Eventually I say, "You know. If you lined up all the hours I've spent sitting on this porch watching the river flow by, I bet it would be weeks of my life." I take another sip of beer before saying "And I don't think any of it was wasted time."

Palka nods his head with understanding, never taking his eyes off the water.

In lieu of paying a percentage of trip costs, Joe and Palka had helped with logistics. Among other things, they'd driven rafts and gear from our friend's rafting company in North Creek out to the Canyon. They'd also been tasked with shopping for food. But, not uncharacteristically, upon arriving in Arizona they'd drunk themselves stupid and were too hungover in the morning to shop for three and a half weeks' worth of supplies. So, also not uncharacteristically, they'd sweet-talked two young women working at the

supermarket into taking over the shopping list for them while they
left to indulge in some hair of the dog.

I wasn't concerned about what we'd do with fifty bunches
of celery. I was concerned about other amounts being wrong. If
we didn't have enough food for twenty-five days, there would be
nowhere along our 225-mile route to resupply.

"It's all good," Joe promised. "We can always eat the extra
salary."

"It's celery, Joe," someone who didn't know Joe very well said.

"Whatever. We'll eat what we got. No worries."

I was worried, but there wasn't time to go through the food or
to go to a grocery store. If we didn't get on the river that afternoon,
we'd lose the permit.

Before we launched, a ranger needed to make sure we had all
the equipment to meet park guidelines. While going through the
checklist, she pointed out that I was one spare kayak paddle short.

"But if we lose or break a paddle, we've got plenty of room in
our rafts for an extra person and kayak," I calmly explained while
my inner critic raged at my total incompetence.

Other people jumped into the conversation trying to help, but in
the end the ranger wouldn't budge on the rules, and I left my kayak
behind in the hands of our second shuttle driver.

For once my inner critic was consoling: *It's not like you could
really paddle anyhow.* True enough. I hadn't whitewater kayaked
since the accident and the Grand Canyon wasn't exactly the mellowest place to restart. Besides, even sitting in my boat on dry land
for a few minutes had been incredibly uncomfortable. I no longer
trusted myself to row a raft through the big rapids, so once all the
gear was tied down and the celery packed, I became something I'd
never foreseen when putting my name on the permit waiting list—I
became a passenger on my own trip. I climbed aboard Joe's raft
and hoped that the girls at the grocery store had done a better job
with the food supply than I'd done with the paddles.

Soon we crossed beneath the Navajo Bridge. Its steel archways,
some 460 feet above us, were the last signs of civilization we'd see

for many days. The walls of Marble Canyon grew taller around us. The burnt red of the rocks blocked out all but a sliver of the blue sky. My friends began to show familiar signs of falling under the spell we called "Canyon magic." Smiles spread wider and bodies grew looser. But unlike other trips where Canyon magic had taken me as well, something inside me fought it, as if I had an autoimmune disease and my body was attacking what was healthy instead of what was not.

By Day Two, I gave up on the idea that I might enjoy the trip and tried to focus on making sure everyone else had fun. Unfortunately, I didn't have any more success with that. I worried that everyone would hate me for inviting them on the worst Canyon trip ever. Starting with the celery at the put-in, I'd been in a constant fight with myself not to cry over every problem. It was only Day Three when I lost that battle. I was sitting in a raft, replacing a neck gasket on a dry suit for one of the river newbies. I'd repaired many gaskets, but that day I kept getting air bubbles in the seal and glue on my hands.

Joe and Palka were sitting in the sand nearby, looking at a river map.

"Where we camping tomorrow?" Joe called to me.

"Shinumo," I replied while trying again to press air bubbles out from the seal.

"We always stay there. How about spicing it up?"

"Sure. Where do you want to stay?"

Joe sipped from his water bottle. "Your trip, Captain. You decide."

I burst into tears.

"Aw, shit. Wha'd I say?" Joe screwed the top back on his water bottle and climbed aboard.

Palka followed close behind. "Whattup, Tamars?"

"I can't do this alone. I need help."

Joe reached for the dry suit.

"Here, lemme fix that shit."

I clutched the dry suit. "I need help running this trip. I'm a fucking wreck. I shouldn't have come but it was too late to back out."

"Aw, shit," Joe said again.

He handed me his water bottle. I unscrewed the lid and inhaled whiskey fumes before taking a big gulp. The alcohol seeped warmly down my throat. I passed it on to Palka and wiped my tears with my sleeve. Dorrie, another good friend from the Crik, climbed into the raft. Dorrie was a kayaker and raft guide with long braids and well-earned shoulder muscles.

She furrowed her brow and asked gently, "What's going on?"

"I'm sorry," I said. "I don't want to be like this. I want everyone to have fun. But I can't make all the decisions. I can't."

Palka stretched out his arms and pulled the four of us into a tight circle.

"We gottcha, Tamars, don't we?"

"We gottcha," Joe said.

"We gottcha," Dorrie agreed.

It had been so long since we'd all been together. I'd forgotten how much I loved my Adirondack family, and how hard they were willing to work to help one of their own. A warmth spread through my whole body like the one the whiskey had brought to my throat.

My friends didn't just watch my back, they made sure I laughed and had moments of fun. They were truly amazing. Yet, I still woke every morning counting down the days. In previous years the deep canyon walls had acted as a barricade blocking out all that was wrong in the world, but now those same walls felt like they were trapping me in.

We were well into the second half of the trip and had already run most of the big-name rapids: Hance, Granite, Hermit, Crystal. But the most notorious—Lava Falls—waited just a few miles ahead. I was rowing Palka's raft. The Colorado's famous rapids were dispersed among many miles of flatwater, and although I didn't trust myself in those rapids, I did enjoy rowing the flats. Nervous laughter from first-timers mingled in the air with the Canyon veterans' combat stories about Lava Falls. Good energy coursed through the group. I missed having that feeling myself, but the relief of knowing everyone else was excited brought me a calm contentment.

Far above us were the first signs of the black basalt rock, remnants of the lava flows from which Lava Falls received its name. As we floated farther downstream, the conical shape of a volcano peeked out above the canyon walls—Vulcan's Throne. Soon we came to Vulcan's Anvil, a dark cylindrical rock jutting about fifty feet out of the middle of the river. A few hundred thousand years ago, that cylinder of rock had been plugging the vent of the volcano as the pressure beneath it built and built until the volcano erupted and blasted the plug to the spot it now stood.

"Want to get on the oars?" I asked Palka.

It was tradition for river runners to pay tribute to Vulcan's Anvil. Some people believed that making the river gods happy at the Anvil would help keep you upright on the way down Lava Falls, so tucked in the rock's hollows were small gifts left by past river runners: an assortment of pretty rocks as well as human-made objects like jewellery, Kinder Egg toys and notes. Palka and I put our hands against the ancient geological specimen and said our silent thank yous for having the opportunity to be there. Just past the Anvil we could already hear the thundering of Lava Falls, even though it was still about a mile away.

I'd swum out of my kayak at Lava Falls more times than anyone should before finally paddling it successfully. On my first Canyon trip I'd made it through the biggest parts of the rapid, only to flip and swim as I was pulling into an eddy near the bottom. On my second trip, Palka and I had both swum mid-rapid and ended up together in that same eddy.

"Fuck this," I'd said to him. "We can do this. Let's hike our kayaks up and try again."

"You go ahead," Palka had said. "I'm happy here."

I'd hiked back up, only to swim it a second time that day. The silver lining of that experience was that it made me confident that the rapid was fairly safe to swim, so on my third trip, when I'd swum it for the fourth time, the only thing I'd feared hurting was my ego. Finally on my fourth trip, when I'd flipped once again, I'd rolled up and continued paddling to the end, feeling an immense sense of oneness with the rapid. But now, as Palka's raft passenger, I didn't have danger or pride to worry about. I felt like luggage.

"Ready, Tamars?"

"Let's get it, Palkas."

Without the usual butterflies I assumed there would also be none of the feelings of reward at the end. But as the first big wave crashed over me, I felt Palka's energy as he cranked on the oars. It was contagious. I hollered out a "Yeehaw!" and Palka responded with a "Wahoo!" I looked around and appreciated how different Lava Falls looked from the higher vantage point of a raft. Wave after wave bounced us around. We assumed silly positions for our friends taking pictures from shore. At the bottom, Palka pulled into the same eddy we'd both swum into years before. We high-fived. It wasn't quite the same as navigating the rapid myself, but I felt a glow of happiness. The river still held magic.

Later that afternoon I sat by the side of the river with Joe, gazing up at the Canyon walls.

"I'm the luckiest person," he said.

Over the years I'd heard Joe say that countless times. I responded the way I always had: "No, I'm the luckiest person."

Early on we used to treat our back-and-forth almost like a competition, backing up our statement with facts: good families, growing up in safe places, good health, good friends, so many opportunities to paddle and so on. But we'd stopped doing that, or at least stopped making those statements out loud. Joe put his arm around me. I thought about the truck accident and how luck had protected me from death, paralysis and the unimaginable feelings that must come with ending someone else's life.

I leaned my head into Joe's neck and watched the brown river flow by.

"So lucky," I said again.

His beard hairs tickled against my forehead as he nodded in agreement.

At Whitmore, Joe and I hiked up the dry wash and picked a spot to stash a few gifts for Drifter.

"So next time he comes back, he'll know we were thinking of him," Joe said.

Inside a small gap in the rocks we placed a tin of Drifter's favourite tobacco, a nasty porn magazine—like the ones I used to find stashed in our trailer at the Christmas tree stand—and a note from Joe and me. The whole idea was ridiculous. We would never be able to explain to Drifter exactly where we'd left the gifts and we didn't even put them in a plastic bag to protect them from the elements, but we missed him. Our North Creek family had been a tight one. Now people were branching off. Drifter had a new family of his own. Joe and I were happy for him, but it was the end of a certain kind of carefree friendship.

"Fucking breeders," Joe said.

"Fucking breeders," I agreed.

Even though I'd been waiting for the end of the trip, I'd still expected to feel sadness as we drove away from the river. I didn't. That probably wouldn't have felt so bad if there'd been something I was looking forward to, but all I was looking forward to was the absence of something.

"I need to do something new with my life," I said to Dorrie as the van bounced up the rutted road away from the river. "It's time for a change."

She smiled sympathetically and squeezed my arm. Neither of us could have any idea that change would come looking for me the very next day.

We were unloading the trailer when my phone rang. After three weeks on the river it was surprising to hear my ringtone. Even more surprising when I saw Graham's number.

"Hey!"

"It's Graham." Despite caller ID, he always announced himself. "What are you up to?"

"Just finished a Grand Canyon trip."

"I know that much. That's why I'm calling today. I was waiting for you to get off the river."

I froze, certain he had bad news. I hoped his dog Koots was okay.

"What are your plans after Flagstaff?" he asked.

"Back to Whistler. Working at the cross-country place."

"Cross-country skiing, eh? Sounds lame."

"I like it."

"How about coming to Nelson to look after the office while I take my family to Hawaii? When I get back, I'll send you to the Galápagos and see how you like working there."

"Are you serious?"

"I'd come up with something better than that if I wanted to mess with you."

"I won't be back in Whistler for another few days."

"Can you be in Nelson within a week?"

I did the calculation. "Yes."

I thought of something else. Since Graham had started running trips in the Galápagos, several of my co-workers had hoped for an opportunity to go. But for one specific reason, I'd never considered that he'd send me. I said, "You know I don't speak Spanish, right?"

"Neither do I. Keep me posted on your ETA."

CHAPTER 16

Galápagos Islands, Ecuador
March 2009

Heat radiated off the tarmac as we descended the airplane steps, and humid, salty air wrapped around us. The cacti lining the airstrip stood tall as trees and appeared to have trunks covered in brown bark. The guests and I would soon learn that their height and tough skin were evolutionary tactics to protect the cacti from hungry giant tortoises. To continue eating the cactus pads, which kept getting farther from the ground, the tortoises adapted by developing longer legs and necks. It was a slow-motion evolutionary competition.

We followed the crowd toward the open-air terminal, stepped on mats that disinfected our shoes, then proceeded to where a large-bellied man dressed in matching bright-white shorts and golf shirt held a sign saying "Nakamura." The Nakamuras were a cheerful, tanned California family of five, with three "kids" in their twenties.

"Welcome to the Islands," the man with the sign said.

He was the licensed Galápagos naturalist guide who'd lead our trip. I was worried about what role that left me, even though Graham had told me multiple times not to be. "Our guests are concerned about the Latin American reputation of doing everything mañana. You're there to make sure things work on a more North American schedule," Graham had said. "Just being a presence on the boat is usually enough to make that happen."

After a job where a typical day meant preparing three meals, setting up camp, washing dishes and in between all that squeezing in some rafting, I wasn't sure how to deal with my vague new role.

"I'm sending you because you get it. You understand what I want on my trips," Graham had said. "And remember, this isn't even a true work trip for you; it's a familiarization trip. Don't stress yourself out. You're going to the Galápagos. Enjoy the adventure."

With the naturalist leading the way, we boarded a public bus that wound through an arid landscape dotted with cacti, scraggly bushes and skinny trees. The bus let us off by a dock where sunlight danced across water the same turquoise as Chilko Lake. Chilko visitors had often said it looked tropical, but to me turquoise represented glacial cold. I couldn't wait to jump in and have my mind changed about that.

Sea lions lounged everywhere. One was even spread across the bus stop bench. With sea lions came sea lion scat. Unsurprisingly, it stank of rotting fish.

"What a smell," one of the Nakamura brothers said.

"That's the smell of the Galápagos," the guide replied proudly. "You'll get used to it."

Another man dressed all in white drove a yellow Zodiac up to the dock. He had a face like Robert De Niro in his thirties—only with a moustache and dark-brown skin.

"Hola," he said.

"This is Antonio, the second mate," the guide told us.

Antonio smiled, revealing teeth as white as his shirt and one shiny gold cap. He motored us to the *Amazonia*—a seventy-two-foot sailing catamaran we'd call home for the week. The captain and the other three crew welcomed us with Ecuadorian smoothies known as batidos. The boat's deck was as sparkly white as the men's outfits. Coming from a job and lifestyle where running water (of the plumbing sort) was rare and sleeping in the dirt was common, this squeaky-clean world made me feel like I'd fallen into a detergent commercial.

That afternoon, the Zodiac, which we now knew as the *panga,* brought us to a sprawling white-sand beach. Marine iguanas with salt-encrusted faces warmed themselves on outcroppings of dark lava rock. Sally Lightfoot crabs skittered around showing off their bright-red-orange shells and blue bellies. We donned snorkelling gear and immersed ourselves in the warm water. Fish of all colours, shapes and sizes darted around. I swam around mesmerized by the parade of colour until I realized everyone else had returned to shore.

"Wasn't that awesome?" I asked, pulling off my flippers and joining the others.

"It was all right," Amanda, the Nakamura daughter, said. "A little murky."

"You haven't snorkelled much, have you?" one of her brothers asked.

"First time," I admitted.

"It gets better," the guide said.

I'd thought it was fantastic, but as the trip went on we snorkelled in water so clear it seemed we could see for miles. We were often surrounded by dense schools of surgeonfish whose flickering lemon-yellow tails hid sharp spikes that protected them from predators. We learned that damselfish maintain algae "farms" and watched as the small brown-bodied fish with neon-blue eyes and fluorescent-yellow lips moved urchins the same size as themselves off their crop. We saw colourful parrotfish whose fused teeth create what's often referred to as a "beak-like jaw" but to me resembled a bucktoothed grin. We learned those teeth were perfect for biting algae off dead coral, and that any inedible reef material they swallowed was ground up and pooped out to become the beautiful white sand we enjoyed digging our toes into.

Fish were only a part of the sealife we saw. Marine iguanas propelled themselves forward in the water with their tails. Penguins chased our flippers. Baby sea lions engaged with us in somersault competitions. Giant turtles surprised us with how gracefully they moved through the water. We swam with a school of golden rays whose silhouettes gave the impression of an escaped load of enchanted laundry. And of course we saw whitetip sharks, blacktip sharks and Galapagos sharks. None of which displayed any interest in eating us.

On the arid rocky terrain of North Seymour Island, we stood among hundreds of the Galápagos's iconic blue-footed boobies— white-and-brown birds whose webbed feet are, as their name suggests, bright blue. It was mating season and the male boobies were dancing up a storm: spreading wings, pointing beaks, showing off feet and gifting the ladies with sticks and pebbles—all in hopes of hooking up. Although it's well known that Galápagos fauna evolved without land predators and therefore lacked any fight-or-flight response, I still hadn't expected these birds to be so indifferent to our presence. The only time they seemed bothered was if one of us accidentally got between a male and the female he was trying so hard to impress. When that happened, we could almost feel him roll his eyes as he stomped around us annoying human obstacles to resume showing off. And while the male boobies danced on land, male frigatebirds sat in the nearby low trees trying to attract mates by puffing out their balloon-like red throat pouches, flapping their wings and making drumming sounds with their beaks.

"Is it just me," I asked, "or does everyone feel like they've entered a fantasy land?"

"We've already seen so much," one of the guys said. "I'm not taking my camera out again unless there's a penguin riding on the back of a giant tortoise."

"While carrying a Sally Lightfoot crab," his brother added.

Not wanting to miss anything, I went to bed late each night and woke early. I made sure to take care of my back by welcoming the rising sun while doing Pilates on the freshly cleaned deck. My back was feeling better, but I knew if I really wanted to heal, I shouldn't allow myself to miss even a day of my exercise ritual.

At night while we sailed, I lay on a deck chair looking at the stars and listening to the squawks of swallow-tailed gulls—the world's only fully nocturnal seabirds—as they flew alongside us hunting for fish and squid churned up by the boat's wake. Before going to the Galápagos I hadn't thought I knew anything about the night sky. But I must have unknowingly absorbed something during all those summers of sleeping beneath it, because I noticed that everything looked different at the equator—the most obvious differences being that the Big Dipper was upside down and for the first time I could see the Southern Cross.

Perhaps it was the heat. Perhaps it was the twice-daily snorkelling. Or perhaps it was just all the fun I was having. Whatever the case, my back pain decreased, the idea that life was worth living grew and sexual thoughts crept back into my consciousness. The latter involving Eduardo, the boat's engineer. While the other four crew members always smiled at the guests and dressed in their freshly pressed whites, Eduardo pouted and after the first day switched to old T-shirts streaked with grease from the machine room. He certainly wasn't as welcoming as the others, but I couldn't help noticing those dark eyes and high cheekbones. However, my lack of Spanish and his lack of smiles deterred me from trying to speak to him.

Passing through the lower deck one evening, en route to my nightly stargazing ritual, I saw Eduardo sitting alone at one of the two dining tables. I smiled at him. He waved me over and gestured for me to sit down. Butterflies fluttered in my stomach.

"You first trip to Galápagos?" Eduardo's deep voice and Ecuadorian accent sounded sexy as he concentrated on getting each word out.

I was relieved he spoke some English. "Yes, it's wonderful. But I need to learn Spanish."

Eduardo smiled. His teeth were intensely white in contrast with his caramel skin. "I be your teacher."

He pointed to himself, said the Spanish word *maestro* and got me to repeat it. He then pointed out several other objects and had me repeat their Spanish names as well.

Mesa.

Escalera.

Panga.

The captain stepped outside and looked at us in a way that made me feel I'd been caught doing something other than learning that *mesa* meant "table" and *escalera* meant "stairs." I excused myself and went up said stairs to check on the night sky.

The following evening brought change to the routine. Instead of sailing through the night, we would anchor in Puerto Ayora, the biggest town in the archipelago with around ten thousand residents. From the upper deck, Amanda and I watched the town's lights grow brighter in the darkness. Diego, the *Amazonia*'s bartender, approached us. His unusual pale-green eyes stood out against his mocha-coloured skin and earned him the nickname El Gato, the cat. He spoke by far the best English of all the crew members. "Are you going out in Puerto tonight?" he asked us while looking mostly at Amanda.

"Maybe," Amanda said. "Where should we go?"

Amanda's family was already in bed when she and I took a water taxi into town. Green lights lit up the wharf. Couples walked hand in hand eating ice cream, kids roamed in herds and men played Ecua-volley—a local version of volleyball. A tramcar with little carts that looked like cartoon insects whizzed by toting happy children. It felt like a county fair, but it was just a regular evening in Puerto Ayora—where it seemed like everyone's main focus was on enjoying life.

Amanda and I walked past restaurants with candlelit outdoor patios, an internet café and a few souvenir shops full of items adorned with pictures of giant tortoises, blue-footed boobies and hammerhead sharks. Then we saw the bar Diego had recommended: Limón y Café. Two of the bar's four walls were fashioned from fishing nets, making the space neither fully indoor nor fully outdoor. The doorway continued with the ocean theme, as it was crafted from the jawbone of a whale. Both locals and visitors crowded the dance floor. Amanda and I had taken only a few steps inside when a table of Americans asked if we wanted to join them. They worked on a research vessel and had plenty of stories to tell.

We were into our second round of litre-sized Pilseners, the national beer of choice, when Diego and Eduardo entered through the giant jawbone. Diego came to say hello, while Eduardo just nodded and went to sit at the bar. I continued to drink and chat with Amanda and the researchers. Now and then I glanced at the bar. Every time I did, Eduardo was looking my way. Amanda elbowed me. "Go say hi."

It was unprofessional to flirt in front of guests, but Graham had said I wasn't really working that trip. Besides, I was already being unprofessional by letting Amanda see me looking at him so frequently. "I'll be back in a minute," I said.

"What drink do you like?" Eduardo asked.

"I have a beer at the table."

"You only drink beer?"

"I like whiskey sometimes."

A highball glass filled to the brim quickly appeared in front of me.

"I see in Galápagos you like your drinks small," I said, and quickly wondered if my sarcasm would be understood.

But he laughed. A quiet, low laugh. And I felt like he'd opened a door by sharing it with me.

We talked about his family history. He was a third-generation Galapagueño. His father and grandfather had been fishermen, as had Eduardo until he got his first job on a tourist boat. Despite the language difficulties, we kept talking. And drinking.

That night, after Amanda went to bed, Eduardo joined me on the deck chairs for my evening stargazing. Using a combination of words and gestures, he asked why I always looked at the stars. I tried to explain how seeing the constellations from a different perspective made me appreciate some of the wonders of our world. He didn't understand my slurred words, and my drunken philosophizing didn't make sense anyhow. He leaned closer and put his soft full lips on mine, gently prying my mouth open, letting me taste the sweetness of his tongue. Months worth of dammed libido flooded out. My hands explored the muscles in his back and arms. I'd forgotten what it was like to touch another human like that. We had drunken, dizzy sex under the foreign night sky.

Afterwards we lay holding each other on the deck chair. Eduardo asked, "You like Galápagos?"

"I love it.".

"You could stay and be my wife."

Normally a comment like that would send me scurrying faster than a cockroach when the lights switch on. But in that moment, it didn't sound half bad. In that moment, everything about Eduardo and the Galápagos felt right.

"See you tomorrow," I said.

We kissed once more before I stumbled back to the small room and bunkbed I shared with Amanda, and he to the even smaller room and three-tiered bunkbed he shared with Diego and Antonio.

My next two days were spent snorkelling, hiking and watching wildlife. And my nights were spent with Eduardo. There wasn't much private space on the boat, but he knew it well enough to introduce me to some secret spots.

The final morning of our trip arrived too soon. I hugged each crew member as we said goodbye. When I got to Eduardo, he held me tight and whispered in my ear, "Fuerte."

I knew *fuerte* meant "strong," but I wasn't sure what he meant by it. Were his feelings for me strong? Was he referring to my carrying the guests' bags despite protests from the crew? The shower in my room was less than stellar—I hoped it wasn't a comment about my scent.

Fuerte. The word became an instant hit on the playlist of orphan words running through my head.

From a plexiglass phone cubicle in Quito, I dialled Graham to check in.

"How was the trip?" he asked.

"Amazing. So...do you really need me back at the office right away?"

Before I'd left for Ecuador, Graham had created a job for me where I'd rotate between trip leading in Ecuador and covering for him in the office so that he could go out on trips more often.

"You just started this job and you're already trying to get out of it?" He sounded amused.

"I want to go to Spanish school. I'd do a much better job down here if I spoke Spanish."

Graham sighed. I pictured him in the office shaking his head. The guests always loved the South American trips Graham led and he probably knew ten words in Spanish, most of which had to do with ordering drinks.

"I'll check my calendar." The clicking sounds of a computer mouse came through the receiver. "I need you back by April 18."

That was two and a half weeks away. "You're the best," I said.

"Yeah, yeah. Just don't forget to come back."

The Ecuadorian city of Manta doesn't have cute bamboo huts, colonial architecture, lush forests or tall mountains. Hence most North Americans skip Manta, and because of that most Manta residents don't speak English. Making it an excellent place to attend Spanish school.

To make the most of my language learning, I signed up to stay in a private home. My host—a woman in her sixties—spoke no English. When she handed me two keys and told me what they were for, I had no idea what she was saying. She tried charades. I didn't pick up on them. Eventually she waved me outside to demonstrate which key opened what. Every detail went like that. My head hurt by the time she showed me to my room. I was sure she felt the same way.

I'd signed up for Spanish classes in the afternoons and surf lessons in the mornings. During my first Spanish lesson, the teacher pointed at pictures and rattled off words while I tried to listen, but the background noise in my head moved to the foreground. I worried I would never pick up the language. On the other hand, I didn't stress at all about learning to surf. Starting at age thirty-six and with a back injury left me no hope of ever becoming an advanced surfer. Instead of being discouraged by that fact, it set me free. Even just paddling out in the early morning light, among pelicans fishing for breakfast, felt rewarding.

Growing up inland, I'd always been wary of oceans. The water made my skin sticky and itchy. It was undrinkable. It was home to biting and stinging creatures. It could carry a person away, never to be seen again. Somehow, though, just a week of snorkelling in the Galápagos had neatly dissolved all those years of ocean distrust and replaced it with curiosity. While on the *Amazonia*, my interest had centred on what was living in the water. In Manta it expanded to wanting to understand the water itself. Surfing, like paddling, relied on being able to read the water. And I soon discovered that also like paddling, if I read the water right, surfing made me feel like I could almost fly. One day I noticed that the salt water didn't even make my skin sticky or itchy anymore.

When I'd first told my mom I was going to Ecuador, she was too worried to be happy for me. A week into my stay in Manta I called to check in. I told her about Spanish school, about surfing and about life in Manta.

"Some man started talking to me on the street the other day but I didn't understand, and when I told him that he yelled at me because he thought I was lying and just being rude."

"Why would he think that?"

"With my tan, everyone assumes I'm Latina. Which is a privilege usually. I went to a tourist town on the weekend and all the other gringos were getting hassled by people trying to sell them stuff while no one said anything more than hello to me. It was great."

"Are you using sunscreen?"

"60 SPF, several times a day. Anyhow, that guy yelling at me put me in a bad mood, and when I got home, the woman I'm staying with asked what was wrong. I told her I was frustrated that I was spending so much time on homework and still not learning anything."

"What did she say?"

"She laughed at me."

"She laughed at you?"

"Yeah. She doesn't speak English, so I'd told her that in Spanish."

My mom and I laughed together. These days my mom normally found something to worry about, no matter what. The outgoing mother of my childhood, who'd happily driven Mara and me around in a seat-beltless car with doors that swung open when she cornered too fast, had grown much more apprehensive with age. But now she surprised me with a hint of her former self. "I think it's great you're doing that. You sound so happy."

For the first time in what seemed like a very long while, I was enjoying doing things for their own sake, not because I thought they'd help me get back on the river.

"Yeah, even with strange men yelling at me in the street, it's pretty awesome here."

CHAPTER 17

Nelson, BC
April 2009

I wasn't back in Nelson long before my relaxed contentment in Ecuador seemed a distant dream. In Canada, problems felt more real. I worried about my time with Eduardo and our decision not to use condoms—or rather the lack of a decision to use them. I was on the pill, so pregnancy wasn't an issue, but one day I read on the internet that the HIV rate in adult Galapagueños was almost 15 per cent. (In retrospect, I doubt that number was accurate but I did read it and believe it at the time.) I went to the clinic.

The day before my results came in, Nelson was enveloped by a cloud. I walked up the steep tree-lined streets until the neighbourhood ended and the forest began. I followed a trail and walked even higher. Eventually I came up through the cloud. Above me was endless blue. Below, a soft blanket of white. I felt alone in the world. I noticed a bead of water clinging to a fir needle. The droplet reflected the blue of the sky, the green of the tree and the white of the clouds below. The perfection of the natural world held inside a tiny package. Looking at the drop, I thought of all the beauty around me that I missed when I wasn't looking hard enough or when I hid inside, too afraid to even try.

The test came back negative. My luck had come through again. Eduardo wasn't the first man I hadn't been careful with. It was easy to blame alcohol, which usually played a part, or the way sex felt without latex. But the bigger issue was that aiming to enjoy the present without thinking about the future had a negative side. When running a rapid, I always put on my life jacket. I needed to start treating sex with that same consistent caution.

CHAPTER 18

Galápagos Islands, Ecuador
July 2009

I returned to the Galápagos in July, to work on a different catamaran. The *Valkyria* was twenty-two feet shorter than the *Amazonia*
and considerably more cramped. I didn't have a room or a bed. On
clear nights I spread my sleeping bag out on the deck to sleep, and
on rainy nights I crammed into the small indoor eating area with
whichever crew members weren't sailing the boat. The men and I
lay around the table on padded bench seats, our feet criss-crossed
over each other as we slept. It was a fast-tracked way to get to
know people. I quickly stopped being shy about my faltering Spanish, and through badly conjugated sentences and mispronounced
words, the five men working on the *Valkyria* became my friends.

A few weeks later, work brought me back to the *Amazonia*.
At the airport, I immediately spotted the moustached man who
reminded me of Robert De Niro. "Antonio!"

He waved and hurried over to me and the guests. "Tamarita!"
Antonio hugged me like an old friend. He escorted us to the dock
where Diego met us with the panga.

"Welcome back, Tamarita," Diego said from under a wide-
brimmed straw hat that looked like something an elderly woman
had left behind.

We loaded the guests and motored toward the *Amazonia*. My
stomach clenched as I wondered what Eduardo's reaction to me
would be. The captain and his first mate welcomed us aboard with

the customary snacks and cold drinks. Diego caught me glancing around and whispered in my ear: "Eduardo was fired. He works on another boat now."

I felt both disappointment and relief. I wanted to see him again, but I was also afraid. Although this wasn't my only travel fling, being with Eduardo had somehow felt different and I had no idea if he felt the same way. I didn't ask Diego why Eduardo had been fired. I just nodded, then circulated to make sure everyone was enjoying their batidos.

I went back and forth between working on the *Valkyria* and the *Amazonia*. Although I sometimes felt like a third oar following our ship's naturalist, after a while I got to know the islands well enough that I could offer a few unique experiences to the guests. I rented us mountain bikes to ride down muddy mountain roads. I got to know fishermen I could hire to take us to a little-visited, but really cool, snorkelling spot. I even taught a few very-beginner surf lessons. At night while the boat sailed and my guests slept, I usually stayed up late with whichever crew member was steering the ship. My Spanish improved as I learned about the men's wives, children and ambitions. I learned the boat had to have GPS, but no one used it. Carlos, the first mate, was teaching me to follow the stars. I didn't feel connected to the job itself the way I had with rafting, but I began to feel that even without the river, there may be somewhere I could belong.

CHAPTER 19

Nelson, BC
August 2009

Between trips, Megan and I had both been staying at Graham's house. The night I returned from Ecuador, Graham mixed drinks for the three of us. "Why didn't Hitler like gin?" he asked. When Megan and I didn't respond he said, "Because it made him mean."

I went to bed after one drink. I tried to blame it on the bad jokes, but really I wasn't feeling well. I never got sick in Ecuador, but whenever I came back to North America I had a day or two of stomach upset. Graham and Megan tried to pressure me into drinking more, but I was done. In retrospect, I think they were trying to loosen up the mood to tell me their news: they had become a couple.

I didn't do my part that evening in making it easier for them to share that info. Instead, I found out a few days later after they'd left town. Megan had asked me to help with a photobook she was working on. But when I tried to open my email account on the computer she'd been using, her inbox popped up first. I should have closed it right away before looking, but I didn't. Next to the subject headings were the first words of each message, and I saw the start of a message from Graham that I wasn't meant to see.

If only I had let them tell me, I imagine everything would have been different. We would have laughed about their age difference, their size difference and the whole boss-dating-the-employee thing. Then we would have moved on. Instead, Megan was furious with me—convinced I'd gone into her account on purpose. *No shit she doesn't trust you. First you nearly kill her in an accident and now you find out about her personal business through her email.*

And if Megan didn't trust me, I couldn't imagine that boded well for my friendship with Graham. I'd already stopped going to North Creek, which left me feeling cut off from those friends. I'd stopped guiding, which meant I barely saw Chris. And now I felt on the verge of losing Graham, my mentor and friend for so long. And losing my friendship with him would certainly affect my relationship with his family. Aside from taking care of his dog, I'd spent a fair bit of time over the years with his wife and kids. One night recently his thirteen-year-old daughter had called me to ask if I could pick her up from a sleepover she didn't want to stay at. It had made me feel like part of their family.

The next time Graham and I met up was near Chilko Lake. After a quick hello, we got into his truck and bounced along the rocky road discussing work stuff. He stopped in front of a cattle gate. I got out to open it.

When I got back in Graham said, "You know, this is the first time you've ever greeted me without a hug."

It hadn't been intentional, but he was right. Even the very first time we'd met in person, at a campsite along the Kicking Horse River, we'd hugged.

Graham began talking about what was happening in his life and I began feeling less afraid. He cared enough about our friendship to want me to understand.

We arrived at our staff house and the whole crew was there. Megan tried to avoid me, but eventually I asked if we could go outside for a moment. I'd meant it to be just the two of us, but Graham saw us leave and came out too. I explained to Megan what had happened, but she just shook her head. Graham hovered over us, wanting everyone to get along; he even volunteered that he'd accidentally opened my inbox a few times when trying to get to his. But Megan didn't believe I hadn't tried to get into her email. She was a reasonable person, though, and agreed we had to at least be courteous to one another. We went back inside to where the rest of the guides were trying on a bunch of funny old hats someone had found. We joined in on the game, as though everything between us was okay, and at the time I still had hope that it would be.

CHAPTER 20

Galápagos Islands, Ecuador
December 2009

Just before Christmas, the *Amazonia* was anchored in Puerto Ayora. After dinner, the guests and I strolled the main drag, where lit-up models of Santa Claus and snowmen stood unbothered by the equatorial heat. As we walked, I said hello to the people I knew. As I was passing by the whale-jaw entrance of Limón y Café, Jorge, the bartender, spotted me. He came out to ask if I'd be by that night. I said I probably would. The guests and I continued past the large public dock with its lime-green lighting to the very end of the *malecón* and the small dimly lit water taxi dock. One man was already waiting. He turned to us and I saw it was the naturalist from the *Valkyria*. We hugged.

A guest said, "You know so many people here. Is it hard for you to leave and go home?"

Before I could answer, the naturalist said, "Ecuador is her home."

It was only 7 p.m. when I left the pharmacy. Everyone warned me women shouldn't walk alone in Quito at night. But at the equator, half of each day is night. Besides, there were still plenty of people out as I walked toward the hostel, swinging my shopping bag with shampoo inside.

A man of about twenty wearing a black sweater made eye contact with me. He pulled colourfully wrapped candies from his bag and held them up like he wanted to sell them. I shook my head and kept walking. He moved closer, reducing the space between us on the wide sidewalk. I swerved toward the buildings to get away from him. He moved in closer. I sped up. He came after me. He stretched out his arms. I tried to twist away, but he pushed me into a doorway. A taller, skinnier man appeared beside him.

"Give us your money," the shorter one said in Spanish.

"No."

Because of the threat of getting robbed, I didn't carry much cash. But I was angry that they were doing this to me, and I didn't want to give in.

A middle-aged man walked by. I called to him to help me. He looked at the sidewalk and kept moving. The candy man reached for my pocket. I swung my shopping bag and hit him in the head. He backed off for a second.

"*Ayuadame!*" I yelled to people passing by.

No one stopped.

"Help me!" I tried in English.

The two men took turns reaching for me while I swung my shopping bag at their heads. The taller one grabbed the bag. The shorter one reached into the kangaroo pocket of my hoodie. I punched him in the chest and he pulled his hand back, ripping off the whole pocket and tearing a line up the front of the sweatshirt. He held my cell phone high to show his friend—like he'd captured some great treasure. I nearly laughed. I'd paid less than twenty bucks for it and had used it well. If these guys had taken a moment to look at the phone they would have realized it wasn't worth anything to them. But it did have all my Ecuadorian contact numbers.

The men started to run off with my phone. I chased them. They turned into a dark alley. Away from the sounds of the busy street, the slap of my flip-flops rang loudly in my ears. I stopped—realizing the stupidity of what I was doing. I didn't even really need the phone. I just hated thinking they had targeted me because I was a woman alone who looked weak. I turned around and walked the rest of the way back to the hostel, feigning confidence. Fighting the urge to look over my shoulder every few seconds.

Inside the hostel, an American man read in a chair by the door. He looked up when I came in. Noticing my ripped sweatshirt, he asked what happened. I told him the story.

"As a woman, you really shouldn't go out alone after dark."

The hammerhead circled so close I saw its eye rotate in its socket, trying to keep me in its view. On two previous trips I'd been excited to glimpse that distinctive silhouette far below me, but as a snorkeller I'd never dreamt of seeing one of these prehistoric-looking sharks close up. Now we were surrounded by a whole school. My pulse accelerated—with exhilaration, not fear. There was no history of hammerheads attacking humans in the Galápagos. I looked into the shark's eye, and for a moment we were locked in one another's world, two dangerous species making a connection in which neither of us was afraid. It felt similar to the high we experience when we travel far from our own culture and feel accepted into a community so different from our own. Perhaps these feelings come from a constant desire to fit in; if we can connect with another culture, or even another species, surely we have the ability to connect with our own. I held my breath and immersed myself as long as possible in the shark's world.

"How many do you think there were?" Justin, one of the guests, asked as we climbed back onto the *Amazonia*.

"Twenty," a second guest answered.

"No, there were at least fifty," a third guest said.

"I counted thirty-five," the guest who worked as an accountant stated with finality.

We had stayed in the water longer than scheduled and had yet to finish rinsing salt from our masks when the crew raised anchor to set sail for Puerto Ayora. On each trip, we spent only one night in town and the crew were eager to get there. They worked six weeks on, two off, and during the six on, the night in Puerto was the only time all week they saw their families.

As soon as we were secured in the harbour, some of the crew left for shore. The guests and I enjoyed batidos, and Justin told a funny story about working the night shift at a bakery and trying to discover exactly how much jelly filling a batch of doughnuts could hold. The story was interrupted as one of the crew members held his phone out to me and said in Spanish, "It's for you."

"Hola?" I asked tentatively.

In Spanish, a deep voice said, "Will you meet me tonight?"

I stayed quiet.

"It's Eduardo."

I stood and walked away from the group. Since my first trip to the Galápagos, I'd crossed paths with Eduardo twice. Once just for a few seconds—his panga had passed by our anchored boat and he'd yelled out to me and waved. More recently we'd run into each other on the street. I'd been with a guest, so we'd spoken only briefly. Both times had stirred up old emotions.

I was so taken aback to hear his voice that I didn't know what to say. He interpreted my pause as confusion about who he was.

"It's Eduardo," he said again, still in Spanish. "From your first trip on *Amazonia*," he clarified, in case I thought it was a different Eduardo, and by then I did know two others.

"How did you know I was here?" I asked, keeping the conversation going in Spanish.

"I told Carlos to tell me when you came back."

Carlos was the first mate.

"Meet me tonight," Eduardo said.

I looked around the deck at my guests. I always went out on the nights we were docked in Puerto, but in the past I'd either had guests who went to bed early—which this crew didn't—or I'd invited them out, which in this case seemed inappropriate. My job was to make sure guests were having the best time they could, not to use their vacation time to go out on the town without them. And ditching these guests to go on a date seemed in especially poor taste since I suspected Justin had a crush on me. There was no doubt I should say no, but memories of Eduardo's soft lips and strong-but-gentle hands circled through my head. "We'll be done dinner by 9:30," I told him.

It was almost 10 when we finished dinner. In the Galápagos, that meant I was still on time. I told my guests I would walk them to the water taxi dock and then I was going to meet a friend before returning to the boat myself. To my relief, they all seemed fine with that. Along the way, we ran into Eduardo. I introduced him to my guests and told him I'd meet him soon.

The guests and I continued toward the dock and Justin asked, "Will you be out late?"

"Not too late."

"We sail at three, don't we?"

"That's hours away."

"Maybe you should come back with us now."

"We're just going to have a couple of drinks and catch up. I'll be back on time."

For someone like me with all the dance skills of a drunken hippo, merengue was much easier than salsa. With salsa, I was expected to execute moves, but in merengue Eduardo held me so close there was no room to show off my rhythmically challenged steps. When the merengue changed to eighties pop, we went to the bar where Jorge poured us stiff drinks.

"What happened?" I asked pointing to Eduardo's nose.

It was slightly swollen with a horizontal cut across the bridge.

Eduardo shook his head like he was embarrassed. "I was doing jumps in the dirt on my motorcycle and I missed. It looks bad, doesn't it?"

"It looks Canadian. When I was a kid all the hockey players' noses looked like that."

Eduardo laughed. I liked his laugh. We spoke mostly in Spanish with some English words tossed in. Sometimes I'd stumble over my words and he'd help me out. Other times I'd ask him to speak slower or repeat or explain what he'd said. He was patient, and I eventually worked up the courage to ask him something I needed to know. "I heard you're married. Is that true?"

"Yes."

I felt a small stabbing pain.

"I'm sorry I didn't tell you. It's a bad marriage. We're getting divorced."

"Oh," I said, not convinced.

"We've been having problems for a long time," Eduardo continued. "After the *Amazonia* I found a job doing day tours. I thought our marriage would be better if I spent more time at home. But that only made it worse, so I went back to a regular boat. We kept trying to stay together for our kids, but whatever I do, I can't make it work."

He looked like he was going to cry. I didn't know what to say. I felt bad for him, but I was also upset he hadn't told me. Then again, I hadn't asked, and in the Galápagos it certainly wasn't the norm to be single in your thirties. Jorge knew how to help our situation. He poured us each a shot of tequila and made sure the next song was merengue. We danced and drank until I no longer questioned whether being with Eduardo was right or wrong. He pulled me outside and kissed me.

"My cousin owns a small hotel up the street."

Before I said anything, he added, "Let's stop at the store so I can buy cigarettes."

"Good. I'll buy condoms."

"You don't have to." He kissed me lightly. "I have some with me."

We walked up the street holding hands. My heart fluttered like a teen about to make out with a boy I'd had a crush on for months. We stopped for cigarettes, then continued on our way.

It was late and no one answered the door at his cousin's hotel. We rang the bell at another hotel. An old man unlocked the heavy gate to let us in. The high-security gate was a strange match for the hotel it protected. Inside our room, the sheets were threadbare and the single mattress caved in in the middle. The walls, which looked like they were once white, were yellowish and the paint was peeling in spots. The only light was a bare bulb hanging from the ceiling. It looked like a caricature of a bad hotel room. But we weren't there for the atmosphere.

He held me, and for a moment we just stood there. Then we were kissing again. Then we were lying on the mattress, urgently pulling each other closer.

"The condoms," I said.

"I don't have any."

"You said you did."

"We don't need them."

I felt awkward telling him we did. I hadn't cared last time. I didn't want to bring up HIV, I didn't want it to sound like I thought he had it.

"I don't want to get pregnant."

"I don't have any."

"I'm going back to the boat." I started to get up off the bed.

He pushed me back down. I tried to shove him away. He took my hands and held my arms above my head. I tried kicking him. He pinned me down. I jerked around, trying to loosen his grip so that I could get away. He was far stronger than me. He tightened his grip.

"Stop! Please stop!"

He held me down as I wriggled around. He stared me right in the eye. The gentle look he'd had when he'd laughed or corrected my Spanish had vanished.

"Let me go."

His grip tightened around my wrists and he used his knee to push my legs farther apart. I tried to fight him. He kept his eyes locked on mine. The anger I saw in them was chilling. I felt him push inside me.

"Please stop."

He stopped for a second and then thrust into me again as hard as he could.

"Don't!"

He kept going. Eventually I stopped fighting, thinking that maybe the fight was what turned him on and if I lay still he would lose interest. But he kept thrusting and looking at me like I had done something unforgivable. I looked away to the bare light bulb hanging from the ceiling. *What did you expect coming to a place like this with a man you barely know?*

He drove into me again and again while holding my hands above my head. I thought about how it felt. It didn't hurt, but I was amazed at how something that my body had craved with such intensity could create no feelings of pleasure. I was relieved that it didn't.

Eduardo's thrusting grew faster. He closed his eyes. He pulled out and ejaculated beside me on the mattress. "You won't get pregnant," he said with disgust.

He let go of my hands and got up off the bed. I stayed where I was. I felt numb. Eduardo went into the bathroom and turned on the shower. Soon, steam escaped from the doorway. I found myself thinking how strange it was that a dive like that would have hot water, a rare luxury in the Galápagos.

I forced myself to get up and put on my clothes, but I didn't leave. I didn't want to wake the old man to open the gate. If he had to open it again a few minutes later for Eduardo, he would know something was wrong. Puerto was a small town. I didn't want people talking about me. I waited for Eduardo to finish showering.

When he came back into the room, he wasn't surprised to see me still there. He picked his clothes up off the floor and dressed.

"Give me your phone," he said.

I didn't ask why. I just handed it to him. He added his number and handed it back.

"Call me the next time you're in Puerto," he said.

We rang the bell at the gate and waited in silence until the old man appeared in his bathrobe. He barely glanced at Eduardo but kept his eyes glued on me—full of disgust. I thanked him for opening the gate and wished him good night. He grunted.

Eduardo was staying at a friend's place in the opposite direction of the water taxi dock. Before we parted ways, he looked at me and said again, "Call me next time you're in Puerto."

I looked at my watch. "I need to go."

It was almost 3 a.m. when the water taxi dropped me off. A crew member was always assigned to night-watchman duty when we docked in Puerto Ayora, and that night it was José Daniel. He held out his hand to help me aboard, then laughed at what a mess I was.

"You Canadians like to drink."

He told me in Spanish that I looked like I'd had a fun night. He said whenever I went out the crew worried I wouldn't make it back by sailing time. They were impressed I always managed to get in right before 3.

"Your guest stayed up until 2, waiting."

I assumed he meant Justin—José Daniel never bothered to learn the guests' names.

"I'll see you in the morning," I said.

He looked surprised. The previous time he'd been on watchman duty I'd stayed up with him, laughing and chatting and even taking him up on his dare to jump into the harbour.

"You're not going to look at the stars?" he asked.

Since I'd started coming to the Galápagos I'd made sure to take at least a few minutes every night to appreciate the sky.

I shook my head. "I'm tired."

The first rays of sun shone through the porthole over my bunk. Every morning on the *Amazonia*—no matter how late I'd gone to bed or how much I'd drunk the night before—I'd always gotten up to do Pilates before the guests woke. There were many things in life I couldn't control, but making a daily effort to keep my back strong was one thing I could. That morning I considered staying in bed until breakfast time. *It's just one day. One day off won't matter.*

Then, from somewhere in my memory, came the word Eduardo had said to me at the end of my first trip. *Fuerte.* Strong. I still wasn't sure what he'd meant by it. But I knew what I wanted it to mean to me. I hauled myself off my bunk.

Outside, I said good morning to Antonio and Carlos, who were giving the boat its usual morning scrub. I found a dry corner and did my Pilates routine. When I was done, I added a little extra: I went to the metal bar where we hung wet suits in the colder months and did as many pull-ups as I could. I thought about how nice it would be to go down a river.

The guests started coming out onto the deck just as I was finishing up.

"Did you have fun with your friend?" one of them asked.

"It was okay."

"I'm surprised you're up so early," Justin said.

"I always get up early," I said. "Gotta prepare for another day in paradise."

In the afternoon, the guests and I lounged on the top deck as the crew sailed the boat to our next destination. My phone vibrated in my pocket. It was Eduardo. My throat constricted. I thought about not answering, but I wanted to know what he had to say. I went around to a narrow space on the boat's port side to answer.

"Hola," I answered. It sounded like a question.

"I'm sorry," he said in Spanish.

I didn't say anything. It was hard to hear him over the sound of the engine, but I didn't want to go inside. I leaned against the shiny white fibreglass of the boat and watched the rainbow of colours flashing in the spray from the pontoon.

"My wife is making it so hard to see my kids and I get angry. But I shouldn't have been like that with you. I want to see you again."

I thought that I should feel outraged at hearing his voice. Or else feel validated that he was admitting wrongdoing. All I felt was numb.

"Tamarita?"

"The boat is motoring right now. I can barely hear you. I have to go."

"Call me when you come back to Puerto."

Fuerte. The word was stuck in my head. I resented the source, but I listened to it anyhow. Pull-ups and push-ups supplemented my daily Pilates routine. I stopped using fins when snorkelling and made myself dive down as deep as I could. None of that would make me as strong as Eduardo or the men who took my phone in

Quito, or any of the strange men I'd begun to find myself wary of. But I needed to try. I wanted to embrace life, not be scared of it. I wanted to be *fuerte*.

A guest named Cindy came to the Galápagos with her sister and a couple of friends to celebrate her fiftieth birthday in late March. Her birthday coincided with the night we were docked in town. The captain brought out his guitar and sang to her. We played salsa music, and the crew took turns dancing with her and her friends. We planned to go out for dinner and then to Limón y Café. I convinced Diego to meet us later at the bar.

Cindy and her group weren't just interested in ticking animal sightings off their list, they were also interested in the human side of the Galápagos. Instead of going to one of the tourist restaurants along the *malecón*, I led them up the hill to where there were no T-shirt shops or internet cafés. Tiny cookshacks lined both sides of a narrow road and plastic tables and chairs filled the centre of the street. Children played tag and jumped rope while their parents lingered at the tables. Voices spoke over each other and pots clattered on stoves. The smell of freshly cooked seafood was everywhere. We borrowed water glasses to drink the cheap bottle of wine we'd bought at a tienda along the way.

"To Cindy!" We clinked glasses.

"I can't think of a better place to spend my birthday," Cindy said.

After dinner, we walked down to Limón y Café and met up with Diego. We danced so much that everyone's faces shone with sweat. Eventually Cindy decided it was time to call it a night.

We walked to the taxi dock, but by the time we got there Diego and I had decided we weren't ready to go back yet.

Cindy hugged us both. "Don't stay out too late."

We returned to Limón y Café where Jorge poured us shots. We were on the dance floor when Eduardo came in. His eyes were on us as Diego and I danced. When the song ended, he weaved his way through the dance floor. Every muscle in my body stiffened.

"I didn't know you were back," Eduardo said.

It had been six weeks since I'd seen him. Diego moved off to find a new dance partner. I wanted to ask him not to go, but I knew that would only cause more problems.

"Why didn't you call me when you got into Puerto?" Eduardo asked.

"I don't have your number. I lost that phone." It was true. I'd forgotten my phone in an airport security tray. But I didn't know why I was offering excuses.

Diego started dancing with someone else, and Eduardo put his hands gently in mine. From his years as a fisherman, his hands were rough and callused. Just like Drifter's and Kevin's. Despite myself, I felt turned on.

"I'm sorry," he said.

Eduardo started to lead and I danced as well as I could, although even after so many nights at the Limón, I still couldn't get the moves. I met eyes with Diego. Eduardo spun me around to face the other way.

"When you are in Galápagos," he said in English, to make sure I understood, "you are mine."

I laughed.

"You are mine," he said again.

If I had been watching another woman in my shoes, I would have told her to walk away. But I wasn't watching someone else, and my mind and body were throwing around so many different signals I wasn't sure what to do. I couldn't understand how my body wanted this man again. Did I really have so little self-respect? On the other hand, didn't walking away equate to running away? Running away would mean I was scared. I wanted to overcome my fear. I wanted to prove to both of us that I was *fuerte* and could do what I pleased.

Eduardo took me to a construction site that his family had something to do with. We started kissing and holding each other. In the bar I had convinced myself that not being afraid to be with him would make me feel strong. But kissing Eduardo among the two-by-fours and buckets of nails made me feel I'd become the kind of woman I'd never thought I'd be: the one who got a black eye and went back for more. I'd never understood why some women would put up with that kind of treatment. I wondered where the confident woman I'd once been had gone. I wanted to leave the construction site. I wanted to leave the archipelago. I wanted more than anything to run a river. I was sure my old self was waiting for me at the bottom of a rapid somewhere.

"My boat's sailing soon," I said.

I was scared Eduardo would try to hold me back but he didn't.

"We can go to the water taxi together," he said.

When the water taxi pulled up to the back of the *Amazonia*, Carlos was standing on the deck holding Diego upright. Carlos, who I'd always gotten along with very well, glared at me as I climbed onto the boat. Diego vomited copiously overboard.

"What did you do to him?" Carlos asked.

"Carlos," Eduardo called out from the departing taxi.

Carlos looked up at the water taxi and the two men waved to one another. When Carlos looked back to me, his glare had turned even colder. He shook his head in disgust. I wondered how much he knew.

"Why is he wet?" I asked, turning my thoughts back to Diego.

Carlos mimed Diego falling off the boat.

I didn't think he'd drunk that much. It hadn't been that long since we'd parted ways. How had I not noticed he was in such bad shape? "Are you going to be okay?" I asked Diego.

He smiled weakly and slid to the floor. I sat beside him. During the time Diego and I had worked together, our friendship had bloomed. We'd had serious talks about family and politics, and shared crazy nights of dancing and ripping around the winding streets of Puerto Ayora on his scooter. I got along well with all the men on the boat, but of all of them Diego was without a doubt my closest friend. I couldn't believe I'd left him when he'd needed me.

In the morning, Diego was still throwing up. He was shockingly green for a dark-skinned man. The other crew members and I tried to cover for him by doing his chores while he sat on an upside-down bucket in the back of the tiny galley. Diego had come out on a work night only because I'd asked him to. At least if I'd stayed with him, I would have seen he was getting too drunk and brought him back to the boat. But instead I'd left him, and for the worst possible reason.

No one said it, but we all knew he would likely lose his job. It was a job that paid well and allowed him to take good care of his family. It was also a job he enjoyed. I couldn't get anything right. I crouched beside him. He traced his finger along a vein running up my forearm. "Do you run on alcohol instead of blood?" he asked. "How can you feel okay?"

I wanted to hug him and take care of him. I wanted to say how sorry I was. I smiled sympathetically. "In Canada, they teach us to drink."

CHAPTER 21

Nelson, BC
April 2010

"Thanks for coming down," I said.

"Thanks for the car," Soren replied, flashing his usual huge grin.

I'd loaned Soren my car while I was away. In exchange, he'd driven it to meet me at the Spokane airport. I tossed my bag into the back, then slid into the driver's seat.

As we drove, I shivered. "It's cold here in the north."

"Nah, you're just getting soft," Soren assured me.

I couldn't argue. I wore a fleece with a couple of layers underneath while he was warm in just a T-shirt.

When we got to the Canadian border, the guard flipped through my passport. "How come you travel to Ecuador so often?"

I'd been searched at borders a lot. Probably more than anyone I knew. But over the years I'd developed a couple of strategies to cut down on that problem. The one I was about to launch into involved me boring the customs officer with long-winded answers, which often resulted in them waving me through after a question or two.

"Well," I began. "I work at an adventure tour company as both the operations manager and a tour leader. When my boss decides he needs to get away from the office and go somewhere fun, I come back to Nelson and take care of the company. Then when he returns I get to go back to the Galápagos and work as a tour leader on sailboats down there."

Instead of looking at me with the glazed-over eyes I was expecting, the officer mulled over my words. I readied for him to pull us off to the side for a search.

"So, you're telling me you get paid to sail around the Galápagos Islands?"

"Yes, that's right."

He looked at my passport pages again. I hoped the search wouldn't take long. With his eyes still on the stamps, the border guard said, "And I stand in a box all day. Which one of us did something wrong?" Then he let us through.

Once the windows were rolled up, Soren laughed and said, "You have to love your job just for reactions like that."

"For sure," I agreed.

The next morning, Graham and I sat at his computer racing through office stuff before he and Megan left on their next trip. They'd moved themselves and our office into a house just north of town. When the tea kettle whistled from the kitchen, Graham stopped talking shop to ask: "Want some rooibos?" A hot drink sounded great. Despite my warm clothing, I was chilled.

We went to the kitchen. While we waited for the tea to steep, he grumbled about how many pairs of shoes Megan had packed. "She's bringing two pairs of high heels."

From the next room Megan responded, "We're going to Argentina. I will be tango dancing. And I will not be doing it in hiking boots."

Graham sighed and shook his head.

"Come on, that's reasonable," I said.

Like it was an afterthought, he said, "I scheduled you on a Firth trip."

If we'd already been drinking our tea, I would have spit it out.

"If you want to go," he added.

I jumped up and hugged him.

After they left, I started to feel worse. I couldn't stop shivering and I

185

was so tired I could barely think. I kept waking in the middle of the night shaking and drenched in cold sweat. When I finally dragged myself to the clinic, the doctor figured I had malaria and sent me to the hospital for tests. The real culprit was much less exotic.

"Turns out I have mono," I told Soren when he called the office.

"Mono, eh?"

I could hear Soren trying not to laugh.

"Yeah, I know. I thought if you didn't get it by the time you finished your undergrad, you were in the clear. Who gets mono at thirty-seven?"

"People who still make out with twenty-two-year-olds?"

"I'm not that bad."

"Uh-huh."

"Fuck off." I told myself fatigue stopped me from coming up with a better reply. But I was laughing too.

In reality, though, it wasn't all that funny. Aside from barely being able to make the eight-step trek from my desk to the bathroom, a dense fog was rolling through my head, making it hard to keep anything clear. I made stupid mistakes. When I had to book a flight, the dates and times looked like a complex calculus problem.

It seemed that half the people I spoke to told me a story of someone they knew who also had mono in their late thirties. Their anecdotes never contained good news. "It was terrible, she took two years to recover" or "It's been three years and he still doesn't have his energy back."

I wondered if I told them I'd lost my dog if they'd all share adverse tales about someone in that predicament too. "Then the dog got hit by a car," I imagined them telling me.

In any case, I stubbornly refused to consider that my symptoms might linger longer than a few weeks. After all, it was only the so-called kissing disease. It couldn't be that bad.

Graham's soon-to-be-ex-wife had kindly invited me to stay at her place, so I wasn't at Graham and Megan's when they got home. When I returned to the office, Graham asked me to follow him. He led me through the master bedroom into the en suite bathroom and pointed over the tub to the picture window framing a patch of forest.

"Nice, isn't it?" he asked.

"Very." Bathing with that view was probably almost as nice as using the groover by the edge of a river.

"Have you been in here before?" Graham asked.

"Yes."

We left the bathroom. He motioned toward the dresser stretching across most of the wall. "Megan's got a lot of stuff. Almost all these drawers are hers. I have practically no space."

"Small price to pay for having a hot young girlfriend," I said, vaguely starting to wonder about the goal of this weird little tour.

Over the course of the day, my mind returned a few times to our morning walk-around. I'd been cleaning up before they came home and had gone into their room looking for a broom. While in there I'd gotten sidetracked by Graham's pull-up bar sitting on the floor—it was the kind that was supposed to fit any doorway. I'd picked it up wondering if I could manage a pull-up or two, but I couldn't get it to fit the doorframe. I wondered if they'd noticed it wasn't exactly as they'd left it, or if they'd spotted a hair I'd unknowingly shed while poking my head into the closet and bathroom on my search. Maybe on our morning tour Graham had been attempting to figure out why I'd been in their room. But I'd never known him to skirt around an issue instead of just asking. Perhaps I should tell him I'd just been looking for a broom? But wouldn't that be a weird thing to say? For years, Graham and all his staff had shared rooms in guide houses and hotels. We'd slept beside each other in vans and tents. I used his credit card and knew his passwords to everything. I couldn't see that he'd care if I was in his bathroom. I told myself my fatigue was making me paranoid and went back to work. But I soon wished I'd faced the weirdness and said something when the moment was ripe.

The day before Graham and Megan left for their next trip, I restocked toilet paper in the bathroom I used. I guess the en suite was running low too, because by the next the morning the rolls

I'd brought in had disappeared from my bathroom. Graham and Megan were already gone, so I headed toward their bathroom to retrieve a roll. I turned the doorknob to their bedroom, but the door didn't open. I tried again. It took a moment for the truth to sink in. *You're such a screw-up. Instead of making things better, you've convinced them that they can't even leave you alone in an unlocked house.*

As far as I knew, this was the first time Graham had ever locked a door inside his own home. I considered talking to them about it, but I didn't know what to say. Instead, I hoped the problem would erode away with time. I hadn't yet learned that trust issues don't work the same way as riverbanks.

On a morning shortly after they returned, Graham said: "Can you stay off my computer today? There's family stuff going on you don't need to see."

Most of the time when I was in the office, I used Graham's computer, but if he was there, I worked on Megan's. So, that day I didn't think twice about using hers.

"Didn't I ask you not to work on the computer today?" Graham asked when he returned.

"I thought you just didn't want me on *your* computer," I said, feeling confused and guilty even though all I'd done was work on reformatting our website.

"Maybe you should just leave for the day."

I'd only been trying to finish my project. But nothing I did was right. The fog in my brain wasn't lifting. *It's been a month since your mono diagnosis. Time to get your shit together and wake the fuck up.*

Graham must have been concerned about that too. One day he asked, "Should I find someone else for the Firth?"

I shook my head fervently. If I didn't take this chance to go on the Firth, I'd probably never get another. "I'll be fine by then."

The internet assured me that most people recovered from mono within two to four weeks. I ignored the parts that said some people can take over six months. And I didn't question whether recovery meant a student was okay to sit through class or a raft guide could row through whitewater for eleven days.

As the rafting season grew near, Graham said: "Once things get rolling, you can either stay in Nelson or we can set you up in the warehouse in the Puddle."

"I'll go to the warehouse."

Graham looked at me like I'd switched languages mid-sentence and he was attempting to decipher my foreign words.

"I'll be a lot more helpful there than here," I explained.

"I agree, but I wouldn't want to live in the Puddle, so I wasn't going to ask you to do it."

"It's where the action is."

Plus, distancing myself from Graham and Megan seemed like the only remaining chance to somehow start building trust with them again.

The moving company we'd shared the warehouse with had left. I repainted the two small rooms they'd used as office space, turning one into our office and one into a bedroom. Despite the bars on the windows, it was a pretty decent space.

"The sunsets from here are outstanding," I told the guides.

They laughed at me until they saw one themselves. The Williams Lake industrial park was a surprisingly good place to watch the sky. Plus, I liked the neighbours. There was a helicopter base next door. At the end of each day the helicopter engineers, and sometimes the pilots, sat outside on lawn chairs drinking beer. I often joined them. We talked about our day and griped about the news, just like a real neighbourhood.

I started going to the Williams Lake pool. On my first day, a man who looked like he was in his eighties shuffled so slowly across the deck I wasn't sure he'd make it into the pool. He did. And on his first lap he passed me. I was likely the only person he'd passed since the Berlin Wall came down. He looked so proud of himself that I thought he might go into cardiac arrest.

After that, I swam every day and started doing Pilates again. At first I couldn't even get a quarter of the way through my Pilates routine. But by the time Chris and I were set to leave for the Firth, I could complete most of it, and I had finally passed the old dude at the pool. Perhaps I should have recognized the fogginess in this thought, but in the moment swimming faster than a mobility-challenged octogenarian seemed like a sure sign I was fit to guide again.

CHAPTER 22

The Road to Inuvik, NT
June 2010

Chris and I had watched a lot of road pass under our tires. Aside from listening to music and gossiping, we also filled the time with debates. There were times when we would passionately debate some political issue on our way to the river, then on the return trip we'd debate it with equal passion, only we'd switch sides, just for variation. To us, that made perfect sense. That was one of the things that had made us good travel buddies.

As we drove north once again, Chris kept trying to lure me into a debate. But my foggy brain couldn't formulate an argument against any of his political opinions, even as they crept increasingly rightward where he knew I'd disagree. Eventually he gave up and switched to complaining about company issues.

"I hate that Graham hires day-tripping guides and just expects me to train them to be expedition guides," Chris ranted for a while, before correctly interpreting my silence.

"Not you," he said. "You know I like working with you."

I nodded weakly.

"You'd think with all the driving we do, he'd at least make sure everyone knows how to change a flat."

I sank down farther in my seat.

"Not you. You've changed flats."

But I only knew how because Chris had taught me.

"Half the guides don't know how to drive with a trailer."

I'd logged hundreds of hours towing a trailer. But you couldn't ask for more solid evidence than my accident that I sucked at it.

"I'm not talking about you. The police report clearly states it wasn't your fault."

I nodded.

"Megan's an adult," Chris said, guessing where my mind had gone. "She chose not to wear a seat belt."

At the next gas stop, Chris offered to get me coffee as he often had before. I declined as I often did. We both smiled, and for a moment everything felt right.

Chris went to the bathroom while I fuelled the truck. In the bed was a Tidy Tank that also needed gas. The tank was new to me. In the past we'd carried jerry cans. I climbed up and unscrewed a cap.

"No," Chris yelled, rushing out of the station toward the truck.

I stood there holding the cap with no idea what the problem was.

"That cap seals in the pressure. We won't be able to pump the gas out now."

"Can't I just screw it back on?"

"No. You've depressurized the system. Fuck!"

I screwed the cap on and tried the pump. It still worked. "I think it's okay," I whispered.

"That's temporary because of the remaining pressure in the system."

Back in the truck, Chris turned up the music. I folded my arms tightly across my chest and stared out the window.

When it was my turn to drive, Chris slept. By the time he woke, we were close to Whitehorse.

"Do you mind driving?" I asked.

"We're practically there."

My hands fidgeted on the steering wheel for a few seconds before I found the courage to say, "I'm not really comfortable driving the trailer through town."

Chris parked by a fishing store. One of the guests—a septuagenarian named Ray—had told Graham he hadn't fished in years and really wanted to catch an Arctic char. Graham had given us a rod and reel and told us to buy whatever else we needed to make that happen.

"That guy is crusty as hell," Graham had said to me after a phone call with Ray.

"Sounds great."

"I mean it in the best way. He's hilarious. You'll love him. You'll probably be shagging him by end of the trip."

"Isn't he seventy?"

"Seventy-two. Think of him as three twenty-four-year-olds. That's perfect for you."

I'd made a face like I'd just smelled someone's hangover fart.

"You're going to love him."

"Is there anything I can do to help?" I asked Chris while he looked at lures.

"Tell me what to buy."

"I don't know anything about fishing."

"Neither do I." The pitch of his voice rose slightly. When I didn't respond he said, "You could pick up the meat order. Do you remember where Ralph's is?"

"You mean drive over there with the trailer?" I asked.

"Well we haven't had a chance to take it off yet, have we?"

I walked back to the truck while reassuring myself that it was no big deal. I'd once backed a trailer up for over a kilometre on a winding logging road. There was no reason I couldn't drive one forward down a few city blocks.

I drove toward the alley the butcher shop backed onto. A car was parked near the entrance to the alley. With the trailer's wide turning radius, I did what I thought was best to avoid sideswiping the car: I stopped in the left lane—giving the trailer plenty of room to turn—and activated my turn signal. I checked the mirrors, saw no cars and slowly steered toward the alley.

The sound of bending metal and shattering glass was like déjà vu. The driver of the old Chevy van that T-boned me bolted out of his door. "Fucking cunt!"

I wished for the weight pushing down on me to finally finish the job and make me disappear. My wish went unanswered. I stepped out of the truck. "I'm sorry. It's all my fault."

The man's van looked undamaged. At least from that event. Dents and scratches adorned its sides, but the front—where his vehicle had met mine—was surprisingly intact. The passenger side of Graham's truck, however, looked like bad abstract art.

"You stupid fucking bitch!" The man waved his arms violently as he screamed.

"I'm so sorry," I said, backing away from the flailing arms.

"What kind of fucking cunt turns right from the left lane? You goddamn whore!"

I continued apologizing. He was right: only a stupid fucking bitch would trash another one of Graham's vehicles. I felt like the dumb cunt he accused me of being. But I also felt relief. On the drive up, Chris had helped me realize I shouldn't guide this trip. Now that I'd crashed another vehicle, everyone else would know that too. Graham would find someone to take my place.

The cops took our statements. The Chevy driver drove away, leaving noticeable quiet in his wake.

"Are you okay?" a young officer asked me as I glanced up the alley.

"Yeah. It's just I still need to pick up my order from Ralph's."

The other officer walked up the alley. Moments later Ralph's assistant appeared with the order on his dolly.

"You're going to drive this truck?" Ralph's assistant asked.

"It's just body damage."

He helped me load the frozen meat into my coolers.

On my way back, I saw Chris walking along the sidewalk. When I pulled up beside him—the truck mangled and windowless on the passenger side—his silence felt like an ice wall. He opened the battered passenger door, wiped crumbled safety glass off the seat and settled in. I told him what had happened, never taking my eyes off the road, as I drove toward our motel. When I was done, I waited for Chris to say he didn't want to work with me. Instead he asked, "Can that van have caused so much damage if it was going the speed limit?"

"It was my fault."

I didn't want to play this game again. Like in the accident with Megan and Mike where people were always finding somewhere else to put the blame. I was the one driving. I didn't want to get out of it. I wanted people to see me for the fuck-up that I was and force me to stop pretending I was a capable person.

"This isn't just dented panels. The frame is completely bent. That would seem to be more damage than there should be if the other driver was sticking to the speed limit."

I gripped the steering wheel tighter. "It was my fault."

"Stop being a martyr for a minute and consider Graham's insurance."

Even if the other driver had been speeding, I had clearly screwed up. I didn't respond.

At the motel, Chris checked us in while I stayed by the truck. I called Mara and told her about the accident. I was practising for telling Graham. I tried to be factual and not emotional. Mara asked a question and I heard the worry in her voice. I didn't want her to worry. I didn't want to be her burden. But I couldn't hold it in. Words and tears spilled over the weir. "No one can trust me. I'm no good. I just want to crawl into a hole and never come out."

"No one was hurt," Mara said in a calm voice. "It was just an accident."

"I cause accidents everywhere. No one should trust me. I can't guide this trip."

"You can. Rivers are something you know."

"I can't."

"It was an accident."

"I can't."

Chris walked across the parking lot.

"I have to go," I told my sister.

With Chris beside me, I dialled Graham. I managed not to cry as I told him what had happened. I expected him to tell me he didn't want me on the trip, but he just asked questions about the truck. When he had the information he needed, I said, "I can't guide this trip. I keep making bad decisions."

"You're just shaken up."

Tears began to flow. "No, I keep making bad decisions. I don't know if I'm still tired from the mono or if it's something else, but I can barely think. I can't do this."

"You're being melodramatic again."

Panic rose inside me. I needed him to understand I was serious. "Please send someone else. I'll pay for their flight to Inuvik."

"There's no one to send."

"Please. There must be someone. I can't do this."

"You can."

Chris spoke to Graham briefly before walking with me toward the motel. "You're a good river guide," Chris said. "There's only one big day of whitewater. And I can help you. If you don't want to run Sheep Slot, I'll hike back up and guide your raft."

I nodded. I tried to stop gasping for air through my tears. I didn't have words to explain to Chris about the fog in my head.

"You can do this," Chris said. "You might even have fun."

I wanted to believe what everyone was telling me. I wanted to believe I was simply experiencing another case of feeling sick before one of my best days. I wanted to believe Graham still knew my capabilities better than I did.

Graham said he trusted me, but he also said not to put my name on the insurance for the rental truck. "You're really upset about the accident. I think it would be better if we have only Chris drive."

I wished he'd just say he didn't trust my driving. I'd been feeling for a while like he didn't trust me, and I was learning to live with that, but I hated not believing him.

We left Whitehorse in the new truck. Chris and I didn't talk much. We mostly stared out the window at the changing geography.

Spruce, aspen and poplar lined the Klondike Highway north of Whitehorse. We crossed pristine rivers and creeks, and passed shimmering lakes, including Lake Laberge—the site of Robert Service's famous poem "The Cremation of Sam McGee."

The Klondike Highway ends at Dawson City, once the epicentre of the gold rush and now famous for the Sourtoe Cocktail. But Chris and I weren't in the mood to see if we could stomach a beverage in which floated a human toe. Instead, just before Dawson, we hung a right onto the Dempster Highway.

The Dempster, a 740-kilometre unpaved road, is Canada's most northern highway and the only one to cross the Arctic Circle. For a while as we drove, time had no measure. Daylight remained unchanged, and as far as the eye could see was a dense forest of spruce trees dwarfed by the limited growing season. Finally the forest began to thin, and seemingly out of nowhere steep mountains shot up toward the sky: the Tombstone Range. The base of the range was a patchwork of colourful lichens, mosses and low-lying vegetation, while high above a rainbow arced over the craggy peaks. On our previous trip I'd said to Chris that the Tombstones looked like somewhere I'd like to hike someday. Passing by again I felt a more urgent pull: I wanted "someday" to be right then. "Can we just stay here?"

Chris looked at me with pity while keeping his foot on the gas.

We were back on one of the timeless, spruce-lined stretches of road when in the far distance we saw movement. Chris stopped the truck.

A wolf was walking our way. Its long, thin legs neither sped up nor slowed down in reaction to our stop. We rolled down the mud-splattered windows and stuck our heads out for a better view but rolled the windows back up again when the wolf sniffed our front bumper. The wolf walked around Chris's side of the car and stared at us through the dirty window. I didn't want to breathe. It sniffed its way around the truck, keeping an eye on us like it wanted to reach across species lines and communicate.

A thought flashed through my mind: *It's here to tell you not to go.* But that idea was crazy. It's easy for humans to find omens everywhere, but the wolf's behaviour was likely far less mystical:

tourists had probably fed it, causing the wolf to associate humans with food. Still, I found it hard to dismiss the idea that our meeting wasn't coincidental.

A vehicle stopped behind us and the wolf trotted toward it, probably hoping for better luck with those humans. Chris started the engine. We looked at each other and smiled. Sometimes a wildlife encounter is like running a river in how it connects you to whoever you experience it with. I felt closer to Chris than I had in a long time.

CHAPTER 23

Inuvik, NT
July 2010

We met the guests in the same hotel lobby as we had on the Firth trip two years earlier. They looked like a fun group. Izzy and Marta were a couple from Vancouver Island; they were there with Izzy's best friend, Phil. Izzy was clearly the driving force behind booking the trip. She was excited about everything whereas Marta and Phil seemed unsure what they'd gotten themselves into. I thought of the Tall Family and how they'd changed their minds about white-water. I hoped we could do the same for Marta and Phil. At first glance Izzy looked like a skinny teenaged skater girl, even though she was in her early forties. Marta was dressed in a cowgirl shirt and hat—and actually looked good in that outfit. Phil was a big outdoorsy-looking guy who hunted and fished. He'd met Izzy while working at the mill where she'd been the first-aid attendant. We also had a father-daughter duo enjoying bonding time before she started her sophomore year of college. Our sixth guest was Ray, the septuagenarian Chris had bought fishing lures for. Unlike the other guests, he'd driven to Inuvik instead of flying—all the way from Jackson, Wyoming. He was tall, with a thick grey buzzcut and notably good posture for an old guy. Ray looked strong for a man his age—especially a man who, according to his pre-trip forms, had multiple health problems and two fake knees. The guests sat on couches asking questions, except for Ray who stood and listened—quietly accepting the gear we handed him.

After the meeting, Chris and I were sorting through the trailer when Ray approached us. "Here," he said in his crackly voice and handed us each a Leatherman multitool and a portable knife sharpener. "Your tip. Might as well give 'em to you now so you can make use of 'em."

Chris and I were both thankful for the useful, and not inexpensive, gifts. We were also both surprised; it was the first time either of us had received a tip pre-trip.

Our first morning on the river, I was up early topping off the air pressure in my raft with the barrel pump. Ray trotted down the bank from where we'd camped. Most of the guests were still asleep. Ray already had his tent rolled and his dry bag packed.

"Here, kid. Let me help you with that." He climbed into the raft with me.

"Thanks, Ray, but you're a guest."

"Just give me the pump, Buttercup."

I decided not to fight with my elders and handed him the pump. I switched to strapping down gear. I noticed his pumping technique. "Looks like you've done that before," I said.

"Every morning on the Grand Canyon."

"When were you in the Canyon?"

Ray smiled wide enough that I saw the gold fillings in his molars. I hoped that in the future his memories of the Firth would make him smile that same way.

"Eighty-three," he said. "Guy I knew guided there. Invited me along as a swamper. Topping up rafts was part of my job."

"An amazing stretch of river," I said.

"You got that right. You know, I was a raft guide like you once."

"Really?"

"In Montana. Long time ago."

Topping up the rafts became Ray's morning job on the Firth. I appreciated the help more than I admitted. The back strength I'd built in the Galápagos had dwindled during my mono-induced rest.

Rowing was harder than it had ever been. I was happy to hand off pumping duties.

While preparing rafts, Ray and I chatted a lot. Some of the things he said were thoughtful and interesting, but he also said a lot of things I found offensive. Many of his views were racist, homophobic and/or sexist. Yet, the more I got to know him, the more I liked him. Which made me question my own morals and beliefs. The one thing that made me feel better about liking him was the fact that I wasn't alone—everyone on the trip liked Ray.

During my many months away from rivers, I'd spent an extraordinary amount of time thinking about why I missed them, yet the Firth still surprised me with all its river-magic tricks. The way the remoteness caused the group to begin bonding right away. The way it quieted everyone so that we had time to use all our senses. I heard ravens making different calls from the ones farther south in BC. I felt the pureness of the breeze—much cooler this time than on our last trip. I sensed the tiny vibrations travelling through the shafts of my oars as the blades pulled water. I even enjoyed the familiar, slightly mildewy scent of my old life jacket. Unfortunately, I also found myself in a vicious circle: rowing exhausted my muscles, making my back too achy to sleep well, leaving me even more tired the next day. And although the fog in my head sometimes lifted, it never went far. I was constantly afraid I would do something wrong.

Chris didn't think it was appropriate for us to wear our dry suits. Unlike the more whitewater-intensive trips we did, on the Firth we didn't give the guests wetsuits. If the air was cold, they wore rain pants, rubber boots and either floater jackets or regular life vests over rain jackets. Since my early paddling days I'd had it ingrained in me to always dress for an unplanned swim. It bothered me that we chose not to do that on the Firth. But we weren't the only company to run trips on that river, and everyone dressed their clients the same way. I conceded to Chris that I was probably being overly concerned, but I planned to wear mine.

"Even with a pro deal," I told him, "it's the most expensive piece of clothing I've ever owned. I like to show it off when I can."

"You being dressed for a swim while they're not doesn't make us look good."

"Oh, come on: a big black-and-purple Gore-Tex bag with legs and arms that are too long makes everyone look good."

Chris looked less than amused.

"The cold is fucking hard on my back," I told him. "My dry suit keeps me warmer and drier than my crappy rain suit."

Chris let the subject drop. I remembered when he used to see me as someone who had his back. Now even keeping myself warm made me a burden to him.

The trail was steep, and Ray leaned heavily on his walking stick. I hung back with him while Chris went ahead with the rest of the group. While we hiked, Ray told me about going through chemo a few years before. He'd been in remission long enough to start believing he was safe, but eventually the cancer had returned. Instead of starting chemo again right away, he'd put it off to come north on a river trip—something he'd wanted to do for a long time.

"So, how come you never got up here before?"

"Well, Buttercup, sometimes we put things off longer than we should."

I asked about chemo, wanting to understand more about how it felt. He preferred telling me about the attractive female nurses at the clinic. We stopped for a break. Ray poked at a plant with his walking stick.

"Wild onion," he said. "Taste it."

I plucked it from the ground and inspected the flower and the slender leaves.

"Taste it," he said again.

My botany skills weren't fantastic, but I had an idea of what it was—and that idea wasn't wild onion. Before I had a chance to take out my field guide, a swarm of mosquitos found us. I placed the plant carefully in my backpack and we carried on. Soon after, Ray spotted a Dall sheep grazing on a distant hillside.

"Beautiful animal," he said.

Its white fur stood out against the patch of greenery it was grazing on. Its long, curled horns made it look regal—like it was wearing an elaborate crown.

"Beautiful," I agreed.

"You know, kid, I've killed every type of wild sheep there is in North America."

I knew Ray was looking for a reaction. He was correct in thinking I was disgusted by trophy hunting, but if I was going to argue with him, he'd already expressed views I'd found far more upsetting than that one. Ultimately, though, I saw no reason to argue with him at all. Not because he was a paying customer and it was my job to get along with him or because he was an old man with cancer, but because nothing I said would change his mind. I'd witnessed his disagreements with other people, and I knew that once the argument reached its peak, he'd hold up his offensive traits like a badge of honour for a life fully lived. "You haven't seen what I've seen," he'd say.

When I didn't react to his sheep-killing comment, he said: "You know, I don't tell many people that. That kind of hunting isn't so popular anymore."

"Ray, has the fact that something isn't popular really ever stopped you from saying you did it?"

Ray chuckled. So did I.

We slowly made our way up the slope and finally reached the long ridgeline at the top where Chris and the others were enjoying the view and taking advantage of the breeze blowing away the mosquitos. It had been two years since I'd seen that landscape. I was struck once more by the vastness—how it seemed like our view stretched out across an infinite distance, yet aside from our little camp we saw no sign of human life. It made me very aware of how alone we were, and how much Chris and I were responsible for.

Descending was harder on Ray's knees than climbing. It wasn't long before the others disappeared ahead. When we finally arrived at the bottom of the hill, I thought we were done with the challenging part. But what had appeared from above to be level ground now revealed itself to be a large expanse of hummocks, small earth mounds created by freezing and thawing in the layer of ground above the permafrost. It was ankle-breaker terrain. Ray and I walked side by side, and all I could do was hope for the best as I watched him carefully place his feet around the bumps in the tundra. I could see he was aching, but he didn't complain. We talked about Ray's career with Wyoming's electrical company and how he'd enjoyed climbing poles to remedy wiring problems. He told me he'd grown up in Chicago and that his sister and her husband still lived there.

"What made you leave Chicago?"

"Too many Blacks."

I forgot about not arguing. "Ray, you can't judge people by the colour of their skin."

"Well, Buttercup, you'll be happy to know it didn't help. After I moved to Jackson, all the spics started moving there. You can't get away from those people."

"Ray!"

"You haven't seen what I've seen, kid. You haven't seen what I've seen."

We walked in silence for a while. I wondered once again how I could like someone who said things that I so fundamentally disagreed with. Then I questioned if I disagreed as much as I wanted to. I hated admitting it to myself but since the evening those men had ripped my sweatshirt and stolen my phone, there was a certain street in Quito I'd tried to avoid even in daylight. It wasn't the busy street where my phone had been taken, but a side street where I often saw groups of young men who looked like they shared the same minority ethnic background as the men who took my phone. And since that night with Eduardo at the hotel, I'd been wary of being alone with any man I didn't know well.

I fought against both those fears. There had been many times in my life when people who had just met me had automatically made assumptions about me based on my being a Jew or being a woman or, when I was growing up in Montreal, on my speaking English as a first language. I knew what it felt like to have people judge before they knew me at all. I knew that on a larger scale that type of judgement had caused many of my grandparents' relatives to be killed in the Holocaust. I knew that that type of judgement continues to cause genocide in the world today—as well as great inequality right here in Canada where, among many other racially motivated problems, Indigenous and Black people are at a significantly higher risk of police brutality than white people.

Because I knew those things, I'd forced myself to walk down that side street in Quito to prove I was wrong to be scared, that those men were just like any other groups of men. Nothing bad had happened when I did. I'd also forced myself to accept an invitation to a campfire from a man I knew only from the waves we shared each time I passed by the building where he was rethatching the roof. I'd been scared as I'd approached the fire, seeing almost entirely men sitting around it. In the end, though, I'd had fun and the men had made me feel very welcome, not threatened. I was ashamed of fearing people because of their ethnic background or their sex. Like running rapids, I was finding that by confronting what I was afraid of, I could see that I didn't need to be so scared. And facing my fears left me feeling more alive than hiding from them did. That being said, much like with whitewater, I was still scared in a way I hadn't been before.

Perhaps I was just making excuses for both of us, but as Ray and I made our way through the ankle-breaker terrain, I realized the more I got to know him, the less I believed his hateful words represented how he truly felt. It seemed to me that many people who spoke about the importance of racial equality weren't actually willing to put themselves in any sort of personal risk to stand behind those words. We may know discrimination is wrong, but how many of us would have the guts to stand up to a gun-toting cop who was using what looked like more force than necessary to restrain an Indigenous man? We all know it happens, but it's much safer to think that this time there's a reason for that force. But I couldn't picture Ray turning a blind eye. Ray seemed like that one guy in the crowd who would always try to help someone being wronged. And then if he were thanked for the act, he'd probably pretend he somehow didn't help on purpose. I'd known him only a few days, but it was becoming clear to me that his offensive old-man persona was just a role he was playing. I wasn't the only one hiding behind a facade.

When we were almost back in camp, I asked, "So, did you enjoy the hike?"

"Buttercup," he said, "it was something I wanted to do, so I'm glad I did it. But," and he shook his walking stick at me for emphasis, "don't ever ask me to come on a hike with you again. I need a rest."

He went and sat down on one of the chairs facing the river. I took the "wild onion" out of my pack, along with my field guide. It didn't take long to find what I was looking for.

"What did I ever do to you?" I asked Ray, trying to sound angry as I approached him.

He looked taken aback. I waved his "wild onion" in the air. "Death camas," I read from the guidebook: "These plants should be considered poisonous to all livestock and humans." I looked up from the page. "Were you trying to kill me?"

The creases around the outer corners of Ray's eyes deepened. He laughed so hard I saw the gold fillings in his teeth once again.

Our next campsite was a long, thin stretch of sand. A cliff at the downstream end of the campsite housed an eagle's nest in one of the crags. The adult eagles were off looking for food, and every once in a while we'd see the baby eaglet's head pop up and look around.

Ray suited up in his fishing hat and vest and walked to the upstream end of the beach. Chris and I watched him cast while we prepared dinner.

"That scene looks like the cover of an L.L.Bean catalogue," I said to Chris.

"That's probably the only time anyone will say Ray looks like a model."

When we saw the rod bend as Ray's line went taut, the entire group turned to watch. The fish put up a good fight. When Ray eventually landed his Arctic char, we all cheered. He didn't hear us because of the sound of the river, but he carried it back like a little boy with his first trophy.

"How's that knife sharpener working, kid?" he asked.

"Haven't tried it yet." I felt bad admitting that, but I wasn't going to lie.

"Where is it?"

I took the sharpener from my dry bag and handed it to him. He used it on the longest knife in our kitchen box, then touched his thumb to the blade.

"Sharpener works good, Buttercup. You should try it."

The knife was sharp, but Ray's fish-cleaning skills were not. Blood splattered across the rocks. Chris and I worried about attracting wildlife, but we didn't want to stop Ray and neither of us knew how to clean fish either. Eventually Izzy helped him. The char had been female, and Ray came to the kitchen holding up the red-orange cluster of her egg sac. "I want to eat the eggs. That's what the bears like best."

Ray was fascinated by bears. On his drive to Inuvik, he'd taken a substantial detour to Prince Rupert looking for spirit bears. He told us he'd even seen two. Which was very unusual.

We cooked up the fish and everyone had a piece.

"Ray," I said, "this is the tastiest char I've ever eaten."

I sautéed the char's eggs like Ray wanted. He ate them, although I don't think he liked the taste as much as he'd hoped. Perhaps it was like he said after the hike—he was glad he did it because it was something he'd wanted to do. I knew as well as anyone that what we think we want often doesn't turn out to be the best thing for us—but that doesn't stop us from trying.

While Chris and I tidied up after dinner, Ray hung out with us in the kitchen, drinking green tea from his oversized mug with the Mayo Clinic logo. He and Chris discussed Canadian politics. When Quebec sovereignty came up, Chris commented on my growing up in Montreal.

"That's where you're from?" Ray asked, to make sure.

"That's where I'm from."

He took a sip from his mug and looked me over. "You're not too bad for a frog."

I wondered if I should bring up being Jewish to see what he'd say about that.

On the morning of the big whitewater day, I secured gear in the stern of my raft while Ray pumped air into the bow.

"Why'd you stop guiding?" I asked.

"Money. Rich college kids started showing up, offering to work for next to nothing. The boss wanted to drop my pay. I couldn't live on what he offered."

I nodded, unsurprised. Money was often the reason raft guides left for other jobs.

"Graham pay well?" he asked.

"You looking to get back into it?"

"Don't be a smartass, Buttercup."

Ray kept pumping. After a moment or two he said, "Money's important. A person should be able to buy their own piece o' dirt."

"I'm happy without owning land."

Ray took a break from the pump and looked at me.

"Just remember, kid, you gotta look out for yourself."

He and I were still in the boat when a wolf appeared on the opposite bank. I waited to hear if Ray had anything negative to say about wolves—how they were a nuisance to ranchers or something like that, but he stayed quiet. He got out his camera and took a few pictures, although mostly he just watched the wolf. He looked like he was in awe. It was only the third time I'd seen a wolf. It crossed my mind that there was symbolism in seeing two wolves on one trip. But I caught myself before falling too deeply into that line of thought. We just happened to be where wolves roamed, especially while caribou were migrating through the area. The wolf stopped to look at us. I wondered if it had ever seen people before. I wondered what it thought when it saw us. Perhaps it wondered if we had some spiritual message for it. After a few moments of staring at each other, the wolf moved on and we went back to getting ready for the day ahead.

Everyone was by the water as we strapped the last of the bags into the boats.

"What raft should I go in?" the college student asked Chris.

"You can all go wherever you want."

I looked up from the bag I was securing. It was the big white-water day. The day Chris had promised to help me with. I hadn't spoken to him about it again since leaving Whitehorse, but in all the time Chris and I had spent together, that was the only time I'd ever broken down like that in front of him. I'd assumed he'd remember that whole scene. I'd also assumed that "help" meant he'd make sure I had strong paddlers for the rapids.

Ray was a good paddler for a man his age, but he was still an old guy with a dry bag so full of meds it looked like he'd robbed a pharmacy. Still, I would have chosen him over Phil or Marta. They were excellent company but they were both scared of even the smallest riffles. In the end, it didn't matter which of those three I wanted least, because I got them all, while Chris had Izzy and the father-daughter team—three healthy, gung-ho paddlers.

Ray had told me that morning to look out for myself. I considered starting by voicing concerns about my crew. But no one would trust me as a guide if I told them I was too weak to take certain paddlers. I reminded myself of the last time I was on the Firth. I had been scared, but at Sheep Slot the line on the river had revealed itself to me, telling me what I needed to do. That day had been the kind of day that kept me coming back to the river. It was a day when timid guests had been transformed into whitewater enthusiasts. Because we were going to enter the same stretch of river, there was reason to believe it could turn into a similar kind of day.

Between camp and Sheep Slot were no real rapids, just a lot of winding river with current pushing into each bend. I searched my memory for information on that section, but the water felt pushier than I remembered and the current harder to read. I kept to the slower water on the insides of each turn, giving myself more time to react if anything came up. Chris's raft moved faster than mine. He wasn't trying to outpace me—he was rowing casually, but his casual oar strokes had more power than I could muster. I was so tired I imagined tucking my oars under my knees, closing my eyes and letting the current do with me what it wanted.

Chris disappeared ahead of me. I moved into the faster current hoping to catch up. Around us the landscape slowly changed into a low canyon. We rounded a few bends, moving more quickly, but I still didn't see Chris's raft. Around another corner we were met by the sounds of Sheep Slot Rapid ahead. I rowed toward the left shore, where we planned to scout from. But the current was stronger than I'd realized and it kept pulling us to the right.

"All back!"

Phil and Marta were in the bow. I saw their paddles barely pulling water. I couldn't see Ray's paddle behind me, but I didn't feel any power from his stroke. We were still far from the canyon wall, but to not hit it we needed to get out from the current pushing us in that direction. Fighting the spasms in my back, I pulled the oars as hard as I could and tried to coach my paddlers to do the same. "All back! Dig those paddles in!"

The current continued carrying us forward, oblivious to our fight. I kept hauling on my oars with everything I had and hounding my guests to paddle as hard as they could.

"All back!"

We moved closer to the canyon wall, close enough to see details in the texture of the sedimentary rock. I still held some hope we wouldn't hit it, but I angled my boat so that if we did, we'd do so with the bow. Hitting the wall sideways at that speed would almost certainly cause the current to pull down on the side of the raft not against the rock, flood in over that edge and overturn us almost instantly.

"Dig those paddles in! All back!"

There wasn't enough power. The rock wall loomed. I put my oars in for another stroke. But this time, instead of yelling for my guests to do the same, I readied them for the hit.

"Get down and hang on!"

Our boats were equipped with luggage racks—U-shaped lengths of aluminum tubing clamped to the oar frame at one end and strapped down to the bow at the other. We used them to tie the dry bags in. The crunching sound that the aluminum tubing made as it hit rock caused every muscle in my body to tighten. At least we'd hit bow first. We were still upright. I fought to keep our angle, hoping the current would move us along the wall and release us only a few metres away, but I quickly lost that fight; the current spun us sideways and pinned the right side of the boat against the wall.

"Over right!"

We needed to quickly move weight to the side of the boat that was against the wall—the high side—or the current would pull the low side under. I jumped from the middle of the raft to the right side. Marta was already seated on that side, but Ray and Phil—who each weighed over two hundred pounds—were both on the left.

"Phil, move to the right side of the boat."

Phil looked at me with wide, scared eyes.

"Please," I begged. "We'll flip if you don't."

Phil draped himself over the dry bags between him and Marta. At least he was off the far-left side, which would win us a few more seconds. I turned to look at Ray and couldn't believe what I saw. Ray was not only still on the left-side tube, he was standing upright on it and using his paddle to try to push us off the wall—thereby putting even more pressure on the side we desperately needed to lighten. It was an incredible display of balance for an old guy with artificial knees, but I wasn't about to praise him for it. It was all I could do not to swear at him.

"Ray, get over to the right side!"

Ray looked at me and kept standing there, pushing against the canyon wall.

"Ray, please!"

"We're going over," Marta yelled.

I turned toward the bow. The front left tube was being sucked under by the current. Water was pouring in.

"Over right!" I tried one last time. No one moved. I watched the left side of our raft disappear beneath the water. As that side was pushed farther under, the right side heaved up out of the river and the floor of the raft flattened against the canyon wall. The raft froze in that position. For a second it felt like we were going to stay vertical, pressed against the wall. Then the raft shifted again. Dry bags and ammo cans swung on their tethers. They knocked heavily against my head and body as the boat went all the way over. I was enveloped by the icy-cold water. Everything went dark and quiet.

CHAPTER 24

Firth River, YT
July 2010

When the river allowed me back to its surface, I inhaled a big breath of air, then grabbed for my whistle to signal Chris. But my whistle was gone. It had ripped right off its cord. Chris's raft was tied up on the left shore. He and his paddlers were already out of the boat getting ready to scout Sheep Slot. They hadn't yet realized we'd flipped. Phil and Marta floated downstream of me, holding hands. I yelled for them to swim toward the left shore. I looked around for Ray but couldn't find him.

Our raft was upside down and still clinging to the canyon wall, as the current gradually inched it off. I swam into some slack water and slowly fought my way upstream in the direction of the raft, hoping the current would shake it loose so that I could ride it downriver. Without a boat I wouldn't be much use to other swimmers, but with a raft—even an upside-down one—I might be able to get to the others and pull them out of the turbulent water.

The current finally freed the raft. To my relief, Ray floated out from behind it.

"Swim, Ray!"

Ray turned his head toward me. I pointed to the left shore where Chris and his crew were back in their raft, pushing off from shore to help.

"Swim that way!"

Ray turned his head away from me and floated effortlessly toward Sheep Slot. I took a stroke in his direction but then stopped. Without a raft, I wouldn't be any use to him. I swam toward my boat instead.

Both the raft and I were moving downstream, and although the distance between us was shrinking, so was the distance between me and Sheep Slot. I had to decide: swim the rapid and potentially get recirculated under the raft, or get to land. I swam hard toward the right shore, managing to get out just before the rapid began. I couldn't see my guests, but Chris's boat was somewhere downstream in the rapid. *Please find them all.*

My raft had floated into the rapid as well. The canyon walls weren't very tall—less than fifty metres—but they tightened up around the river downstream, leaving no place to move along the shore. I followed a game trail that took me higher up the canyon. At the top was a clear view of the rapid: glassy tongues of grey-green water rushing over rocks, frothing holes, crashing waves. But no sign of Chris's raft or any guests. Beyond Sheep Slot the river flowed briefly through a smaller rapid and then turned ninety degrees. I assumed everyone must have rounded the corner. I ran to the bend. From there I could see several kilometres downstream. Still no one. *Where are they?*

I saw my raft upside down in an eddy on the other side of the river. As quickly as I could, I descended the canyon to the water's edge and then slid into the river. I swam using an upstream ferry angle. I felt like I was on a treadmill and would never get there, but when I finally arrived on the other side I wasn't too far downstream of the raft. Using the uneven surfaces of the canyon wall as handholds, I made my way upstream to the raft and climbed onto its exposed underside. Kneeling to keep myself steady, I pushed against the canyon wall, trying to force the boat out of its spot. The raft moved but quickly rebounded to its original position. I tried again. The same thing happened. I tried different angles, but the result was always the same. One of the oars was probably wedged in the rocks below and I had no way to get it out.

I looked downstream. Swimming would be the fastest way to go. But swiftwater rescue courses had instilled in me how easy it was to transition from rescuer to victim. Swimming alone in unfamiliar whitewater seemed like a textbook method to fast-track that transition. Instead of jumping in, I climbed the rocks to the top of the canyon and began running downstream. I soon found it was much faster to run in the grassy interior than along the craggy edge. I made a pattern of running for a few minutes through the grass and then detouring to the edge to look for signs of our crew. Each time I looked over the edge of the canyon and didn't see anyone, another layer of regret built up for having wasted so much time trying to free my raft.

I saw a Canadian flag in the distance: the Sheep Creek ranger station. I envisioned Chris and the guests inside, warming up under blankets, drinking steaming mugs of hot chocolate. I ran a few more steps in that direction before detouring for one more look over the rim.

There was a hint of bright yellow. Chris's raft. They'd pulled into a small cove I hadn't been able to see from the river bend. I made my way down the steep terrain, sliding part of it on my butt. I could hear Chris talking about sending people to look for me.

"I'm here," I called.

Chris ran over before I made it to the group. "Phil's hypothermic. We couldn't find Ray's pulse when we pulled him out. Izzy and I resuscitated him and he's holding on, but he needs a heli. I think one of his lungs has collapsed."

I didn't have time to react emotionally. "The ranger station is just downstream."

"How close?" Chris asked.

"Five minutes."

"Round up as many people at the station as you can and call for a heli from there. We need to evac them both."

I looked to where Ray lay with Izzy leaning over him. It was incredibly lucky to have a professional first-aid attendant on the trip. Our eyes met. "He didn't have a pulse," she said. A frightened child briefly peeked through her normally ultra-cool expression.

I climbed back up the hill and ran for the ranger station. The ranger was there with three student researchers—two women and a man. They looked stunned by my sudden appearance, but in moments they were gathering blankets and a backboard. There was a satellite phone in Chris's raft, but the reception would be tricky in the canyon, so I used the ranger's sat phone to call Parks Canada in Inuvik and arrange a helicopter evacuation. As the five of us ran back to the scene, the male researcher told me he was certified as a lifeguard. He seemed eager to put his first-aid training to use.

By the time we got there, Marta, Phil and Ray were all out of their wet clothes, with the latter two wrapped in sleeping bags. We placed Ray on the backboard and added wool blankets over top of the sleeping bags. Marta appeared unscathed. Phil was sitting and talking, which was encouraging. Ray's skin was tinted blue and his breathing was laboured, but his lungs were exchanging enough air to allow him to complain. "I'm cold. I'm cold. Rub me." The two young female researchers worked at warming him by placing their hands under the blankets and rubbing his arms and chest. *At least that'll put a silver lining on the dirty old man's day.*

I tried using our phone to reach Inuvik. The canyon wasn't very deep, but the phone still couldn't pick up a satellite. I climbed to the plateau to call.

"How much longer 'til the damn helicopter gets here?" Ray asked.

"Half an hour," Chris answered.

"You told me that half an hour ago."

Every ten minutes or so I called Parks Canada in Inuvik. Each time I called I was told the heli was still on the ground. They'd never had to do an emergency evacuation in the park before and rounding up people and equipment was taking time.

There wasn't enough room to land a helicopter in our tiny cove, and we worried that moving Ray would exacerbate his internal injuries. I climbed back up the hill to ask Parks if the heli could come equipped with a longline to evacuate him. Ten minutes later, when I went up to contact them again, the heli still hadn't left. I went back down to tell Chris. After another ten minutes I climbed back up. Parks told me they weren't able to get a longline.

If you hadn't asked, they would have been in the air twenty minutes ago. Every minute counts.

I slid back down the slope to Chris. "We need to move him."

Chris didn't want to put Ray in a boat where he could easily be bounced around; instead, he wanted us to carry him up the slope. I understood Chris's concerns but I'd been up and down the slope several times and had seen what the river looked like downstream.

"Even if we rope him," I said. "It's going to be almost impossible to carry him up there smoothly, plus I'm scared we'll drop him. I think our best bet is to move him by raft. There's no whitewater between here and Sheep Creek."

We loaded Ray as gently as we could. Chris took Izzy and the ranger as paddlers. I walked with the three researchers to Sheep Creek. I stood in the water to help catch the raft and bring it gently to shore. Everything went so smoothly it seemed we had made the right choice.

We carried Ray up from the river and set him down on dry, even ground. I climbed a hill to call Parks again. "How long?" I asked.

"Another hour."

Fuck!

Chris stood at the bottom of the hill looking up at me, waiting for an answer. I yelled the news down to him. Chris's entire body slumped. He shook his head and walked back to Ray. The Parks guy started asking me a bunch of questions about Ray. I told him I had to go.

"I'm cold. I'm cold. I'm cold," Ray said over and over.

After all that running around, inside my zipped-up dry suit the temperature felt like I was hosting a Bikram yoga class in there. I unzipped. It went against current first-aid protocol, but I planned to get under the blankets with Ray and share my body heat with him. Before I had my arms out of my sleeves, Ray closed his eyes and stopped complaining.

"Ray?"

Nothing.

"Ray!" Izzy yelled in his face, like an angry drill sergeant.

No response. Izzy secured a mask over his nose and mouth and gave him two breaths.

"No pulse," Chris said.

They began CPR while I retrieved the automated external defibrillator (AED) from Chris's boat. We stuck the adhesive pads to Ray's bluish bare chest. Chris pressed the button.

"No one should touch the patient," the robotic voice told us.

Everyone moved their hands away from Ray while the AED diagnosed him. We were all perfectly quiet, like we were giving the machine silence to concentrate.

"No shockable rhythm detected. Continue CPR."

That wasn't how it worked in first-aid courses or even in the movies. In those cases, the machine always administered a shock.

Izzy gave Ray two breaths. Chris performed thirty chest compressions. The cycle continued until the AED voice once again informed us that it was time to diagnose the patient.

I was sure it would find a rhythm this time, that the previous time had just been a mistake. Again it told us, "No shockable rhythm detected."

Izzy blew two more breaths into the mask over Ray's face. The student researcher who was also a lifeguard took over for Chris on the chest compressions. Each time we stopped for the machine to diagnose I felt hope, but after each diagnosis the machine repeated "No shockable rhythm detected. Continue CPR." We switched out whoever was doing chest compressions and kept going. At one point I looked up and saw two Dall sheep on the cliffs above us. A mother and her baby.

"Ray, there are sheep watching us," I said. "Don't you want to open your eyes and see the sheep?"

In wilderness situations, thirty minutes is often considered the time to stop CPR and accept that the victim is dead. At forty minutes I was pumping Ray's chest when pink foamy liquid spewed from his lungs up through the mask and hit Izzy in the face.

"We're done," Chris said.

Forty minutes without a heartbeat and now Ray was a biohazard. It was time to stop. But I didn't want to. I didn't move my hands from his bare chest. I closed my eyes, held my breath and waited to feel movement under his cool, soft skin. When I had to breathe again, I opened my eyes and looked into his face, expecting him to give us a sign he was still alive. A sign the AED was wrong. That Chris was wrong. That it wasn't over and we should keep going. His face didn't look like the face of a dead man. The dark circles beneath his eyes hadn't been there this morning, but he still looked like Ray. Living, breathing, offending-everyone Ray. I imagined the young man he'd once been. It wasn't difficult to see his younger self just below his wrinkled skin. I imagined him full of energy. Running rivers, crashing through waves. I couldn't understand how every drop of that energy was gone. How does energy disappear?

Chris and Izzy were looking at me. Waiting. I slowly lifted my hands from Ray's body. Someone pulled a blanket over his face.

Within minutes, the ranger came down the hill toward us. He'd been talking to Parks. "They want you to keep doing CPR."

"It's over," Chris said.

"They want you to keep going," the ranger said again.

"No." Chris shook his head. "It's over."

The helicopter hadn't received that message. When it landed, two young male Parks workers bounded out like characters in an action movie about to save the day.

"It's too late," Chris told them.

For a moment no one seemed to know what to do. Then the doctor who had flown in with them left to examine Phil.

After we explained the situation, one of the Parks guys asked, "Where's the stuck raft?"

"I'll show you," I said.

Before leading the two of them and Chris to the raft, I looked back at Ray's body, still strapped to a board and covered in blankets. He'd been such a big man, but now he looked so small and alone in this vast wilderness. It felt wrong to leave him by himself like that. But I did.

It took all four of us and a rope system to free my raft from its hold.

You should have realized how stuck it was right away. You wasted too much time.

The helicopter left with Ray's body. Bob, the airplane pilot, flew in to pick up the rest of us, including the ranger and researchers. Parks Canada wanted us all in Inuvik for a debrief.

We flew over open meadows and rounded mountains. I thought about all the swiftwater rescue and first-aid courses I'd taken that had emphasized the safety of the rescuers first. I realized too late those rules were meant for responders swooping in on an accident already in motion, not for the person responsible for the accident. I should have stayed in the river and swum for Ray. I didn't actually believe I could have helped him without a raft, and there was a good chance he would have pulled me under in panic, but at least I would have tried. And if I'd died, it would have been while attempting to help someone else, not disappearing from the scene only to reappear too much later, unscathed. And even if I hadn't swum after Ray, once I'd realized my raft was stuck in that eddy I could have braved the river then instead of taking the land route while leaving Chris and Izzy to clean up my mess. I should have swum. Especially in that dry suit that had made it so easy for me to get to shore.

Guides in colourful dry suits had always reminded me of cartoon superheroes. But it took more than a suit to turn a coward like me into a hero. Although apparently a suit was all it took to turn me into a survivor. I was just wearing the right clothes. I hadn't suffered at all. I didn't deserve to be okay.

CHAPTER 25

Inuvik, NT
July 2010

That first night back in Inuvik I dreamt Ray was pulling me into his grave. I fought back, but he kept pulling and yelling, "It's you who belongs in here, not me."

I woke knowing he was right.

A dry bag could hold up to only so much time underwater. Like everything else from my raft, Ray's bag was soaked through. I removed his belongings one item at a time. I wrung out his long underwear, T-shirts, pants and socks and draped them around the bathroom. The sound of water droplets hitting the tub and the floor grew louder with each piece of clothing. It echoed off the ceramic-tiled walls. When all his clothes were hung up, I sat on the lid of the toilet and listened to the orchestra created by the drip-drying of a dead man's clothes.

Graham kept in close contact with us. After one conversation, Chris got off the phone and told me, "Graham spoke to Ray's sister. She asked if he'd had a good trip and Graham told her he had. When he told her about Ray catching the fish, she was happy. She said Ray had said before he left that catching an Arctic char was something he really hoped to do."

I smiled at the memory of Ray dressed like he was on the cover of an L.L.Bean catalogue, reeling in his fish.

"When Graham asked what she wanted us to do about his truck

being in Inuvik she said, 'That old rascal. He couldn't have died any farther away.'"

Chris and I laughed. We were short on things to laugh about, so we took advantage when an opportunity came along.

A young RCMP officer with a long ponytail came to the room to fill out an accident report. The officer was gentle with me, like she thought I might break. I recounted the events of that day. When I got to Ray floating toward Sheep Slot, she asked, "Do you think he was suicidal?"

"No."

"He doesn't sound like a man who didn't know how to help himself."

The question bothered me. Ray had needed chemo, but instead he'd scheduled a rafting trip to a place he'd always wanted to go. He had given Chris and me our tips before the trip started—something neither of us had experienced before in our many years of guiding. Ray seemed set on crossing items off his life list: seeing a spirit bear, driving the Dempster, hiking a challenging trail, catching an Arctic char and eating its eggs. And I was pretty sure he'd heard me telling him to swim, yet he'd made no effort at all.

I felt like a traitor thinking those things. Like I was trying to absolve myself of responsibility. Then I remembered Ray lying on the backboard, yelling at us. I said to the officer, "He was so mad that the helicopter wasn't there. He didn't want to die."

"It's not uncommon for suicidal people to change their minds."

"Ray wanted to live."

"How long did you know Mr. Huber for?" she asked.

"Six days."

"That's all?"

I recalculated the dates in my head, then nodded.

"It sounds like you knew him for much longer."

"That's how life is on river trips."

Bob flew Chris and me back to Sheep Creek, along with the ranger, the researchers and the two Parks workers. The Parks guys helped Chris and me roll our rafts and pack the gear we'd left behind. We made several trips with the ranger's ATV, transferring equipment to the landing strip. At one point I was alone by the water where Sheep Creek drains into the Firth. I looked at the cliffs where the ewe and her lamb had watched us fail to save Ray. I looked at the spot where he'd lain as we'd pumped on his chest. Where the electronic voice had repeated again and again, "No shockable rhythm detected."

I turned my eyes toward the Firth. Greenish water gushed over rocks, creating a small glassy wave not far from where I stood. I wanted to jump into the river and flow down with it to the sea. The river wouldn't judge me or know not to trust me. The river would just continue journeying past whatever was in its way in its relentless pursuit to reach the ocean.

I should have been thinking of Ray, but instead I thought of myself. I thought of how I would never again battle the wind in the braiding channels of the delta. Or sing sea shanties with guests while pulling a raft through the lagoon. I wouldn't camp among the ghostly white driftwood shelters. Or swim in the cold salty water of the Beaufort Sea. I wouldn't even see the waves around the next corner. I stared at what was in front of me. I tried to paint as many of its details as I could into my mind so that I could bring this last river with me wherever I went.

We'd left the river with six days worth of food remaining. While four of us moved gear, unbeknownst to us Bob was looking through the food supplies and doling out duties to his co-pilot, the ranger and the researchers. By the time we returned to the cabin, he had orchestrated a gourmet dinner.

"It's important to bring some normalcy to the situation," Bob said.

Bob was known to be one of the best fixed-wing pilots in the Arctic, which meant his schedule was always full. He could have easily hurried us back to Inuvik to pilot another flight and make more money. Or he could have gone home early to his wife who he spoke so highly of and to their Pomeranian, who apparently had several outfits to match Bob's. But instead of doing either of those things he rooted through coolers, gave instruction on chopping and cooking vegetables, and did a perfect job of seasoning and grilling steaks—all to return some normalcy to the lives of a few people he barely knew.

The ten of us sat around the cabin's long wooden table. We ate, drank wine, even laughed. And we talked about Ray. Bob understood a lot about the importance of enjoying life. He was quietly teaching us what he knew.

I didn't look forward to leaving Inuvik. In Inuvik I didn't have to tell anyone what had happened—everyone already knew. Under the midnight sun there was nothing left to hide. But after a few days of tying up loose ends with Parks and the RCMP, the time came for us to go. Graham told Ray's sister we would bring the truck down for her. I offered to drive, but Graham said he'd fly up another guide to do it instead.

"You're too shaken up to drive," he said. "If something were to happen, you wouldn't be able to forgive yourself."

I wanted to tell him: "If I was ever going to total someone's vehicle and not feel that bad about it, it would be Ray's. I already made sure he wouldn't need it anymore." But of course I didn't say that.

"Have you spoken to your sister?" Chris asked as we drove out of Inuvik toward Whitehorse.

"No. Have you called Joni?" I asked about his partner.

"Last night."

"That's good."

"You're going to have to talk to someone eventually."

I nodded.

Two counsellors had been moderating the Parks Canada debriefing session. After the debrief, the counsellors had approached me, voicing concerns that I wasn't expressing my emotions. It seemed Chris agreed.

"I'll call my sister when we get to Whitehorse," I said.

"You can talk to me."

I should have taken that opportunity to tell Chris how sorry I was for the situation I'd put him in, and how grateful I was for all he'd done for me. Chris was one of the best co-workers I'd ever had, and while he'd been dealing with the problems caused by my capsize, I'd been off running through the tundra instead of by his side where I should have been.

I stared out the window. After a while I said, "I don't feel the emotions I should."

"There's no right way to feel."

It was cheesy, but what else was he going to say?

"I'm angry," I said.

"At me?"

"At Ray."

All the calmness in Chris's expression disappeared.

"He was seventy-two fucking years old. You can't be mad at him. He was just doing what came naturally."

"I know."

I wasn't angry for the reasons Chris likely assumed, like ignoring my "Over right" command and trying to push off the canyon wall. I understood why Ray might have done those things. I was mad at Ray for dying. Everything would be different if he had just stayed alive.

"If you're angry at anyone, it should be me," Chris said. The way the sun shone through the driver's-side window caused his red beard to look like it was made of fire.

My mind had indeed tried placing the blame on Chris. There were things he could have done differently. I had also tried pinning it on Graham. But the blame wouldn't stick to either of them. How could they have known how cloudy my brain was or how weak my body was? Yes, I had certainly expressed doubt about my ability, but self-doubt was as much a part of me as the mole above my right eyebrow. Why should Graham and Chris have thought this time was different? When Graham had asked if he needed to find someone else because of my mono, I'd assured him I would be fine. Why would he have doubted me? I had said in Whitehorse I didn't want to go, but no one had physically forced me onto the river. Graham had said there was no one else, but if I'd broken an arm, he would have had to find someone to replace me. It was my fault for not explaining how serious my problems were. It was my fault because as scared as I'd been, part of me had still selfishly wanted to get back on the river. On the morning Ray had died, no one but me had stopped me from saying I needed stronger paddlers. And there was no reason I couldn't have spoken to Chris about that the night before; he'd always been willing to help me in the past. More than anything, neither Chris nor Graham had been the ones rowing my raft when it crashed into the canyon wall. I looked at Chris and his flaming-red beard.

"I was the one holding the oars."

For a long time after we were both quiet, watching the seemingly endless expanse of dirt road meander through the low trees.

Chris and I had barely finished unpacking from the Firth when it was time for me to leave again. I had a trip to lead in the Galápagos. Just as the river doesn't stop for emergencies, life continued rushing along after Ray's death, complete with guests expecting to go on tours. The plan was for me to drive from the Puddle to Seattle and fly to Quito from there. On the way to Seattle I would stop in Whistler to visit my sister.

My mom was also visiting Mara. They were both in the living room when I came in. Mara in a chair by the fireplace. My mom in the corner of the L-shaped couch. She had her feet crossed under her, just like I often sat.

They both already knew Ray had died, but being with them in person made me feel I was expected to talk about his death. Talking about it with family was different from talking about it with anyone else. For the first time since the accident, I cried.

"I don't want to waste my life being depressed anymore," I told them through my tears. "I'm so tired of feeling guilty about everything. I feel like I don't have any more room to take this guilt on. I just want to take advantage of being alive."

My sister looked happy I'd said that. My mom pulled her feet in tighter and nodded like she wanted to encourage me. Her face looked frightened. She was probably scared for me, for my road ahead, but at the time I wondered if she was scared *of* me. I couldn't blame her. I was scared of me.

When I checked my email that evening there was a message from Graham:

Tamar
We'll have a debrief when I get back, but it would be help-
ful and appropriate if you talked to Izzy, Marta and Phil
as soon as possible. I would suggest a call to check in and
let them know that you are sorry about the accident and
following events. During my discussions with each of them,
they all voiced a concern that you have not really apologized
to them.
  Apologies are not an admission of guilt but can do a lot
to mend fences. Do it when you are ready. :)
Cheers,
Graham

I'd wanted to apologize to everyone on the trip, but I'd been scared of exactly what Graham suspected—that it would look like an admission of guilt. I'd been ready to own up to my own guilt, but I'd worried about the legal ramifications for Graham. I should have talked to him about that. I emailed him back to see if he had their phone numbers. I was relieved not to get a response. Writing was less scary.

Dear Izzy, Marta and Phil,
While it would be appropriate to call each one of you indi-
vidually, and I could make all sorts of excuses why I'm

emailing instead (for instance: I'm not at the office and don't have your numbers), the truth is that I'm too scared to call. I'm not very good with my emotions and I suspect that if I called I would either get very stoic or totally break down and be incomprehensible—either way, I don't think I would really be able to get across what I would like to.

Graham said you mentioned that I haven't yet apologized. I know I shouldn't have waited for him, or any of you, to say something, as I definitely owe you all an apology—I have found this situation very difficult and since getting off the river I feel like I haven't been reacting as I should. But I want you to know that I am very, very sorry. I'm sorry that Phil and Marta had scary cold swims. I'm sorry that Izzy had to watch two people so close to her swim and I'm sorry that she felt guilty about it. I'm sorry Phil had hypothermia and that he got water in his lungs. I'm sorry about Ray. I'm sorry you all had to be on a trip where someone died. I'm sorry that Izzy got hit by bodily fluids. I'm sorry I didn't get to you guys sooner—I thought I could get my raft out of the eddy and that would be the fastest way to get down to you, but I couldn't and in the end I wasted a few minutes trying when I could have spent them running. I'm sorry that you took off time from work and spent all that money and only got half a trip. I'm sorry we didn't see muskoxen or caribou or bears. I think the three of you are so awesome and I'm sorry that we will probably never get to be friends. I'm sorry I flipped the raft. I'm sorry for so many things, and I'm sorry I've taken so long to tell you this.

On the other hand, I'm very thankful Izzy was so incredible and pulled Marta in and resuscitated Ray and so much more. I'm very thankful for all the help that Marta gave in the first-aid situation. I'm very thankful that Phil didn't give up and got out of the river okay. And I'm also thankful for how great you guys were before the accident, and for the laughs you gave us afterward. I'm especially thankful that *even though you didn't get to swim in the Beaufort, you still got to go home.*

I hope so much that you will all be able to continue on many adventures without the memory of this river accident holding you back from anything.

You are three wonderful and special people and I wish you all the best, and, once again, I'm sorry.
Take care of yourselves,
Tamar

The words didn't live up to what I wanted to say. But they were the best I could do. Breath held, as though readying to remove a Band-Aid, I pressed send.

In Graham's next email, he thanked me for sending the apology. It seemed the three guests had appreciated receiving it. I was happy for that, but reading his message made me realize that none of the three of them intended to respond to me. There was no reason for me to expect they would, but still, my body wilted into my chair.

Although I'd apologized to Graham on the phone, I emailed him to tell him once again that I was sorry. He responded quickly:

I know you are. Nothing more needs to be said. Shit happens. How we deal with it will define us. You need to allow yourself to let it go. Ray was a cool, no-nonsense man and would tell you to let it go.

CHAPTER 26

Galápagos Islands, Ecuador
July 2010

The transition from Arctic Circle to equator was a quick one. My sister was worried about me guiding again so soon, but even though Ray was gone, I was still here. What else could I do but carry on? And I figured being around people who had no idea what had happened on the Firth would make it easier to do that.

I met my guests at the Quito airport. A family of four from Texas. The parents were both doctors and looked like the TV version of an ideal American couple. They had a son and a daughter aged twelve and fourteen. We chatted a lot in the taxi on the way to the hotel. They were very friendly and asked interesting questions about the upcoming trip. I did my best to answer and not get too distracted by the inner workings of my mind as it relived the images of the dark circles under Ray's eyes, the sound of the AED repeating "No shockable rhythm detected" and the cold smoothness of Ray's motionless chest beneath my hands.

"I'll see you in a few hours," I said once they were checked in.

I walked to my room, thinking about what a nice family they were and how they were so ready to have a trip of a lifetime. Once I was changed and my teeth were brushed, I got into bed and pulled the covers over my head, hoping whoever was in the room next door wouldn't hear me cry. I had meant what I'd said to Mara and my mom. I didn't want to be depressed anymore. I didn't want to let life pass me by. I agreed with Graham that I needed to allow myself to let it go. But I had no idea how to do that, especially when I didn't deserve to go on living a normal life. I wasn't a good person. Whenever I thought I was doing the right thing, it turned out to be wrong. I didn't believe anyone should trust me, and I didn't know if I'd ever again be able to trust myself.

We flew from Quito to Baltra Island in the Galápagos. Once we made it through the arrivals line, I spotted Antonio. When I'd first come to the Galápagos, Antonio had crossed over our language barrier to make me feel like part of the crew. Usually just seeing him across the airport felt like being welcomed home. This time I was scared to talk to him. If Antonio could understand people so easily without language, he might look at me and see I was responsible for a man's death. And although that might be pushing past his sensing abilities into clairvoyant territory, he'd probably already decided I wasn't someone he could trust after I'd been such a bad friend to Diego.

When Antonio saw me, he flashed his usual big smile. "Tamarita!" He stretched his arms out to hug me.

His warm welcome brought me unexpected hope. Perhaps in the Galápagos I could be the person Antonio remembered. Perhaps I could somehow let everything go.

Our first stop was Bachas Beach, where Pacific green sea turtles dig their nests. When the babies hatch, they usually dig their way out at night, as darkness is their best protection from becoming a predator's hors d'oeuvre. Because visitors are required to be off park land before sunset, we were usually left to imagine what a newly hatched turtle looked like as it experienced its first glimpse of the outside world. But on that first day back in the Galápagos, a ruckus erupted behind us while we were watching flamingos feeding. We turned to see a frigatebird harassing a great blue heron. After a dramatic fight, the heron finally let go of what it had in its beak. The frigatebird swooped, grabbed the falling object and flew off with it, but not before we saw that the treasure the birds were fighting over was a baby sea turtle. We went to get a closer look. Soon another tiny turtle poked out from the sand.

"Aw, look how cute it—" The sentence wasn't even finished before the heron grabbed the turtle in its beak, shook it until it stopped moving and choked it down before another frigatebird showed up and stole its snack.

"That was horrible," Leah, the fourteen-year-old, said.

"That's part of life," her mother, Brooke, replied. "Survival of the fittest."

It seemed everywhere we went on that trip we saw death. Aside from the baby turtles, we also saw a baby iguana meet its end and we came across a dead baby sea lion on the beach. Each time Leah expressed being appalled, her mom reminded her that death was part of the natural cycle of life. With my near-constant thoughts of the circles under Ray's eyes, the mechanical voice of the AED and the cold smooth feeling of the skin on Ray's unmoving chest, I was more thankful for Brooke's reminders than Leah was. But despite all that, they were having a great time and I couldn't help but get swept up in their excitement too.

One evening at dinner, I told the family: "You've got choices for tomorrow. We can ride horses up to a caldera, go see the Wall of Tears, get some surfboards and play at the beach or take a boat to a place called Los Tuneles and go snorkelling."

"What would you recommend?" Brooke asked.

"Los Tuneles."

The trip to Los Tuneles involved a ride in a local fisherman's boat—a small fibreglass skiff that looked like it wouldn't take much to break in two. The route was often rough, culminating in a surf landing that had made more than a few people lose their Galápagos tan. But the snorkelling was phenomenal. I explained all this to the family.

"We're in," Brooke said.

"Okay, but when you see Dario's boat tomorrow, remember you booked through an adventure tour company, not a luxury tour company."

"Adventure is what we're here for," Rob, the dad, assured me.

I was excited to go back to Los Tuneles—especially since I assumed Graham wouldn't want me working for him much longer and this would likely be my last trip to the Galápagos. But that night I questioned why I hadn't suggested a different activity. I barely slept, overcome by an ominous feeling that something would go terribly wrong. The same sort of feeling I'd had driving to Inuvik and the same sort of feeling I'd experienced the morning I'd flipped Graham's truck. If I'd listened to my gut those times, trouble and tragedy could have been avoided. On the other hand, I knew very well that if I'd spent my life obeying bad feelings in my gut, I would have also avoided almost every activity that had made my life worth living. I didn't know what was the right thing to do.

In the morning, the fishing boat puttered up to the *Amazonia*. It was navy blue on the outside and a cheery turquoise on the inside. Not that there was really an "inside"—like most Galápagos fishing vessels, it was a basic open skiff with wooden benches down the port and starboard sides. Dario was at the wheel. His biceps bulged under his T-shirt and he had the weathered skin of someone who'd spent his life in the sun. He was a man of few words and much knowledge. Despite our conversation the night before, Rob and Brooke looked at Dario's boat with contrived smiles.

Once we'd boarded, Dario did something I'd never seen him do before: he handed out the life jackets he normally kept tucked away. Safety measures were always a welcome addition, but I wondered if the seas were bigger than usual and if Dario was also worried.

The water was rough and the little boat was put to the test, repeatedly catching air off the tops of waves, then smacking down into the troughs. Wind whipped our hair. Salt water splashed over the sides of the boat, soaking us from head to toe. It was so much fun that I forgot my worries of the night before. I forgot about truck accidents. I even forgot about Ray. Then I looked behind me and saw young Cole clinging to his mother. Anxiety crashed down on me. In the distance, I saw the break we would have to cross. A barrier of waves, each over ten feet tall, crashed violently into the shallows. I faked a smile and pointed to the break: "That's where we're going!"

Rob laughed. He thought I was kidding. Dario slowed the engines.

"We're not really going through that?" Rob asked.

"We sure are!" I checked that everyone's life jackets were still secure.

Dario motored slowly toward the break. Then he gunned the engine. The hull sliced through the top of a green wave. He slowed again before climbing the next wave. Fast and slow, fast and slow, Dario worked his way through the green waves until the huge breakers crashed just ahead of us. I glanced at Dario. He looked like his world had shrunk down to his boat and the water in front of us. We idled. I felt the boat rise from a wave building below us, then watched it crash just ahead. Dario accelerated. I held my breath. In just seconds the break was behind us. He'd timed everything so perfectly we weren't even splashed. It was like the parting of the Red Sea. Dario: the Galapagueño miracle worker.

Amid an underwater landscape of tunnels and Dr. Seussian rock formations, we snorkelled with turtles, penguins, sea lions and diving blue-footed boobies.

Later, when we got back to the *Amazonia*, Brooke said, "That was like a dream."

"The snorkelling was cool," Cole said. "But the boat ride was my favourite part."

The rest of his family agreed. I was glad I hadn't listened to my gut.

CHAPTER 27

Williams Lake, BC
August 2010

I hadn't seen Graham since before the Firth. When I returned to Williams Lake after the Galápagos, he was away again. I assumed he was waiting to let me go in person. In the meantime, I resumed my office duties. On the day he returned, I was anxious. I had no idea how our conversation and, more importantly, our friendship would proceed.

"I read the comment Brooke left on the Facebook page," he said. "Well done."

Brooke's posting was reminiscent of Michelle's email: an encouraging message delivered just as the job they'd praised me for was about to reach its end.

We talked about office stuff, then Graham said, "You're holding it together really well. Better than I thought you would be."

Chris had said something similar the day Ray died, when we were on our way to get my raft with the Parks guys. Chris had meant it as a compliment. I wasn't sure if Graham did.

"You know he's here, right?" Graham asked.

"Ray?"

"They FedExed him. The delivery woman nearly fainted when I told her what was in the box."

I pictured him in a foam cooler—like for halibut, only Ray-sized. I wondered what the FedEx lady had thought might be in such a large package.

"He's in there?" I asked, glancing out the office door into the vast warehouse. How long could a body stay in FedEx packaging? Was that legal?

"He's here in the office," Graham said.

I looked around the small room where I'd spent the past few days working.

"Half of him, anyway."

I thought I might gag. Graham pointed to a cardboard box, slightly smaller than a loaf of bread. I felt like an idiot. Of course, he'd been cremated. I had noticed the box a few days earlier and briefly wondered what was in it. I was glad I'd ignored the urge to shake it.

"Small box," I said.

"His sister and brother-in-law took the other half."

I'd sat at a computer for almost a week with half of Ray over my shoulder.

"Did I tell you what I'm going to do with him?" Graham asked.

"Serve him up in blender drinks?"

Graham shook his head. "That's for when I die. I'm not giving that to anyone else."

"What are you going to do with him?" I tried to sound enthusiastic.

"Stuff him in a dead salmon."

I waited for more.

"He loved bears, right? So, in September up at Chilko, I'll stuff him in a salmon so that a bear will eat him. I figure that would get the crusty bastard pissed off."

I smiled at the thought. The crusty bastard would certainly have approved of the plan.

Graham and Chris both thought I was holding it together well. But not everyone agreed.

"You don't sound good. I don't think you should stay there," Mara said over the phone.

I had expected Graham to tell me it was time for me to find a new job. When that didn't happen, staying felt like the right thing to do. After everything I'd done wrong, I didn't want to leave if Graham still needed me. However, Mara wasn't the only one who thought I should go.

"You need to leave the Puddle," one of the heli guys said while we drank end-of-day beers on the lawn.

"Why?"

"You're depressed."

"I didn't know you were a psychiatrist as well as a helicopter engineer."

"I don't need clinical training to see you're depressed. I don't know what happened between when I met you and now, but something changed and living in that warehouse by yourself isn't helping."

Over the past three years I'd cried far too often, but not one of those tears had been shed since this last visit to the Galápagos. I'd figured that was a sign I was getting better. But with both the engineer and Mara telling me otherwise, I began to think maybe they were right. Maybe it was time to leave the warehouse. Graham was away and unreachable. Since he'd initially given me a choice of working from the Puddle or Nelson, I assumed he wouldn't care if I worked from Whistler.

I didn't think working from Mara's house affected my job. I continued answering emails and working on a custom itinerary for a Baja trip. So, when Graham returned to the connected world, I was taken aback by his disappointment in my move.

"But in the spring you said it didn't matter where I worked from."

"It would have been best if you'd waited to tell me before you left."

A few days later he called again, unhappy to find that when I'd left the warehouse I'd taken everything I had with me. Once again, I didn't understand why that made a difference. Everything I owned fit easily into my car. The days of being on the same page as Graham felt like an ancient memory.

"I didn't know if you'd want me back," I explained. "If you'd like, I can be there tomorrow."

"It seems you've already made your decision."

The last thing I wanted to do was let Graham down, but that's exactly what I kept doing. I was still the same lucky person I'd always claimed to be to Joe—only over the past few years that luck had shifted to come at the expense of those around me.

Not long after that phone call, Graham and I spoke again. I said, "Maybe it would be best if I stopped working for you."

"I've been thinking that too. But I didn't want to push you out. I wanted it to be your decision."

We agreed I'd work a few more weeks until early September when business slowed. A low-key ending to over eight years at a job that had been my world.

After I was officially done, I sent Graham a final invoice for my office days and the Galápagos trip. He didn't pay it right away. Unlike after the accident with Megan and Mike, I asked him again. It wasn't about the money. I just wanted him to tell me if he wasn't going to pay me. It was my last chance to know what he really thought. If he blamed me for what happened, I wanted to hear him say so. I kept pressing him. He deposited money into my account. He never said it was my fault.

CHAPTER 28

Churchill, MB
October 2010

Stomping snow off my boots, I opened the door to the helicopter base office to hand over waiver forms from the tour company I now worked for. JT, a lanky helicopter engineer, was finishing telling a story to the base manager. "And then we raced the wheelbarrows right down the middle of Kelsey Boulevard," JT said, bouncing with his usual vigour.

"Uh-huh." The manager sounded bored. She'd spent most of her fifty-something years in Churchill and was interested in trap-lines and hunting, not the drunken shenanigans of seasonal work-ers. I, on the other hand, felt the opposite way. "Sounds like fun," I said.

JT threw up his hands in exasperation. "Tamar, you were there! C'mon, you don't remember?"

Since arriving in Churchill I'd rarely woken up remembering how I'd gotten home. "I need to start drinking less," I said.

"Hell no," JT responded. "Polar bear season and booze go together like cops and doughnuts. You just need to start remem-bering more."

Between early October and late November, polar bears gather near Churchill, Manitoba, waiting for Hudson Bay to freeze so that they can get out on the ice to hunt seals. In a strange coincidence, right after I'd stopped working for Graham, the polar bear tour company I'd worked for as a cook two years before had called to see if I could fill an opening in their operations department. By then I'd thought a lot about Graham advising me to "let it go." Mostly I'd realized I didn't think I could. I felt like I carried Ray with me everywhere. Instead of futilely battling that feeling, I'd decided to try to take Ray on adventures he'd enjoy. Working in the "Polar Bear Capital of the World" fit the bill.

Part of my job was scheduling helicopter tours, and I spent a lot of time at the heli base. Drinking after work with the helicopter crew quickly became part of my daily routine. Sort of like in Williams Lake, only in Churchill we consumed significantly more. And with temperatures that occasionally dipped to forty below zero, we didn't put chairs on the lawn.

The pilots had to stop drinking at least eight hours before flying, but JT and I had no such rules to abide by. Hanging with him was like doing shots from the fountain of youth. I felt like I had years earlier, when the future looked long and full of promise and the baggage I carried hadn't held the weight of a dead man.

JT and I were caught up in a bender like I hadn't experienced in years, and my body was giving me signs it couldn't continue like that for much longer. On the final day of bear season, I vowed not to drink until at least Christmas. I wasn't alone. Even the indomitable JT said, "It's time to go home. My liver needs a rest from this crazy town."

I returned to Whistler wanting to keep the positive energy I'd found in Churchill while living healthier. I skied, did Pilates and went to the pool and the gym. I ate well and abstained from alcohol. But I quickly learned that staying sober meant the past was always with me. I heard the AED's voice saying, "No shockable rhythm detected." I saw the blood in Megan's hair. I felt Ray's smooth, cool skin as my hands rested on his chest, waiting for a sign that a miracle had happened and he was still alive.

I'd believed I was telling the truth when I'd told Mara and my mom I was too filled with guilt to take on any more. However, I'd since discovered I was like an empty bucket into which guilt had poured like sand. When the sand had begun spilling over the rim,

I'd thought I'd taken in all the guilt I could fit. But it turned out guilt also came in liquid form, and there was plenty of room in the bucket for the sand to absorb that as well.

Spring neared. I got a landscaping job. Working outside without being responsible for people's lives sounded perfect. But hours of mowing and weeding left me too much time to think. And days of mowing lawns were punctuated by calls from one of my oldest friends, Liane. My parents were getting older and my mom was experiencing health problems. Liane lived in Montreal and saw them often. She wanted to keep me informed of how they were doing. I appreciated how much she cared but knew it should be me spending that much time with them. My whitewater career was over. I was mowing lawns for just over minimum wage. I was already planning to go to Montreal in September for Liane's wedding, and the more I thought about it, the more it became clear that once I was there I should stay. All I could recall doing in my adult life was causing death and destruction. It was time for me to do the right thing.

CHAPTER 29

The Road to Montreal, QC
August 2011

With my driving history, it seemed wrong to be eager to follow that yellow line again. But a cross-country road trip felt like pure freedom. My first stop en route to Montreal was Boise, Idaho, to see an old North Creek guiding buddy who'd moved there a few years before. The kayak I hadn't been able to take on my last Canyon trip had found its way into his garage. And it seemed like a good time to finally pick it up.

To my circle of friends, Idaho was even more famous for whitewater than it was for potatoes, so even though it had been forever since I'd paddled, we decided I couldn't visit without kayaking. My friend chose the Class II–III Main Payette just north of town. The drive to the put-in took us alongside the river most of the way. I could see for myself how benign the rapids looked. Still, my mind was filled with images of getting stuck in logjams and being recirculated endlessly in holes.

We slid our kayaks into the water. Sun glinted off the little riffle in front of us. I took a deep breath and paddled out of the eddy. Soon we were crashing through wave trains and paddling around holes. I felt like I was exactly where I was supposed to be.

While I was in Boise, another old North Creek friend contacted me to say that once I was south of the border, I ought to visit him in Telluride, Colorado. So I did. My friend took me offroading in his beat-up SUV. We careened along cliff edges and descended hills that made us feel like the vehicle was going vertical. We stopped to explore an old mining tunnel, where even just a little ways in it felt claustrophobic. We tried to imagine what it must have been like deep inside the mine with only an oil-lit headlamp for light. That night we went out drinking and dancing until the bars closed. After too brief a sleep, we set out to hike one of the surrounding peaks. Between the altitude, the hangover and my general fear of scrambling up loose scree on exposed mountainsides, I spent much of the climb feeling on the verge of passing out or throwing up. But standing on the summit beside a good friend and gazing out at the wide-open vista of the surrounding mountains made our mission worthwhile.

The North Creek crew had spread far, and before leaving Telluride, Dorrie got in touch and invited me to visit her in Santa Fe. I'd never been to New Mexico, and Dorrie and her new puppy proudly showed me around the trails and adobe neighbourhoods of her new home.

Saying goodbye to people I loved had never been easy, but I noticed on this road trip that it had become even harder. I'd come to realize parting ways didn't only mean I wasn't sure when we'd meet again, but if. I left Dorrie and drove through Texas in 110-degree heat. In Oklahoma, I was the only camper in a state park with a brick-red sandy beach. While treading water in the warm lake, I watched sunset transform the blue sky into a thousand hues of pink and red. For a few enchanted minutes, the ground, the sky and the water were all painted from brushstrokes using the same corner of Mother Nature's colour palette.

I kept driving east, to Memphis and the kitsch of Graceland. I wanted to visit the Outer Banks of North Carolina, but a hurricane named Irene was heading that way, so I turned north instead. Irene flooded towns and blew down trees and powerlines across the eastern states. I followed behind her, seeing the aftermath of her destruction while I met with beautiful sunny skies and not a drop of rain. The experience felt like a metaphor for my life.

My last stop was only a few hours from Montreal, in northern New York State, where Joe was living aboard a small sailboat on

Lake Champlain. We sailed until just before sunset. Joe was stoked that after two and a half decades of vegetarianism, I'd joined him in becoming an eater of flesh. He cast a line in an attempt to catch us a fish for dinner. But his line never went taut. "Nothing's been bitin' since that bitch Irene churned up the water," he said.

We ate a dinner of plain couscous and raised our cans of PBR, "To being lucky in life."

In the morning Joe and I jumped off the boat and swam in the cool lake. Then he took me flying in the old De Havilland tail dragger he had bought.

"I can't believe you own a plane," I said.

"Neither can the lady at my bank. When I applied for a loan she said, 'Mr. Whiting, have you looked at your tax return? How can I possibly give you a loan?'"

We both laughed. Joe had so much charm, I wasn't surprised that he'd found someone else to loan him the money.

"I'm the luckiest person," he said.

"No, I am." Despite all that had happened, in that moment I meant it.

We flew above Lake Champlain and the rolling Adirondack mountains, where the sugar maples had begun lighting up the forests with their blazing yellows, oranges and reds. Joe eased the tail dragger back down onto the runway, smooth as could be. When we came to a stop, we looked at each other and both said, "Not bad for a guy who failed high school math."

I wanted to stay on my road trip forever. Living the highlights without having to put down roots. People say you can't run away from your problems. I believed I could. As long as I never had to stop.

CHAPTER 30

Montreal, QC
September 2011

I moved into a studio apartment not far from my parents' place and started looking for work. No one wanted to hire me. I kept trying. After sending out over fifty résumés I finally landed a job with a dog-walking service.

The dogs greeted me for each walk with wagging tails and sounds of canine joy. They made me laugh out loud every day. I grew so attached to them, some days I wondered if I was the one who was most excited for our walks.

But away from doggie love, life in Montreal was challenging. It had been over a year, but I kept hearing my raft's aluminum baggage frame crunching against the canyon wall. I'd see Ray floating toward the rapid. Over and over I'd feel his cold, unmoving chest. Each morning I'd wake with a horrible feeling in my gut. I'd have to talk myself out of the idea that it was a premonition I was going to crash my car and kill the dogs. But the hardest thing to deal with was failing at the reason I'd moved to Montreal; I was struggling too much with my emotions to be of any help to my parents.

I wanted to be a better person or at least a different person. I tried meditation, swimming, vitamins. Liane put me in touch with a young female psychologist. She was kind and gave me homework to do. Keeping track and writing stuff down felt like tangible steps to getting better. Unfortunately, liking her and doing my homework weren't enough. Several times, the psychologist suggested taking antidepressants. I said no. I had taken a single one a few years before and become so anxious I'd spent an entire night trying to convince myself not to dive headfirst out my window. My physician had suggested I at least try a second day, or another type of medication. But I was scared of screwing up my mind even more than it already was. Besides, I didn't believe my problem was chemical. My problem was that I kept fucking up.

"But when I asked if you had suicidal thoughts, you told me no," the psychologist said.

"I don't."

"Imagining putting a knife through your temple is a suicidal thought. As is picturing driving your car into an oncoming truck, or over a guardrail."

"But I don't want to kill myself. What I want is to stop wasting my life. I want to take advantage of being alive. I don't know why I picture stuff like that."

"People experience suicidal ideation when they're overwhelmed by negative emotions. You're picturing a way to get away from those feelings." The psychologist saw my panic rising and added: "Many people have thoughts like that, and the vast majority don't act on them. But you should definitely pay attention and tell me if they get worse."

The suicidal images soon progressed from a few times a day to a few times an hour and then to a few times a minute. I continued walking the dogs and having friendly chats with other dog walkers. I spent time with Liane and my parents. I smiled a lot. I appeared normal. I just happened to have a weird habit of seeing every sharp object as a way of ending my life. I moved my kitchen knives from the rack on the wall to the back of a drawer.

One day while looking through my parents' storage locker I found pictures from my university days. I called up my old roommate and we laughed while remembering those times.

"Do you know where Geoff is?" she asked.

"I tried to track him down about two years ago, but I didn't have any luck."

Geoff was a musician from Vancouver who'd stayed on our couch whenever his band played in Toronto. Eventually the band had become fairly well known and could afford nice hotel rooms, but Geoff had still preferred our shabby apartment.

I got off the phone and googled Geoff. A Facebook memorial page came up. A posting stated he'd been "fighting his inner demons for a number of years, and they finally got the better of him."

I called my old roommate to tell her Geoff had killed himself almost two years before.

"I can't believe he'd do that," she said.

I remembered entire days when Geoff didn't want to leave the old grey couch we'd rescued from a street corner.

"Are you crying?" my friend asked.

I hadn't seen Geoff in several years. But I found it hard to accept that I would never see him again. I dreamt about Geoff that night. He was sitting at a table in a café. There was an empty chair beside him. I walked toward him. He looked up at me and gestured for me to sit in the empty chair. "I've been waiting for you," he said.

I had a similar dream the following night. And the night after that. When I saw the psychologist next, I told her I would try the antidepressants.

On medication I found it more challenging to fake being okay. The pills had a strange effect on me. Several times a day it was like a black veil descended over my eyes. I kept taking the meds, hoping I just needed to get used to them. After two weeks I felt like I was only getting worse.

"You're having a bad reaction," the doctor said. "Stop taking them. There are lots of other antidepressants to try."

I stopped, but I didn't try another drug. I also stopped seeing the psychologist and looked for a different path.

In April I told my parents, "I think I need to leave Montreal."

"To do what?" my dad asked.

"I've been looking at a sea kayak guide course in Tofino. It's in May. I think I'm going to do it and then try to get a job there."

"Are you sure? We're really enjoying having you here," my dad said.

Despite all my failures, my dad was saying they still loved me. Yet, what I heard was "You're failing us by leaving." I thought about Geoff. I had to go.

I emailed résumés to kayaking tour companies, hoping to line up work once I finished the course. After my experience job hunting in Montreal, I was amazed to receive replies from most of them. It felt like a sign I was taking a step in the right direction. A company not far from where the course was being held sounded like a good fit. I sold my well-loved hatchback and flew to BC.

On the west coast of Vancouver Island, rainforest spills into the ocean. Moss-covered cedars and hemlocks, giant ferns and salal bushes all lean across sandy beaches and over rocky cliffs, reaching toward the ocean as though the vast forests aren't big enough to contain all that lives there. Layers upon layers of plant species grow atop one another, sometimes in symbiotic relationships and other times attempting to hijack nutrients or get closer to the sun. Sandwiched into those layers are insects, arachnids, worms, giant slugs, birds and mammals who have all figured out where to sleep, eat, hide, hunt and mate within this dense growth. Past the edge of the woods, the ocean teems with just as much life. Sea otters, who were all but wiped out in the area a hundred years ago, have made a successful comeback and wrestle and nap amid the bull kelp. Porpoises and seals hunt for herring. Transient orcas hunt for the porpoises and seals. Rafts of seabirds congregate, calling out loud messages to one another. Jellyfish and nudibranchs of different colours, or sometimes no colour at all, swim using the unique motions adapted for each species' shape. The list goes on. The West Coast breathes life.

The kayak guide course had our small group of five paddling along this vibrant coast by day and bivouacking on different beaches by night, inhaling the salty air and listening to the change of tides.

For the first few days, all of that was more than enough to keep me thinking I was on the right track, even as my back ached and my mind dipped its toes into murky waters. But as the days rolled forward, those dipped toes became feet, and then my mind waded in farther, until I was once again over my head in an ocean of dark thoughts. I increasingly imagined fatal scenarios on the water, often where I could have done something to help but failed to. I had waves of being completely unable to focus. Using the compass and map would be easy and logical one day, but the next it felt like I was trying to teach myself quantum physics.

Despite these recurring mental power outages, I was passing the skills modules as we got tested. Then, on the last full day of the trip, we stopped at a picture-perfect sandy beach to unload our camping gear. Once camp was set up, we returned to our kayaks. The plan was to practise surf skills. The surf wasn't particularly large, but I couldn't stop picturing the other students flipping, slamming their heads into the ground and injuring their spinal cords. I didn't want to be there when it happened. I didn't want to fail to rescue them.

"I can't do this," I said to my instructor.

"Of course you can," she said.

"I can't."

"This is well within your skill level." She seemed confused about why I was doubting that.

These were the last skills we had to check off the list to pass. If I didn't get back in my boat, I wouldn't pass the course. I wouldn't get that job. I would have wasted all that money. And I would be back to not having hope for the future.

"I can't."

I asked Mara if I could move back in with her. The whole way back from Vancouver Island on the bus, the ferry and the second bus, suicidal images intermingled with reruns of the rafting accident with Ray and the truck accident with Megan and Mike. Over it all, my mind kept repeating: *You're broken.* In Whistler I got a job in a kitchen and quit a week later. The invisible weight grew heavier. Mara seemed scared to leave me alone in the house. One day while she was out I became scared to be alone. I kept picturing knives in my temple. Guns in my mouth. Ropes around my neck. The images wouldn't stop. *You're broken. You're broken. You're broken.* I walked to the emergency room at the clinic. The nurse asked what was wrong. I said I felt depressed. She asked more questions. I didn't know what to say. She assumed I wanted to speak to the doctor. The doctor offered a prescription. I didn't want it. He seemed irritated. He asked the same questions the nurse had. I still didn't have the answers.

"Clearly you're not comfortable talking to men."

I had no idea why he said that.

"We could send you to the psych ward in the city. But they'll just give you drugs. That's what they do."

I didn't say anything. I wanted him to send me. I wanted to explain that the drugs wouldn't scare me so much if there was someone to make sure I didn't hurt myself. I wasn't sure why I still cared, but I didn't want to lose the fight like Geoff had. I couldn't say the words, though. The doctor gave me a reference for the counselling clinic and I left.

At the clinic I discovered that during the time since my previous experiences with therapists, I hadn't magically transformed into a better patient.

"When was your last relationship?" the psychiatrist asked.

I thought about my long-but-not-monogamous relationships with Drifter and Kevin. I thought about the lodge chef I'd had a passionate summer romance with, that we'd agreed ahead of time would end with the rafting season. I thought about the boy from Newfoundland with the crazy hair and beautiful smile. My relationship with him had been as close to a classic relationship as I'd ever had. But it had also been a very, very long time ago—the soundtrack of our life together had been filled with grunge. Kurt Cobain had still been alive. My mind moved to more recent times and I thought about whatever it was I'd had with Eduardo.

"What do you consider a relationship?" I asked the psychiatrist. "It's not a trick question," he said.

When the next questions didn't go any better, the psychiatrist said, "I can see you don't like talking to men."

I wondered if the ER doctor had written that in my report. I wondered if it was true and I just didn't realize it. The psychiatrist arranged for me to see a female psychologist. I tried to take a different route with her than I had with therapists in the past. Instead of wading through questions I didn't have answers for, I planned to lay out all my dirty laundry right from the start. But when I tried to tell her what was going on in my head, she told me I was too emotional.

"Try picturing big glass jars," she said. "Picture them in any colour you please. Now imagine putting each of your emotions in its own jar and sealing it up. Really picture it. Next week we'll see if you're ready to take one out and examine it on its own."

I had no idea what she meant.

I thought about cutting myself open to let all the negative sludge inside me bleed out, but cuts leave scars and I didn't want people to see the physical evidence of how crazy I'd become. Instead, I did something I hadn't done in years. I went home and ate far too much, then I went to the toilet and pushed my finger down my throat. It took some trying before everything started to come up. I hated myself for being so wasteful on top of everything else, but I kept forcing myself to bring up more, hoping that along with the vomit, I'd scour and spew out whatever it was that had gone so rotten inside me.

Despite all the badness, I did finally have something to look forward to. I'd put together an application for a master's writing program and to my surprise I'd been accepted. School would be mostly online, but to start there was a two-week summer program on campus. I thought the psychologist would be happy for me, but when I told her she said, "I don't think you're ready. Have you thought about postponing it?"

I didn't look into postponement. The future was so uncertain that I felt anything I didn't do right away would probably never happen.

In summer school I wrote about my first time guiding for Graham. It had been an exploratory trip that was part of the guide school he ran, and I had assumed it was the unofficial test to see if I had what it took to work for him. Guiding the Ram River had been a totally different world from guiding the Hudson. We'd rappelled our gear and ourselves down three raging waterfalls. There'd been life-threatening rapids and scary near-misses. At one point, a few other guides and I had jumped from a high ledge into our freefalling rafts. The final scene of my story took place after much of our gear had unexpectedly plunged over a waterfall. Recovering it had taken quite some time, and when we'd finally pulled into camp, people had been wet, hungry, tired and cold. We hadn't had time to rest, though; we'd had to collect wood, start a fire and scavenge the waterlogged coolers for salvageable food. I'd started into cooking dinner when Graham had stood among the trainees and asked, "So, who still wants to be a raft guide?"

My hand was the first one to shoot up. "I do!"

Graham had laughed. "Tamar, I wasn't asking you," he'd said. "You already are a guide."

The story I wrote for summer school wasn't very good, but it let me relive a time when I'd still been confident and Graham and I still had many years of rivers and friendship ahead.

During the school year I took two full-time classes. In January, someone in my non-fiction course posted an old picture from a trip she'd taken to Herschel Island in the Beaufort Sea. It was a funny picture of a Twin Otter parked next to a Yukon government sign. The sign showed a pictogram of an airplane inside a red circle with a line through it and the words "This beach is not a designated airstrip" printed below.

I recognized the plane and messaged my classmate asking if Bob had been the pilot. He had. I admitted to her that I was fascinated by Bob and my dream was to follow him around and write a book about his life flying bush planes in the Arctic during our summer and the Antarctic during our winter. Two days after we exchanged those messages, news of a plane disappearing in Antarctica made the headlines. For the first few days, Bob's friends and co-workers had held out hope that he and the others on board were still alive, saying that if anyone could survive out there it was Bob. A few days later his plane was spotted from the air. It was determined that no one could have lived through the crash. The quotes from friends, co-workers and customers backed up what I already knew—he'd been an extraordinary pilot and a well-loved man who'd died doing what he enjoyed most.

About a month later, a student in a different class submitted a story with a character who was a lovable bush pilot named Heath, which was Bob's last name. It turned out the student's husband was a pilot and Bob had been his good friend. I would never get to write the story about Bob I'd hoped to. It made me happy his story was being written in another way.

School reminded me how important stories are for understanding other people and for navigating our own lives. For so many years I'd thought of my life in terms of a novel. School made me open that book again. The more I examined the existing pages, the more obvious it became where the next chapter needed to go.

CHAPTER 31

North Creek, NY

June 2013

Rafting season on the Hudson began early in April when melting snow filled the river to its banks and sometimes beyond. After years of chasing high water, I chose to start work in June—after spring runoff had come and gone. On my first day back, we drove to the river in a school bus I'd painted Smurf blue years earlier. A young guide I'd just been introduced to stood at the front bellowing out a safety talk above the sound of the engine. Fifteen years had passed since I'd given my first safety talk, and this kid was still telling the same jokes.

He wasn't the only guide new to me. After six years away from the Hudson, there were lots of new faces at our company. One of the exceptions was Dave, the trip leader, who I'd guided with for many years. When we got to the put-in, though, I saw that many of the guides I knew from other companies were still there. It was both exciting and terrifying. *You're not the same person they remember.*

I'd told my boss I wanted to see the river again before guiding, so for my first trip of the season I was going as a passenger with a guide named Tim. Tim was in his early twenties and had grown up in the area. I was surprised I didn't know his parents.

"I've heard stories about you," he said.

"Don't believe any of them." A clichéd reply, but I couldn't think of anything better.

On the Hudson we generally paddle-guided, meaning the guide sits in the back and steers with a paddle, kind of like in a canoe. Once our raft was in the water and the four guests were seated, Tim climbed in and sat on the stern tube. I sat on the right side, just forward of him. Tim explained the commands to the guests, and then we practised.

"All forward!"

"Right back!"

"Left back!"

"Get down!"

The shrill of Dave's whistle pierced through the sounds of voices and flowing water. He raised his paddle in the air and all the other guides did the same; everyone was ready to go. Dave yelled, "All forward." He and his crew paddled out of the put-in eddy and disappeared around the corner. One by one, the other rafts followed.

With more first-aid training than most of the guides, Tim had been assigned the sweep position—as I so often had been. Despite the added responsibility, the familiarity of being at the back felt comfortable.

"Hang on," Tim yelled as he spun the boat to hit our first wave sideways. It had been a long time since I'd been splashed by river water that wasn't ice cold.

"Yeehaw," I yelled. "Rafting is fun."

Tim laughed at me. "I'm glad you like it."

We splashed our way through the rest of the Indian River and then into the confluence with the Hudson.

"Damn, this place is beautiful," I said.

Tim looked around. "Not a bad place to call home."

We floated through the small waves of Cedar Ledges and then through the long flat section where the guests jumped in to swim. I jumped in too. I came up beside the raft and grabbed hold of the chicken line, the rope around the perimeter of the raft.

"Need a hand?" Tim asked.

"I hope not." I stretched my body out, kicked both legs at once and hauled myself into the raft. "Had to make sure I could still get back in by myself."

We floated through more flatwater and on past Virgin Falls to the top of Entrance Rapid, the rapid that would take us into the Gorge. At the front of our group of rafts, Dave steered his boat down the centre line. The next two boats followed. A guide with a prematurely greying beard started centre as well, then veered purposely toward a hole on the right. I'd always avoided that hole at the medium water level the river was at that day. I wondered if I'd been wrong about how sticky it was. It still didn't look friendly to me. The guide with the greying beard dropped in sideways. His boat stopped like it had hit a brick wall. He held on tight while all six of his passengers tumbled into the river.

"All forward," Tim yelled. "We have swimmers."

We dug our paddles deep and kept our eyes on the bobbing yellow helmets. We passed the guide, still holding tight as his raft got tossed around in the hole. His beard framed a grin as wide as a teenager's on the day they got their braces off.

We approached a swimmer. I put down my paddle, reached overboard and pulled in a young boy. The kid was barely in the boat before Tim steered us to the next swimmer, a man in his twenties. I pulled him in. Tim moved us quickly to a third swimmer, a girl who looked about twelve or thirteen. She was coughing from swallowing water. When I asked her if she was okay, she looked around in a panic.

"Where's my dad? My dad can't swim, where is he?"

"Another raft has him," I said, even though I wasn't sure.

We had three of the six swimmers. I scanned the water for more helmets and didn't see any. I hoped what I'd said was true. At the bottom of the rapid we approached the other boats.

"I see him," the girl said. "He's there! I see him!"

I felt relief right along with her. The raft with the girl's father had also picked up another swimmer, and the sixth was in Dave's boat. Everyone was accounted for.

The hole eventually spat out the grey-bearded guide and his raft. He soloed his boat to the bottom of the rapid and picked up his guests. His smile had faded slightly, probably for the sake of his crew. Many times an unplanned whitewater swim turns into the highlight of a trip. However, this group looked like they just wanted to go home.

At our post-trip meeting, Grey Beard bragged about his perfect score—rafting lingo for when a guide gets all the guests to fall out but stays in themselves. In my previous years on the Hudson, guides from the other companies had teased my boss for running overly safety-conscious trips. Since that time, my boss had cut down on his river days. In his absence, it seemed things had changed. I wondered if I was too old-school to fit in.

I was scheduled to guide the next day. I woke feeling sick to my stomach. Although that had been a regular occurrence on Chilko trips, the only time I'd felt ill on the Hudson had been when Jose Cuervo had made his rounds the night before and I really was on the verge of puking.

Through the morning rituals of handing out wetsuits and life jackets, I laughed and joked with the guests while images of people disappearing into river holes and not resurfacing mingled in my mind with images of Ray lying unbreathing beneath my hands. As the bus motored toward the put-in, my inner voice grew so loud I couldn't hear the safety talk. *You shouldn't be doing this. Why are you here? Tell them you're sorry but you've changed your mind.* The voice wasn't unreasonable, but how could I stop? I'd accepted the end of my relationships with Kevin and Drifter. I'd kept going without Graham's sarcasm and support. I'd carried on without having Chris to rely on, debate with and care enough to try pushing me toward a caffeine addiction. But every time I heard water running over rocks, I felt an empty space inside me that only the river could fill. I couldn't even look at a picture of a waterfall in a doctor's waiting room without analyzing what line might be runnable. No matter how much I told myself I needed to move on, there seemed no way to be fully alive without the river.

My guests were three couples from Long Island who were all friends. We practised our strokes in the put-in eddy until Dave blew his whistle and all of us guides put our paddles up, ready to go. I smelled dust coming up from the road as the SUV flipped near the Ottawa. I saw Megan's hair red with blood. I heard glass shattering, metal bending and a man yelling, "You stupid fucking cunt." I saw the dark circles under Ray's eyes and felt the cool smoothness of his skin as I pressed in vain on his chest.

Dave left the eddy first. I was so used to being sweep on the Hudson that I watched all the rafts pull out in front of me, and it wasn't until it was only Tim's boat and mine left in the eddy that I finally called, "All forward!"

The current moved us toward the glassy tongue cutting through the top of the rapid. The tongue provided the smoothest entry into the rapid. It was a line many guides took. And for a moment I considered taking it as well, then I threw in a draw stroke and aimed the bow away from that tongue, toward the line Tim had taken the day before and the line I'd always favoured.

"Hang on!"

I spun the boat to hit the wave sideways. We were only a few paddle strokes into a seventeen-mile trip and the guests were already drenched. They looked back at me with surprise. One of them cheered. Then the others joined him.

"Welcome to the river!" I said to them, and to myself.

Every rapid felt like a homecoming. We crashed through holes and waves while keeping everyone inside the raft. I didn't have that ultra-focus of big rapids but I still felt very present on the river, enjoying each splash and bounce. At one point I could almost see Ray beside me, with that smile that revealed his gold fillings. By the end I couldn't believe I'd had qualms about coming back. The way the vibrations of the current travelled from the paddle blade, up the shaft and into my hands made me feel like I'd reconnected with the outside world, instead of hiding in the cocoon I'd spun around myself. I wanted the day to never end.

I was renting a room from my friend Donna, the guide who had been an inspiration to me—both on the river and in life—when I'd first started on the Hudson. Back in the day we had partied a lot. After a first day back on the river in the old days we would have celebrated at our favourite roadhouse or a big camp-fire party with lots of booze and dancing. And Donna and I probably would have started kissing in hopes of getting the whole crowd making out with one another. But now we were older and mellower, and Donna's three-year-old grandson was spending the night. We hung out on the porch enjoying conversation and a few beers while tossing a tennis ball for her dog. It was different. And it felt good.

The next morning I felt sick to my stomach all over again. But again, by the time we arrived at the take-out I wanted to drive back to the put-in and do it all over. I kept reliving the same pattern—beginning my day flooded with images of everything that could go wrong and bombarded by memories of everything that already had. Then we'd get on the river and hit the first wave and I would be just as excited as my paddlers experiencing the river for the first time. I would be reminded all over again that guiding rafts was the best job in the world.

"Eight feet and rising," my boss announced.

Rain had poured down all night, saturating the ground and filling the creeks and streams that fed the Hudson River. Eight feet was akin to springtime high water—exactly the kind of level I had started the season late to avoid.

"We've got a bunch of camp groups, so all those rafts are going to run Riparius to Snake Rock."

At eight feet, the section of the Hudson that we normally ran—the Gorge—developed waves big enough that it felt like we had to take several paddle strokes to climb them. It grew frothing holes that looked like they would pulverize anything that dared enter them. And while the Riparius to Snake Rock section was fun at high water, comparing the two was like comparing an outdoor music festival with the local cover band at the corner pub.

Many of the guides looked unhappy, guessing at their fate as we waited to find out who would be stuck with the camp groups. Our boss handed out trip sheets so that we could see for ourselves.

As he placed one in my hand, he said: "I put you on the Gorge. I assume you want that?"

"Hell, yeah," I said, excited to be one of the chosen few. It was a welcome reminder that although I'd lost Graham as a supporter, he wasn't the only person who'd encouraged me through my rafting career. My boss in the Adirondacks had always believed in me in the past, and this was confirmation that he still did. For a few moments I felt exhilarated, then the reality of what I'd signed up for sank in and my usual pre-river nausea spread from my gut into my throat. I had trouble hearing what people were saying because of all the yelling going on in my head. *Don't do it. Someone's going to die.*

On our drive to the put-in I thought about how I'd come back because I couldn't get over my love of the river. *Is it really love or is it addiction?* I wasn't sure I knew the difference. I wondered if I'd spent my life chasing rivers in the same way that junkies chased the dragon—not the original meaning of the phrase where the opium smoke actually looks like a dragon, but the more common meaning of doing whatever it takes to try to get back to that original high.

My group of six was from Rochester. The woman who planned the trip knew everyone, but some of the group members were meeting for the first time. We started down the river. As usual, I hit the first wave sideways, soaking my passengers. However, I didn't experience the relief I normally did. The level on the dam-controlled Indian River didn't reflect what we'd be up against on the Hudson. When we finally arrived at the confluence, I saw that boulders that had protruded far above the Hudson's waterline the day before were now hidden beneath the flow. *You shouldn't be guiding this. Someone's going to die.*

I followed the raft in front of me. It was headed toward the Welcome to the Hudson Wave—a wave that only blossomed at higher water, so I hadn't seen it in its glory yet that season. Doubt screamed in my head. My stomach threatened to release the breakfast I'd forced myself to choke down.

"All forward!"

We hit the wave square on. Water crashed down over the bow. My guests shouted happily as it drenched them. My stomach unclenched a tiny bit.

We passed through Cedar Ledges and then into the flat stretch where people swim. Usually we stopped at Elephant Rock. At typical summer levels, the rock protruded so far above the water that many guests who climbed it to jump off had second thoughts once they were up there. But on a high-water day like we were having, there was no reason to stop: I had to lean down to touch the top of the rock as we floated by.

We arrived at Entrance Rapid, where Grey Beard had achieved his "perfect score."

"This is the rapid that takes us into the Gorge," I told my guests. "Once we get to the bottom, you'll see the mountains are higher, the river is narrower and everything is a whole lot more fun." It was what I always said, but this time I wasn't sure I believed that last part.

Dave led the way. The three other rafts, including mine, followed his line. We avoided the raft-flipping hole that had formed on the right as well as the raft-holding holes on the left. Toward the bottom, the little wave train that was usually there had flourished into big standing waves. We powered forward, riding the waves like a roller coaster, getting dowsed with each one. My crew was stoked. The screaming in my brain subsided to loud nagging. I took a moment to enjoy the scenery. We were in one of the most picturesque spots on the river: a dark pool of flatwater below Blue Ledges, the hundred-metre-high rocky cliffs that took on a bluish tint in certain light. My guests were having a great time and so far everything at eight feet was exactly as I remembered it.

"The next rapid is the Narrows. It's the narrowest section we'll run today. All that water getting squeezed together creates some really big waves."

I looked around and made sure everyone was listening.

"I'm going to need you to pay attention to my commands and paddle hard. I'm also going to need you to smile."

I received a few questioning looks.

"Our photographer's in there, and if you're not smiling in the pictures it reflects badly on me as a guide. All forward!"

We rode through a wave train at the top. At the levels I'd rafted so far that season, the next move would be to go right to avoid a nasty ledge-hole, with the cheesy and somewhat sexist name Widowmaker. I'd seen some violent flips in that hole, but I also remembered there being times at high water when Widowmaker had turned into a fun wave. Dave avoided it, as did the raft behind him. I eyed it as we got closer. It had a big glassy face with a frothing white top. *Just follow Dave's line.* But I couldn't resist. "All forward!"

It took the guests only two strokes to get us lined up face-to-face with the wave.

"Get down!"

They squatted to the floor. The raft bent and we were showered in white.

Ray, that one was for you.

"Get up! All forward and show off your smiles!"

I pictured Ray in the raft, smiling right along with everyone else.

We paddled hard through the giant haystack waves. My skin tingled. All churning in my stomach had ceased. I couldn't believe I'd ever doubted wanting to be there.

At high water in the Gorge, one rapid led directly into the next. From the Narrows, we continued into Osprey Nest, Carter's, Givney's, OK Slip, Gunsight In, Gunsight Out. The waves and the holes in all of them looked like they were on steroids—just like I remembered from big-water days years before.

Harris Rift was the last long rapid of the day. As we approached it, I blanked on what it looked like at high water. The waves at the top seemed disorganized. I wasn't sure where to go. My heart sped up. I felt sick again. The one thing I remembered for certain was that there would be several holes that could send people overboard for a potentially rocky and dangerous swim. I yelled for an all forward. My crew powered us through a few introductory waves. Then we hit the first big one. We rode to its peak. From up there I could scout the next part of the rapid, if only for a split second. The noise in my head stopped. My focus narrowed. And just like it had so many times before when I'd given it all my attention, the river rewarded me by clearly spelling out my route.

I'd been searching for so long for a way to get back to that focus I'd first found on the river. That connection with the natural world, where everything else ceases to exist. And as usual, in the actual moment I didn't even realize I was there. Because in the moment there was no past and no future. In the moment, my entire world was that stretch of river.

Writing had prodded my return to the Hudson, and on that big-water day I thought I'd found my fairy-tale ending. In my mind, the story was a basic love story: girl meets river, girl loses river, girl gets river back and lives happily ever after. Then I woke the next morning terrified all over again. Being on the river felt like home. Getting there required a daily commute on an emotional roller coaster. After a while, the ride wore me down. I often tell people that after that season I retired for good from raft guiding. But like my other attempts at retirement, that's not exactly what happened.

CHAPTER 32

Bella Coola Valley, BC
September 2019

Sunlight dances across the river water and illuminates the surrounding ice-capped mountains. As I pull back on my oars, I can almost hear Chris and Graham calling me Brett Favre.

While looking for a job the summer after leaving the Hudson, my inner critic had been adamant that I wasn't qualified for anything. My internal streaming service had backed that up with frequent replays of Dr. Briggs, up in Williams Lake, informing me that McDonald's was hiring. Then a friend forwarded me a help-wanted ad for bear-viewing guides. I wasn't sure I had the skill set for that line of work, but it was an outdoor job in a beautiful place, and if nothing else, it was an adventure that Ray would love. And so I applied.

I was surprised and happy to get hired, but in the first few weeks I questioned whether I had the necessary patience to last the season. Hours were spent watching bears do very little. But like sitting on the staff house porch watching the Hudson flow by, I began to appreciate the quiet way nature teaches us. Watching bears interact with each other showed me how to trust and be trusted by them. Once I was through that door, it was impossible not to become fascinated by their world. I loved working at that lodge, but after three seasons my itchy feet got me moving on to another bear-viewing operation. One that offers wildlife watching by raft.

Now, instead of chasing big waves, I run the river in search of grizzlies. And today we have found the biggest one in the neighbourhood. Although at this moment it seems more like he's found us. He's a large male the guides refer to as Bent Ear. It's a nickname he earned in better times, as now all that remains of his pinnae are ragged stubs. In addition to missing ears, his face is scarred and his jaw crooked. Clearly he's taken hits in more than a few fights. But the way the other bears move out of his way leads me to believe his opponents came out looking even worse.

It's my third season on this river, so I should be used to Bent Ear's behaviour by now, but it still makes my heart race. No other river guides I work with have experienced this with him, but Bent Ear likes to engage me in what feels like a game of chicken. Bears have the right of way around here, so when we see one coming up one side of the river, the guides row over to the opposite bank whenever possible. Most bears continue up their side and don't pay my raft much mind. Not Bent Ear. He stops, stares at me and then starts to cross the river toward my boat. I respond by following protocol: pulling anchor and rowing out of his way to the other side. If my crossing doesn't take us too far downstream, Bent Ear will wait until we're settled with the anchor dropped and then start to approach us again, as if testing to see how many times I'll move for him.

Today, as Bent Ear swaggers toward us, I can see how nervous my guests are. They keep glancing over at me, checking to see if I'm going to move us, or pull out my bear spray, or give them some sign that this gnarled bruin is too close. Just like when I used to raft whitewater, I'm nervous too. In a good way. In a way that makes me feel focused and alive. For a moment I wonder if maybe this time I should stay put and see what happens. But I understand the rules, and as this big bear with a lopsided mouth and scarred face gets closer, I pull up my anchor. Bear viewing tends to be a quiet activity, so there's no *yeehaw*-ing or *wahoo*-ing, but the looks on the guests' faces tell me we're all feeling excitement from our shared experience. I row away with the crisp autumn air on my face and a warm glow in my chest and I think: *I fucking love my job.* Bent Ear has won our game once again. And the fact that he has singled me out to play his game with makes me feel like one lucky loser.

I know I came close to not being here. I haven't forgotten about fighting the urge to swerve my car in front of a semi truck or hiding my sharp knives in the back of a drawer. And these days I still sometimes feel that invisible weight pushing down on me. I still see the dark circles beneath Ray's eyes and feel the cool skin of his motionless chest under my hands. Lucky for me I've had lots of guidance to help find my way throughout this journey.

During my last season on the Hudson I'd wondered if what I'd always considered my love of rivers was actually just an addiction. I'm still not sure I know the difference, but what I do know is that while I was busy chasing a whitewater rush, the currents were quietly teaching me an important lesson.

As rivers move toward the ocean, they grow and change. When something tries to stop them, they find a new route down. Sometimes they circle back in eddies and holes—that's part of what creates their character—but ultimately they keep pushing onward. They carve through mountains when they need to. And even when the excitement of their biggest rapids has come and gone, unforeseen beauty still lies ahead.

I look back at Bent Ear. Then I look at my guests and this beautiful river valley. I imagine Ray's gold-filling smile. And I think to myself the only thing I can: *All forward! Fuerte!*

AFTERWORD

I've been made aware that this story still has some unanswered questions. I'll do my best to wrap a few things up.

- I don't believe Ray was suicidal. I believe he gave Chris and me our tips ahead of time because it was a practical thing to do. He ignored my pleas to get to the high side of the raft because he was a stubborn old man who thought he was doing the right thing. And he didn't swim toward shore because he was freezing cold and his clothes were weighing him down. I don't believe that Ray wanted to die on the Firth, but I do believe he was aware of the risks and went anyway because of how alive river trips of the past had made him feel. I'm not trying to absolve myself of responsibility for his death. I was the one holding the oars. I have many regrets about that Firth trip. But I can't deny that I'm honoured to have met Ray, and if I'm going to be carrying the memory of a dead man for the rest of my life, I appreciate that it's a dead man who keeps kicking me in the ass to take him on adventures.
- I don't want this story to make it sound like becoming a bear-watching guide has been the ultimate solution to my mental baggage. I learned a long time ago that when things go very wrong, the culprit is rarely just one mistake. Only after leaving the Hudson did I realize solutions work the same way. As powerful as rivers are, it was naïve of me to think the single act of returning to one

would solve all my problems. But that doesn't mean help was unattainable. Vigorous exercise, immersion in nature, changes in diet, spending time with friends and family, drinking much less, cold-water swimming, neurofeedback, wildlife guiding, finding a psychiatrist who actually listens and just the passing of time have all helped lift the invisible weight that so often pinned me down. As has writing this story. Having to put words on a page in some sort of order, instead of simply enduring the continuous images and sounds randomly jumping through my mind, has made me look at my life differently. I used to try to put myself in Ron Thompson's place. Would I be able to forgive myself? Would I be able to continue living a full life? I didn't think I would. However, writing this story has brought me understanding—which has cracked open the door to forgiveness. I'm not yet all the way through that door, but I am far enough in to think that perhaps Graham was right: *Ray was a cool, no-nonsense man and would tell you to let it go.*

- Graham really did stuff Ray's ashes into a dead sockeye salmon and leave it on the banks of the Chilko for a bear to eat.

- In the end we did have enough food on my last Grand Canyon trip, but despite our best efforts we never finished all the celery.

ACKNOWLEDGEMENTS

Thanks to my amazing agent, Stephanie Sinclair, for taking me on, giving me great advice, and of course finding this book a home. Despite your long list of clients, you continually make me feel like you have all the time in the world for me.

To my editor, Scott Steedman, thank you for delivering your astute advice in a way that gave me lots of room to make changes while keeping the story my own. And thanks so much to all the editing students in Scott's class at Simon Fraser University for your excellent insight. Receiving feedback from an entire class was a really interesting way to be edited, and I'm grateful for your help.

This book was conceived during my midlife-crisis master's degree in creative writing. So a huge thank you to my teachers and fellow students in the Creative Writing program at the University of British Columbia for all that you taught me about telling stories, and also for giving my life some direction when I really needed it. Special thanks to my thesis advisor, John Vigna. You suffered through some pretty terrible drafts and invested many more hours in this story than your contract stipulated; I'm grateful for your guidance. Thanks also to my secondary thesis readers: Ian Williams, you agreed to become a reader at the last minute and gave me lots of valuable feedback despite the short notice, and Deborah Campbell, you not only gave me lots of helpful story advice but you were also the first person to really encourage me to get this book published. I'm still scared of the impact that telling this story will have on my guiding career, but you're right, I probably can't keep guiding forever anyhow.

Larry and Noni Raskin, thank you for offering to read this manuscript early on and for all your time and support. I can't find the words to tell you how much that's meant to me.

Karen Kaushansky, Liane Schinasi and Katherine Muller, thank you for being early readers of, and believers in, this book. And while we're at it, thanks for a lifetime of friendship.

Amanda Phillips, you may not have read any of this book before publication but our years as roommates were like an ongoing workshop in storytelling (drunken storytelling, but storytelling nonetheless). To Nancy!

Thanks to Anna Comfort O'Keeffe for publishing this book and for taking the time to answer my questions. And thanks to Lucy Kenward for copy editing (and for letting me leave a few small grammatical errors as is, so they sound more like me).

Joanne Hoffman, thank you for listening to my stories and helping me feel a little less scared about sharing them with others.

Thanks to my parents for raising me with lots of adventures both in real life and in books, and for never trying to pressure me into a more conventional life or trying to pressure me out of my many "once-in-a-lifetime" opportunities. Thanks to my sister, Mara, for proofreading my stories, giving me a home to live and write in, helping me through my darkest times and, of course, for not pushing me out of the self-opening car doors when we were kids.

I can't imagine my life without all the rivers and the people I shared them with. However, one of the common criticisms I received from early drafts of this story was that I named so many people it was like reading a Russian novel. So with great difficulty I edited out many names of, and stories about, people I've spent time with on rivers. Hopefully some of you are happy to not be in this book (Ohi Johnsen: I'm not sure how you managed to get out of this), but just know how grateful I am to all of you for giving me a life worth writing about. And thanks as well to my fellow Kanawanians who started me on my love of paddling.

Finally, thanks to anyone who took the time to read this book. I hope you didn't hate it.